The Chancellor's Spy

The Chancellor's Spy:

THE REVELATIONS OF THE CHIEF OF BISMARCK'S SECRET SERVICE

Wilhelm J.C.E. Stieber

TRANSLATED FROM THE GERMAN BY JAN VAN HEURCK

Grove Press, Inc. / New York

First Edition 1980
First Printing 1980
ISBN: 0-394-50869-6
Grove Press ISBN: 0-8021-0198-4
Library of Congress Catalog Card Number: 79-52090

Library of Congress Cataloging in Publication Data

Stieber, Wilhelm, 1818-1882.
    The chancellor's spy.

    Translation of Spion des Kanzlers.
    1. Stieber, Wilhelm, 1818-1882.   2. Spies—Germany
—Biography.   3. Bismarck, Otto, Fürst von, 1815-1898.
4. Germany—Politics and government—1871-1888.
I. Title.
DD205.S74A3713   327'.12'0924 [B]   79-52090
ISBN 0-394-50869-6

Manufactured in the United States of America

Distributed by Random House, Inc., New York

GROVE PRESS, INC., 196 West Houston Street, New York, N.Y. 10014

The Chancellor's Spy

PUBLISHER'S NOTE

Some readers may wonder why this gripping and historically significant record was not published long before now.

Wilhelm Stieber was, apparently, convinced it was impossible for a man who had held his high-ranking positions in the police and secret service to turn over his memoirs to the public. He felt it was his duty to keep silent during his lifetime. Moreover, these memoirs were not written with the intention of having them published; they represent, rather, the attempt of a dutiful official to personally justify himself to posterity. For Stieber understood that he was regarded by some of his contemporaries as a "reactionary hunter of men," and by others as a "secret socialist"; thus he drew ire from both the political left and right.

After Stieber's death, his private papers, along with other important legacies (among them, the chair on which Napoleon III was seated when he signed his surrender in 1871), fell into the hands of his son, Paul, who died in 1944. During World War II, Stieber's entire estate was lost except for the single copy of the original memoirs, made by his son, whose heirs offered them for publication in Germany in 1978.

Before the memoirs were published in Germany, their contents were examined in light of the historical literature which devotes ample attention to Stieber. The original nineteenth-century style of writing and expression has been retained in order to preserve the authenticity of the work. Other material published in Germany in 1884, which represents a statistical synopsis of Stieber's years of service, was consulted to ensure the accuracy of the facts.

In view of the political terrorism taking place today, there is no need to emphasize the fact that the private notes of the chief of Bismarck's secret service are of contemporary importance. They are also timely because of the astonishing modernity of Stieber's ideas. Stieber can rightly be considered the father of modern espionage, secret service, and intelligence agencies. The tactics and principles he established, indeed invented, still form the basic operating procedure of everything from Scotland Yard and the FBI through and including the CIA and the KGB.

PART ONE

An INDEX OF PERSONS for *The Chancellor's Spy* appears at the end of the book.

When I was born on May 3, 1818, in Merseburg, Saxony, my father, a tall, extremely imposing man with the unusual Christian name of Hypolith, was only a subordinate official in the Merseburg government.

Nevertheless, we lived on a fairly grand scale; for my mother, Daisy, a strikingly beautiful woman, came from a family of wealthy English landowners who proudly traced their ancestry back to the British national hero, Oliver Cromwell (1599-1658), and who contributed generously to our support.

My father, who adored horseback-riding, had won my beautiful mother's heart in a romantic and adventurous fashion. The carriage in which she and her family were travelling was attacked by highwaymen, and at this moment my father rode up, leading two horses belonging to government superiors that he used to care for to augment his small income.

In the dim light, the marauders may have believed that a number of riders were approaching, or they may have been frightened by the shot fired from my father's hunting rifle. In any case, they all fled as fast as they could, never to return, whereupon my father politely sprang from the saddle to ask the frightened family how they were. They, in turn, thanked him profusely, regarding him as a saviour sent by God.

The eldest daughter, my future mother, was just recovering from the fainting spell that she had suffered when the highwaymen appeared. The first thing she saw was my father standing before her, the saviour who had rescued her from the most extreme peril, the very image of masculine strength. In that moment, she fell passionately in love with him. Only a few weeks passed before my father and "the Englishwoman," as our family henceforward called her, were married, an event that created quite a stir in Merseburg.

In the spring of 1820, my father moved to Berlin, where he was promoted to secretary, and later, to supervisor, in the Church hierarchy. Probably it was for this reason that, after concluding my studies at the famous "Graues Kloster" gymnasium, he decided that I should enter the Church.

Obediently, I began to study theology at the University of Berlin, but no sooner had I started, than I had an experience that was to change the course of my life. A young Swede named Bjerregaard, who had left his homeland and come to Berlin a short time before, was working as a janitor's assistant at the university; and only a few weeks after his arrival, had fallen into bad company.

These unsavory companions broke into and robbed the house of a university professor, although the inexperienced Bjerregaard did not suspect what they were up to. While the thieves were collecting their booty inside the house, Bjerregaard, who had been told that his false friends intended to engage in an amorous escapade with the professor's cook, stood guard outside the door waiting to signal the approach of passersby and enable his friends to get away. The thieves were interrupted at their work and fled, while Bjerregaard, who was innocently following them, was captured by the police who had swiftly arrived at the scene. The young Swede was arrested and charged with burglary.

I had met this somewhat foolish, but obviously decent and honest foreigner, quite by chance. From the very outset, I found incomprehensible and improbable the idea of his having participated in the crime, and, believing him innocent, determined to do what I could for him.

The very first conversation I had with him, while he was in custody, convinced me that this unfortunate man, who was all alone in Berlin, was completely innocent. Thereupon, I contacted the Swedish ambassador to Berlin, and with his help, obtained from Sweden Bjerregaard's past official records. These established that he belonged to a poor, but high-principled family, that his conduct had hitherto been completely blameless, and that he enjoyed the best possible reputation among all those who knew him. Accordingly, I could not believe that this honest young man had sunk so low as to become a housebreaker and a burglar in the few weeks that had elapsed between the time he left home and his arrest in Berlin.

By citing these facts, I was able to procure Bjerregaard's acquittal. Thereupon, the Swedish ambassador, who had attended the Berlin Supreme Court trial and heard my impassioned plea of defense (at that time there were no official defense attorneys possessing an exclusive right to defend their clients, and anyone could defend the accused in court), sent me a letter of thanks, accompanied by an honorarium, that he paid out of his own pocket, to recompense me for my successful effort in the defense of his fellow-countryman.

However, I declined to accept the money, and requested that

the ambassador give it to Bjerregaard, who, after spending several months in police custody, was totally without means. In response to this gesture, the ambassador publicly thanked me in the Berlin newspaper, the *Vossische Zeitung,* for my energetic assistance in restoring the young Swede's honor, and then proposed to the Swedish government that they grant me an honorarium out of state funds. The Swedish government responded at once to this proposal, empowering the ambassador to give me, a young theology student, ten *friedrich d'ors* as an official token of gratitude.

This experience opened my eyes, and made me realize that I was not cut out to be a cleric, but was a natural-born lawyer. Secretly, and without my father's knowledge, I matriculated in law at the University of Berlin, and until 1841, studied law and public finance and administration.

My repeated attempts to get my father to change his mind about my future career and to stop insisting that I pursue my religious studies, failed. All the same, I wished to continue to receive his financial help toward my study of law, which, although I kept it secret, was a necessary preparation for my pursuit of my true and only vocation. Thus, I had recourse to a subterfuge. I copied long passages from the pious sermons in a book belonging to a former fellow-student of mine and placed them in plain sight in my study in my father's house. Indeed, I acceded to the request of a sick minister friend of my parents and preached a successful forty-five-minute sermon in the church frequented by members of the court; the King himself was there. This sermon, whose piquant theme was "What punishments await the Christian for the sin of lying?", visibly moved the congregation.

As I mounted the pulpit, robed in a black gown with a touch of white at my breast, I saw my father and mother sitting beneath me, full of anticipation, in the first row of pews. Then my eyes wandered to the wooden cross above the altar and my thoughts to the Saviour, wondering what He would think of an impostor who proclaimed the word of God in order to wangle money out of the father he was deceiving.

Although rain was pouring down outside, the King appeared. As he was getting out of his simple coach, he had been been unexpectedly drenched, and was now sitting in an armchair with a knitted cushion under his feet to protect them from the cold church floor. Then, resolute unto death, I raised my head and began to preach.

At first my voice was lost in the vast vault of the church; but as my confidence grew, my voice grew stronger, and finally my words went rolling through the arches like the clang of thunder:

"Divine forgiveness will not be accorded you on the flaming day of the Last Judgment—unless you bow to the earth in penitence, unless you sink down in humility and remorse!" I preached.

From the moment he heard the first murmurs from this young preacher who was a stranger to him, the King adopted the expectant attitude of a connoisseur preparing to enjoy an old familiar song that this time will be sung by a new interpreter. And when my voice reached its pinnacle, when it roared triumphantly along the entire width of the nave, intensified by the echo, my father and mother barely managed to refrain from uttering a "Bravo!" that would have been quite inappropriate in this place; in fact, they were almost on the point of bursting into loud applause of the sort one hears at successful performances in the royal theater.

From this moment on, I felt a seductive desire to continue the playacting that was being rewarded with so much approval from the public. Shaking my head, clenching my fists and flinging my arms right and left, I raised myself up, then sank down again and adopted all the dramatic poses that I had frequently observed in preachers.

"If you do not heed the admonitions of the Church," I threatened, "your bones will be broken and your flesh will roast, and it is in vain that you will whine for mercy, for then God will not be merciful!"

While I was audaciously threatening them with broken bones and roasting flesh from the pulpit, a contented shudder was clearly passing through the congregation beneath me. Even the King was nodding, as if he totally agreed with this false preacher who was scattering his wrath among the people. He had leaned back, and suddenly I recognized that he was drowsing with his eyes open. My sermon had lulled him to sleep!

As I came to a halt with the thundering sentence, ". . . and therefore I ask for *mercy* for you all!," the King woke up and surveyed me with as much dismay as I did him, as if he believed I were asking *him* for something. Then he rose and gestured graciously to me, whereupon there was heard the muffled rustling of ladies' dresses and the scraping of boots, and slowly the monarch made his way to the exit, accompanied by his entourage.

The moment I descended from the pulpit, I pressed towards my parents. My father's joy was infinite, but equally infinite were the pangs of conscience I was suffering, and that same evening I confessed my deception.

When my father learned the truth, he broke down, drove me from his house, and refused to contribute financially to the continuation of my studies.

Thus, from then on, I was forced to earn the means of subsistence, and the money for my study of law, by serving as secretary to the criminal court in Berlin, and to the police department. It was in the course of these activities, that I first came into contact with Berlin police inspectors, who took me along when they investigated crimes and arrested criminals.

Suddenly, this adventurous line of work began to seem so much more desirable than my dry pursuits at court, that after I passed my junior barrister's examination (I passed with distinction), I asked permission to become a police inspector in Berlin's Division IV, the criminal division. Police Chief von Puttkamer personally granted my petition, in 1844, after I had been appointed junior barrister.

At once, my work as a police inspector proved unusually fruitful. I succeeded quickly in determining the guilt of all the participants in a capital crime that had been committed in the house of a Berlin banker, after the police had been investigating the case without success for more than eighteen months. When I brought them before the judge, all the guilty persons were sentenced to long prison terms.

A short time later, I succeeded in tracing a dangerous band of robbers who had been hiding for months in the woods near Berlin and for whom an entire company of soldiers had searched in vain. To be sure, this achievement was the result of luck, and I did hardly anything to bring it about. While walking through the woods, I suddenly found myself near a cavern concealed by tree branches. The sound of loud snoring emerged from the cavern. When I looked inside, I saw all the marauders whom we had sought for so long, lying side by side, noisily sleeping the sleep of the just, or rather, of the unjust! Apparently, they had believed themselves so secure behind the impenetrable thicket of branches that they had not posted a watch.

I was able to slip away undetected, and had only to summon the police. Supplemented by a unit of soldiers, all armed to the teeth, the police soon surrounded that area of the woods and were able to surprise and capture all of the men they sought without meeting any resistance.

However, my greatest success in police work was my investigation of the Tomascheck case. Long before I became a police inspector, a master tailor named Franz Tomascheck had insured his life with a Berlin insurance company for the horrendous sum of one hundred thousand talers; he died a year later. Upon receipt of a death certificate duly attested by a physician, the insurance company paid the insurance money to Tomascheck's widow, who then left Berlin for parts unknown.

By chance, I apprehended a Hungarian swindler in Berlin. At his trial, he made the embarrassing accusation that we imprisoned the little foreign rogues, but let the big Berlin criminals go free. When I questioned him, the Hungarian, who had been in Berlin once before, told me that a short time before, he had met the tailor Tomascheck in Bohemia, and that he was quite alive. As far as he knew, this was the same Tomascheck who had had himself declared dead in Berlin some years ago.

I immediately undertook to investigate this puzzling case. Tomascheck's grave was opened at my instigation. All we found in his coffin were his heavy flatiron and several bricks.

Thereupon, I travelled incognito to Bohemia, where, after much laborious searching, I discovered the "deceased" master tailor living in a small town under the guise of a wealthy man of independent means. He was leading a life of comfort and luxury and apparently did not think it possible that his life would be disrupted by a visit from the Berlin police.

I arrested the astonished man and turned him over to the Prussian authorities. His accomplices in his insurance swindle were his wife, who was living with him in Bohemia, and the physician who had made out a fraudulent death certificate for her supposedly deceased husband in return for ten thousand talers—the wages of sin.

On February 24, 1845, I received a letter from Privy Councillor Mathies of the Ministry of the Interior (later, Mathies was, for years, a member of the Chamber of Deputies; and from 1859-1861, was First Vice-President of the Chamber of Deputies; then he became president of the Lutheran Church Council in Prussia), asking me to come to see him the following day on official business. I was asked to maintain "the utmost discretion."

Curious, I complied with the summons from this exalted official. Mathies told me in confidence that the provincial authorities in Silesia had uncovered a conspiracy among inhabitants of the Hirschberg Valley. Apparently, a number of the conspirators intended to overthrow the existing system of government.

Mathies told me that evidence of the sort that would empower the law to intervene had not yet been obtained. Therefore, Count von Arnim, the Minister of the Interior, had suggested that I, the junior barrister who had had so much success in my pursuit of criminals, should be sent to Silesia to conduct a secret investigation of the conspirators and their plans.

At once, I agreed to undertake this mission, and the very same day I had the police issue me a passport bearing the name of Wilhelm Schmidt, a painter who was travelling in Hirschberg and its environs to exercise his art. (In my free time, I actually was accustomed to paint landscapes and portraits, with quite acceptable results.)

The next morning, I left for Hirschberg. There, I immediately contacted the man who had denounced the conspirators to the government, a laborer named Herrmann. I did this very innocently by using him as a model and painting his portrait in my lodgings.

Herrmann informed me that a "workers' conspiracy" existed throughout Silesia. The conspirators intended to dispossess of their property, and if necessary to murder, all the "rich," in order to return to the people the possessions they had stolen. The informer brought me another informer whom a "tall stranger" had asked to join the conspiracy and to whom this stranger had given a written proclamation; he gave the proclamation to me.

This piece of propaganda depicted, in angry terms, the pleasures of the rich, contrasting these with the privations suffered by the poor, and used impassioned arguments to prove that this contrast was not justified by the principles of nature, law or religion. The only solution it offered was to seize all the possessions of the rich and distribute them to the poor. This "new order" was to be achieved through a mighty conspiracy, to which men who shared these views should secretly pledge themselves. The proclamation ended with the following "war song":

> You rich thieves, brood of Satan!
> You greedy scoundrels,
> You stole the people's property—
> Death be your reward.

The style of this manifesto told me that it could not have been written by an uneducated man, and I, in fact, determined that its author was a Hirschberg factory-owner named Schlöffel, a man who was respected throughout the area. (Later, Schlöffel played a decisive role in the revolutions of 1848 and 1849, and then, lived in America as a political refugee.) I also suspected a master carpenter named Wurm, who lived in Warmbrunn, of being at the head of the revolutionary league, and a number of artisans of being ringleaders.

After around eight days of thorough investigation, still in the guise of Schmidt, the portrait painter, and thus totally unnoticed, I had ascertained all the facts, which confirmed the data supplied by my informants, and which established that Schlöffel spent an "inordinate amount of time" with members of the working class.

Of course, in itself, this fact would not entitle the police to intervene. In order to establish a cause for such intervention, I offered the aforesaid Herrmann a substantial sum of money if he would gain entry to the home of his employer, where he was a well-known figure, break into Schlöffel's writing desk, and bring me the contents.

Herrmann actually succeeded in doing this. He waited until Schlöffel's cook was alone in the house and told her that during her employer's absence the factory-owner had told him to change the lock on his desk. To prove his intention he showed her a bag of tools that he had brought along. Once the cook had left him alone in the factory-owner's study, it was easy for him to break into the desk, conceal its entire contents in his bag and bring it to me.

I immediately looked through all Schlöffel's private papers, but I was unable to discover anything definitely incriminating.

Thereupon, I sent a courier to Privy Councillor Mathies at the Ministry of the Interior in Berlin, notifying him of the results of my investigations up to this point. I added that, in my opinion, the suspected conspirators were not yet subject to arrest, because, so far, we did not possess sufficient evidence of their guilt.

However, in response to my message, Mathies immediately sent me orders dated March 10, in which he told me to arrest without delay all the persons I had designated as suspects, especially Schlöffel. Mathies stated emphatically:

"In a matter of such importance it is impossible to allow even one of the suspected conspirators to retain his freedom. Thus, assuming that nothing is discovered that substantially contradicts what you have learned so far, we cannot fail to keep them under arrest until one of them has confessed. Therefore, all the men you have named are to be arrested forthwith and must be brought here at once."

Acting on this order, which was not to be disobeyed, I appealed to the local authorities, with whose assistance I immediately arrested all the suspects. Schlöffel was the only one we failed to arrest, for at that time he happened to be in Breslau. Therefore, I travelled to Breslau and, showing Police Chief von Witzleben the arrest order, asked him to arrest Schlöffel. However, the Police Chief refused, and only after long hesitation did he assign me several police officers, with whose aid I myself undertook to arrest Schlöffel in Breslau. A few hours after his arrest, Schlöffel was transported to Berlin, where the Supreme Court kept him in custody for four months; however, once again, no really incriminating evidence against him was brought to light during this period.

Later, six of the other men I had arrested, including the carpenter Wurm, were charged with high treason. Wurm received the death sentence, and the others were sentenced to a number of years in prison. Later, Wurm's sentence was commuted to life imprisonment, and the amnesty issued in 1848 restored their freedom to all the condemned.

My investigative activities, under a false name, in the Hirschberg Valley, and the arrests I had made there and in Breslau, had attracted the public's attention to me and had caused quite a stir, particularly in so-called "liberal" circles.

During the meeting of the Silesian Provincial Diet, which was just beginning its session and which Privy Councillor Mathies attended in his role as representative of the Ministry of the Interior, Deputy Milde (in 1848, President of the Prussian National Assembly and the Prussian Minister of Commerce) engaged, on April 5,

1845, in an energetic discussion of my mission, and concluded by introducing a motion to ban this kind of "secret police" in our country. However, his motion was rejected and received only four votes.

Nevertheless, in the years that followed, people, particularly the opposition press, repeatedly accused the government of having acted "unlawfully" in the Hirschberg Valley and of having had insufficient legal grounds to make the ensuing arrests. The entire blame for these alleged illegalities was shifted to me, and the government did not consider it necessary to say a single word to inform the public what had really taken place. On the other hand, I myself was not in a position to publish the documents relating to Schlöffel's arrest, which would have revealed that I had merely acted as the agent of those in high office, for it was my duty to preserve the strict secrecy of these documents.

Thus, for years, I was pursued by the rumor that during my investigations in the Hirschberg Valley, I chose, without being authorized to do so, to infiltrate the Schlöffel family under a false name in order to spy on Schlöffel and to discover his allegedly treasonous plans. In reality, I never had any personal contact with the Schlöffel family, and I did not lay eyes on the suspect Schlöffel himself until the moment when I arrested him.

PART TWO

In the spring of 1848, I was sucked into the whirlpools of revolution in Berlin when King Friedrich Wilhelm IV took his unhappy ride through the city, an armband and a cockade in the republican colors—black, red and gold—fastened to his clothing. The monarch clearly hoped that this bold and fearless demonstration and the sight of his own sacred person would prevent the rebellion that appeared imminent among his people. It was in response to the threat of such an uprising that the government took the most perverse countermeasures, which, because of their very absurdity, were doomed to failure; and then, in the moment of greatest danger in March, 1848, ran away like a pack of cowards, leaving their sovereign behind to face the threat alone.

The principal cause of the impending revolt was that the King, after abruptly dissolving a so-called "national constitutional convention" formed by his people, had, in its place and on his own authority, drawn up a new constitution. Although it resembled to some degree the rough draft drawn up by the national convention that he had dissolved, and indeed was even more liberal, the constitution reserved to two houses of parliament, in which the powers then in sway would retain some voice, the right to revise it.

Thereupon, the "democratic" leaders of the people spread their "battle cry" abroad, demanding that no one support these two "reactionary" houses of parliament, because the "national convention" which had the support of the people, and which, therefore, was alone competent to frame a constitution, had been "unlawfully blown to bits" by the King.

It was purely by chance that I arrived on the scene just as the solitary royal horseman, whose ride through the city exposed him to such danger, and at the same time disclosed his ignorance of the world, was surrounded by more and more unruly people, until, in the end, he was in danger of being pushed from his horse.

Determined to do something, I leaped forward, grabbed the black, red and gold banner from an aggressive leader of the noisy rabble, and, waving the banner back and forth, laboriously paved a way for the King's horse through the crowd, who were surging forward with wilder and wilder abandon.

But it was not until I began to yell incessantly at the top of my lungs, "The King is on your side!—Make way for your King!" that I finally succeeded in drawing the rider to safety behind the massive gate of the palace. His horse was threatening to shy at any moment and sweat was running down the King's face. The guards at the gate, who were themselves being buffeted by the crowd, were barely able to close the two wings of the gate behind their monarch. The rumor that began to circulate later, that from the very beginning I rode ahead of Friedrich Wilhelm IV on his "historic ride," carrying a black, red and gold flag, is unfounded, if for no other reason than because at that time I was far from being an expert rider!

The King had barely reached safety when he staggered from his horse and collapsed. I sprang to his side, and, with the help of the soldiers, carried the seemingly lifeless man into the guardroom, and then into a room in the palace where a doctor hurried to join us.

Disconcerted, I watched the doctor pull off the King's beard, which appeared to have been glued on. At this point, the unconscious man awoke and stammered: ". . . The angry crowd, the shying horse! What a role for His Majesty, but never again . . . !" His entire body was trembling. Then he closed his eyes again, and his head fell back helplessly.

"Go away!" the doctor ordered me. "But no—stay and show me your identification!" After I had proved that I was a police officer, he said, in relief:

"I owe you an explanation, Inspector, and I rely on you, as an official in the service of the King, to keep silent about it: Thank God, as you have just discovered, His Majesty did not ride out himself; an artist from the Royal Theater rode in his place."

I stared down at the motionless man, who, even after his artificial beard and hair had been removed, closely resembled the King, not least because of the topcoat he wore. I wondered whether this topcoat belonged to the King or was a theatrical costume. But all I could manage to say was, "Is his condition serious?"

"There's nothing to worry about," the doctor said soothingly, and held a bottle of smelling salts under his patient's nostrils. "Thank God, it's only a harmless fainting spell, quite understandable under the circumstances!"

Shortly thereafter, a servant summoned me to the King's chambers. Dragging his feet as he walked toward me, and looking pitifully pale, the monarch grasped my right hand with both of his. In a weak voice, he breathed: "You have preserved the father of your country from insult and disgrace, if not from something worse! What you did will not be forgotten!" He continued to gaze intently at my face until a glimmer of recognition passed over his features:

"Aren't you that young clergyman whose fiery sermon I heard some years ago, a sermon from which I derived so much edification?", he asked, displaying his amazing memory.

I turned pale, but nevertheless, I manfully told my King the whole truth, confessing how I had deceived my father because he would not allow me to pursue my true vocation, and saying that I was aware of how lawless and culpable my masquerade had been. However, not without pride I added a description of the fruitful work that I had accomplished as a police officer.

"I have heard about those daring exploits," the King acknowledged. "So you are their hero! Well, you yourself bore witness to the fact that I, too, was compelled to put on a masquerade!"

He paused for a moment. "I'll keep your secret if you'll keep mine," he said. Then, squeezing my hands once more, he promoted me from a simple police inspector and junior barrister to the post of head of the Berlin police force! My appointment was to take effect immediately.

In the winter of 1850, I was summoned, in my official capacity, by von Manteuffel, the Minister of the Interior, who showed me, under the seal of the strictest secrecy, a note from the King. It said:

"I believe that Stieber is the man to uncover the web of conspiracies and to destroy and punish the plotters, thus making an example of them, as we have so long desired they should be destroyed and punished. Let Stieber create his masterpiece! I believe that this idea of mine will have important consequences, and desire that you implement it immediately. There is no time to lose! Burn this note. *Vale!* Friedrich Wilhelm."

This note, written in the King's own hand—which, as von Manteuffel later confessed to me, he did not burn—had reference to a series of conspiratorial and treasonous letters that a Rhenish editor named Karl Marx had, for the past two years, been sending from England to a "Secret Communist League" in Prussia. The note also had reference to the recent arrest, engineered by me, of a tailor's apprentice named Nothjung, who was taken into custody because he did not have the proper identification. Nothjung was found to have documents proving the existence of an "International Communist League" whose central office was located in London.

In response to this discovery, the King now assigned me no less a task than to track down this revolutionary league on the spot, and I forthwith travelled to London in a private capacity, carrying the papers of a newspaper editor named Schmidt. Ostensibly I was there to attend a large industrial exhibition.

I spent only eight weeks in London, during which time I very quickly scented out an international Communist conspiracy that had been conducting secret activities for years; had cast its nets over all of Europe, especially Germany, and had attracted countless members in almost all the large cities of Germany, France, Switzerland and England. The goals of the conspirators were the violent overthrow and expropriation of the "bourgeoisie" (a concept derived from the French Revolution), the abolition of the previously existing social order, which was based on "class conflicts," and the foundation of a new society that did not exhibit such conflicts. Their guiding principle, fanatically proclaimed, was: "The time is ripe for the violent amelioration of our corrupt world!"

The members of the German, as well as the foreign, Communist leagues were mostly German, and the command center in London consisted exclusively of German emigrants, most of whom belonged to literary circles. The most eminent members of the London central office were the aforementioned editor Karl Marx, an impoverished and indeed totally destitute man; his friend Friedrich Engels, the son of a Rhenish factory-owner; the Prussian Lieutenant Ernst Willich, who had been suspended from duty; and the bankrupt former student Karl Schapper.

My investigation of Marx revealed that this German exile came from a Jewish family native to Treves, studied philosophy in Berlin and Bonn, and tried to get a teaching post at the University of Bonn, but was turned down because he was of Jewish extraction. Thereupon, Marx became editor of the *Rheinische Zeitung*, in Cologne; and was banished, in 1849, for publishing inflammatory and subversive articles. He fled to Paris; but then was banished from France for inciting to riot; and fled to London; whence he subsequently made repeated trips to Paris, carrying false papers. Marx had a beautiful, much-sought-after wife from an old

Westphalian noble family, with whom he had fathered three daughters. In addition, he had an illegitimate son named Henry Demuth, who was born in London, on June 23, 1851, and whom he begot with Helene Demuth, his family's maidservant.

My investigation of Engels revealed that he was the son of a factory owner from Wuppertal, that he fled to Switzerland after taking part in a "fight" between "Socialists" and the police in Baden, and that he then found employment in a firm in Manchester, England run by business associates of his father. A visitor was fascinated by his first impression of Engels: He was tall, broad-shouldered and blond-haired and possessed an extremely winning nature. In addition, he was passionately devoted to horseback-riding, swimming, fencing and hunting. He wrote a book entitled *The Exploitation of the Working Classes.*

My investigation of Karl Schapper revealed that at the tender age of nineteen, when he was a forestry student at the University of Giessen, he was already a party to a Communist plot framed by the writer Büchner. Then, he participated in the storming by revolutionaries of the main guard-house in Frankfurt; in London, too, he was always prepared to engage in riot and revolution. There, his intimate friend and energetic collaborator was a watchmaker named Moll, a native of Cologne, who, after he fled from Germany and was banished from France, took refuge in England. Schapper and Moll were regarded as professional revolutionaries.

However, a year ago a schism developed in the London command center of the Communist League, because Marx and Engels advocated different views from Willich and Schapper. Marx and Engels wanted to promote moderate principles, whereas Willich and Schapper advocated Communism in its most extreme form. Each group was trying to consolidate its position at the expense of the other and win over adherents from the other side.

All these conspirators, who had fled their German homeland, regularly received letters from German professors, editors, and others who shared their views and exercised influence on the German public. The letters contained extremely precise reports about efforts to overthrow the system in Germany and everything that might contribute to this goal. The recipients replied to these communications with extensive advice and directives.

The reason why these revolutionaries chose London as the headquarters for their "International Communist League" is that they wanted to take advantage of the Britons' noble, liberal and democratic freedoms of association and assembly. They founded a "Workers' Education Association" to recruit and train new members for their conspirational cause and establish, throughout England and also in Europe, branch offices bearing the deceptively pacific name "cottages."

In London I succeeded in locating the headquarters of the Communist League, and I decided to beard the lion in his den.

I had myself announced to the leader of the League, Dr. Karl Marx, as a German editor named Schmidt, claiming that I had travelled from Berlin to London with the express purpose of looking for a young German colleague—who was, to the best of my knowledge, a member of the Communist League—and conveying to him greetings from his family. I chose "Friedrich Herzog" as the name of this fictitious person; the name had simply popped into my head.

In response to this fairy tale, I was, in fact, led in to see Marx. I found a squat, middle-aged man in a dark, threadbare coat with a stiff shirt-front, flowing black hair and a black beard; he looked like a university professor. The only striking thing about him was the penetrating gaze that emerged from beneath an unusually high forehead; a loose cravat like those affected by artists and painters; and a gleaming monocle firmly fixed in the socket of his right eye.

Marx informed me with regret that he did not recognize the name of the man I was seeking; however, he advised me to acquaint a certain Dietz, who was in charge of the League's central records, with the object of my quest, and gave me Dietz's address. I was about to turn and leave, when Marx asked me to stay and began to question me:

"How do you, yourself, feel about our cause?" he asked me. However, then, in the manner of very egocentric people, he fell into a monologue without waiting for my reply.

"Everywhere in the world," he said, "the workers build splendid palaces, but they themselves must starve in wretched cottages. They produce all the goods of life and maintain the entire machinery of the state, but their rulers do not show the slightest concern for them. It is our sacred duty to change that!"

Thereupon, I asked him how, in his opinion, such change should come about. He did not hesitate for an instant: "Through the transfer of all the factories from the power of their self-seeking owners to the workers, who alone have the right to use them."

I objected that to attempt such a change would cause a civil war whose outcome would be, to say the very least, uncertain, because all the power was in the hands of these same owners.

"Not for long," Marx responded confidently. "Time is on our side! The most recent news I have received from Germany indicates that Communists are at work all over the country. In Barmen, the Prefect of Police is himself a Communist, and in Elberfeld, the entire citizenry attended our Communist rally!"

I did not succeed in concealing my astonishment, and I asked Marx whether these middle-class citizens were unaware that they were showing appreciation for something whose purpose it was to forcibly bring about their ruin. "What makes all these obviously unsuspecting citizens attend a Communist rally?" I imprudently cried.

But Marx was not disconcerted. "The cause is the dissatisfaction that is growing even among the middle class," he explained with passion, "the increasing resentment of brutal censorship, feudal arrogance and the omnipresence of spies working for the police!"

As he spoke these words he handed me a small book bound in bright red, entitled *The Program of the Communist League*, which he had written in collaboration with his friend Engels. (These two were the intellectual leaders of the conspiracy.) After the book had been printed by a London firm, thousands of copies were sent into various countries. I reproduce here the salient points of its contents:

THE PURPOSE OF THE COMMUNIST LEAGUE IS:

The overthrow of the tyranny of the property-owners that has reigned until now, the seizure of their property and power by the "proletariat" composed of workers and farmers (in accordance with the manifesto issued by the central office in February, 1848), the centralization of all factories and capital in the power of a "state of workers and farmers." In detailed form, the laws governing the implementation of this program are the following:

1. The expropriation of all landed property by the State,
2. The abolition of the right of inheritance,
3. The monopolization of finances in a state bank,
4. The nationalization of the transportation system,
5. The central management of all factories and real estate according to a plan designed to ensure the good of all,
6. The equal duty of all citizens to work.

As soon as these measures have abolished class distinctions, the public executive authority, with its powers, that has existed up to that point, will be abolished and replaced with a voluntary order of mutual cooperation governed by one law: the welfare of all.

The book ended with the battle cry of the Communist League, which Marx had composed in 1847: "Proletarians of the world, unite!"

I thanked him for the gift and then tried to escape from Marx, but he seemed to want to test me further:

"Are you an editor?" he asked. "For which newspaper?" I named a Berlin medical publication that was not only harmless, but had ceased to be published a short time ago. Obeying a sudden inspiration I added, "I am actually a frustrated physician. That is, I studied medicine until I was dismissed from the university because of my sympathy with revolutionary ideas."

I believed that my remark would elicit a compassionate response from Marx, who had also been dismissed from the university, and that I might thus worm more useful information from this apparently loquacious and guileless man. But his reaction was completely unexpected. For this revolutionary, who, even at that time, was already both famous and feared, replied:

"So you are a doctor? Then tell me, what medication is effective against the pain of hemorrhoids?"

At first, I thought that I had not heard him correctly, but Marx explained to me, without hesitation, that he suffered almost unbearably from this disease, which for years had tortured him so much while he was sitting down and writing that now he would only be able to work standing up, if it were not for the fact that the aforementioned Dietz, a former apothecary, always made up some soothing medication for him.

I made sure that I had understood him correctly by asking Marx again if this Dietz was the same man who was in charge of the League's central files. When Marx replied that he was, my plan was already complete:

After a moment of reflection I asked Marx, as a keepsake, to sign his name in the book he had just given me, a request to which he promptly acceded. Hereupon I finally took my leave, expressing my good wishes for his health and plans.

I swiftly returned to the lodgings that I had taken in a little inn, because identification was not required there. And here, after I had first practiced on another sheet of paper, I wrote in disjointed Roman characters in the empty space above Marx's signature in his book, the sentence: "Please bring me some medication and the files at once!"

I tore the sheet of paper out of the book, and carrying the note I had written on it I went that same evening to Dietz's house, whose location Marx had indicated to me.

There I introduced myself as a German physician named Dr. Schmidt, whom Marx had consulted because he had suddenly begun to suffer severe pain. I said that I had treated him and that he had sent me to fetch the medication that Dietz often prepared for him, as well as the complete files, to which Marx wished to refer while writing something during his illness.

Although I was a total stranger to Dietz, who was an emigrant from Wiesbaden and did not appear to be very intelligent, the note from Marx and my obvious knowledge of the most intimate details of Marx's life—details that I presented with such an air of authority—dispelled any doubts he may have had about my identity. After all, whom else could Dietz have taken me for?

He devoted himself forthwith to preparing the medicinal compound that Marx had already obtained from him so often, and I waited full of anticipation, wondering whether he would be equally willing to hand over to me the register of the Communist League, which had been entrusted to him.

However, he did not do so. Instead he ceremoniously concealed four thick folio volumes, which apparently contained the records I wanted so desperately, in a sack made of strong material, like the sacks in which sailors keep their belongings. Then he insisted that he himself would take the medication and the bag to Marx.

But I had foreseen that such a problem might arise and did not say a word to try to dissuade him. Instead, I helped Dietz to tie up the bag containing the folio volumes, and then accompanied him to Marx's house.

However, when we had reached the stairs, I asked Dietz to wait a little while, explaining that I wanted to see my patient alone first in order to find out if he were able to receive visitors. Dietz complied after a moment's hesitation.

I did, indeed, mount the stairs to Marx's attic apartment, but I paused outside the door without making a sound, and a short time later returned to Dietz, who was waiting on the first floor. I told him that my patient was very weak and was resting in bed, and that he had asked Dietz to give the things he had brought to me, the doctor in charge of his case. Impressed by my self-assured manner, which commanded respect, Dietz actually obeyed.

Hereupon, I sent Dietz away, strongly impressing on him that he should not return to visit the sick man, who needed his rest, until three days had passed; then once again, this time carrying the medicine bottle and the linen bag, I climbed the stairs to Marx's lodgings.

Dietz left the house immediately, and I watched him from an attic window until he was out of sight. Then I left Marx's house with the plunder, of which I had finally succeeded in gaining possession. In order to avoid attracting attention, I walked at a measured pace rather than fleeing as fast as I could.

Carrying my inestimably valuable prize, I swiftly made my way back to Berlin, for I had to take advantage of the time I had obtained by my cunning. After this time was up, my deception would certainly be discovered, and a warning would be issued to all the members of the secret alliance who were mentioned in the register.

The data which I had captured did, in fact, give the Prussian police undreamed-of information about the power and wide dissemination of the international Communist League. At the same time, the police came into possession of precious secret documents contained in another folio volume that the zealous Dietz—intentionally or inadvertently—had given me along with the register.

These documents clearly established that a Communist League whose headquarters were in London had existed since 1847, had contributed decisively to revolutionary movements in Prussia from 1848 on, and since that time, had been represented by secret, so-called "confederations" in the following German cities: Cologne, Berlin, Brunswick, Hanover, Hamburg, Frankfurt-am-Main, Leipzig, Stuttgart. But the documents I had acquired also proved that the Communists had secretly gained a foothold in Brussels, Verviers, Liège, Paris, Lyons, Marseilles, Geneva, St. Gallen, Chaux de Fonds, Locle, Bern, Dijon, Lausanne, Strasbourg, Valenciennes, Metz, Basel, Algiers, New York and Philadelphia. They had more power in France than elsewhere, for here the conspiracy appeared to be both significant and extensive.

Acting on the basis of the evidence I had obtained in London, I now went to Paris in order to look for further traces of the conspiracy. Carlier, the Parisian Prefect of Police, willingly cooperated with me, and I was invited to rely upon the help of the French authorities, whereas while I was in liberal London I had been forced to rely upon myself alone, and, lacking any real authority, had to use trickery to gain possession of the register of the Communist League.

When I arrived in Paris, I seemed to have entered an erupting volcano. Everywhere, fanatical visionaries were hurling the most inflammatory watchwords at the uninformed masses, and everywhere I encountered innumerable turbulent clubs for emigrants, who supported countless different movements. New theories, to some degree fantastic, to some degree designed to aid society in practical ways, continually entered the stream of human thought. Dozens of pamphlets, manifestos, proclamations, programs and counterprograms were spread from house to house. Unrest was most acute in the quarters inhabited by the poor: Here there were hundreds of little societies and groups of conspirators whose heads burned and whose thoughts rumbled with new world-orders.

Never before have there been so many utopian dreamers, eccentrics and fools. Men like Gabet and Proudhon taught the return to "primitive Christianity." They were ardent visionaries who preached, "Jesus was the first Communist; Communism is nothing other than true Christianity," and a certain Louis Blanc even went so far as to say, "Socialism is the Gospel in action." From Robespierre, the leader of the French Revolution, they had adopted the statements that the State must guarantee and organize every man's "right to work"; and that "social science" was the most exalted of the sciences and was destined to replace the politics of the past, which had led astray the fates of nations.

I devoted particular attention to the democratic-republican "Secret League of the Outlawed," which had been founded by German refugees, and from which the most extreme elements had been eliminated, only to establish another league "of the Just." This group, in turn, sought to attach itself to other revolutionary secret societies, especially the "Society of the Seasons," founded by the French Communist Blanqui.

The German Socialist Grün, with the support of his fellow-countryman Eisermann, had become a prominent figure. Both he and Eisermann were adherents of a doctrine that advocated that decisive changes be brought about by cooperative means, whereas the others attacked this "pseudo-Communism," which seemed to them too tame and which they believed would divert them from their primary goal: The complete overthrow, throughout the world, of everything that had existed in the past.

On May 12, 1839, all these conspirators had attempted to bring about a revolution in France, but their efforts went awry. The German leaders of the conspiracy, Karl Schapper and Heinrich Bauer, were captured, and, after a long term of imprisonment, were banished from France. Thereupon, they fled to London. One of the revolutionaries, the Frenchman Blanqui, was condemned to death, but then his sentence was commuted to life imprisonment, and since that time, he had been a prisoner in the French fortress of St. Michel.

A few days after my arrival in Paris, I was in my two-room lodgings, when a strange gentleman was announced: I was told that he wished to speak to me. I invited the stranger into the anteroom, where my well-dressed visitor, a man around thirty years old, introduced himself as a lithographer named Cherval. As a member of the Communist League in Paris, he told me, he had learned that after I had gained possession of the files of the League's central office in London, I had come to Paris in order to encourage the French government to take measures against members of the League.

When I coldly replied that I had no reason to discuss with him the purpose for my visit to France, Cherval sprang from his chair and threatened that I would have to pay with my life if I did not abandon my plan and leave Paris at once. I refused to tolerate this threat and ordered my visitor to leave immediately, saying that if he did not leave, I should have him arrested. Instead of obeying, Cherval swiftly drew a long dagger and proceeded to attack me.

I managed to knock the dangerous weapon out of his hand by throwing a chair at him and then tripped him so that he fell. He fell head over heels to the floor, landing with such force that he lay motionless, apparently stunned, whereupon I attempted to handcuff him. But while I was doing so he regained consciousness and, seeing the handcuffs, began to snap his teeth in all directions like a madman, until I finally succeeded in overpowering him.

Not until I had tied up my attacker did I notice a bleeding wound in the flesh of my arm, inflicted by his teeth. It was not serious, however, and healed in a few days.

Within the hour, I had begun to interrogate the handcuffed

Cherval, a German whose parents had also been German and who had not taken the French name Cherval until he arrived in France. I interrogated him in the presence of a high-ranking French police officer. Cherval denounced a number of his cronies, among them the apprentice tailor Tietz, who was later convicted of high treason by the Prussian Supreme Court of Judicature, as leaders of the Communist League in France. Cherval was moved to this betrayal by my promise that if he told me what he knew, he would not be prosecuted for his attempt on my life.

I kept my promise to him, for the statements of the would-be assassin Cherval led to the immediate arrest of a number of the people he had denounced and the confiscation of all their papers. These papers revealed that the Communist League in Paris was governed by a large directorate divided into three "subcommunities," one run by the Communist writer Scherzer, the second by a master tailor named Reininger, and the third by the fanatical assassin Cherval.

The minutes of their meetings, which we had confiscated, revealed their goals. Almost all the people mentioned in these minutes were Germans who were still unknown to the police, and who, far from being emigrants, were free to return to Germany at any time. In the minutes of one meeting attended by members of Cherval's community, I read, "The present rulers can only be overthrown by violent means, and therefore, all our members must prepare to use violence. We must act without any compunction: arresting all property-owners, confiscating their property and turning it over to men who share our views!"

One characteristic plea was that of the radical Cherval, duly recorded in the minutes, that the people arrested should not be tried in court but should be immediately "liquidated" under the pretext that they had tried to escape. Almost all the minutes had a similar tone.

As a result of the discoveries I made in Paris, most of the members of the Communist League whose names had been discovered were immediately brought to trial in Paris, for their League intended to overthrow the French system of government. Cherval and the tailor Gipperich were sentenced to deportation for a period of eight years, and Scherzer and a tailor named Nette were sentenced to three years' imprisonment.

My investigations in London and Paris, and the evidence I brought back from there, made it possible for the German authorities to arrest all the leading members and agents of the Communist League in Germany. The Court of Assizes in Cologne undertook to investigate no fewer than twelve of them, among them Becker, a Doctor of Law and later Lord Mayor of Cologne; the writer Freiligrath; Bürgers, a man of letters; the cigar-maker Röser; and three physicians, Daniels, Jakoby and Klein, to decide if charges of high treason should be brought against them.

Because it was assumed from the outset that the accused would contribute no information about the acts of which they were accused, and that not many witnesses would be prepared to testify, the court was compelled to laboriously assemble a great quantity of "circumstantial evidence," until some two hundred files had been packed full, and another fifty had been filled with personal data that had accumulated during the time the accused were in custody.

Finally, an indictment was drawn up that comprised several hundred pages. The judges' task was made more difficult by, among other things, the flood of motions that they daily received from the accused, and that they had to deal with in addition to their other duties.

The trial finally took place over a period of five weeks, from October 4 to November 12, 1852. It took days just to read the countless documents and written statements, for the accused repeatedly used lawyer's tricks to attempt to delay the proceedings. These tactics clearly resulted from the clandestine communications that circulated among the accused, despite all attempts to supervise them closely.

Untoward incidents repeatedly occurred at court, and more than once the better-educated among the accused were able to win a round against the exhausted judges.

From the first moment on, the police allowed no doubt to arise as to who was in control of the situation. They surrounded the court building and their security measures were very strict. Throughout the trial, no one went in or came out without their permission; at the entrance, guards searched everyone except the judges, and people were repeatedly searched in the courtroom itself.

Finally, Röser and Bürgers were each sentenced to six years for attempted treason; Dr. Becker was sentenced to five years in prison; several of the other accused were sentenced to three years in prison, and several were acquitted. The accused might perhaps have been able to mitigate their punishment if they had been willing to give evidence. But despite all the evidence against them, they obstinately refused to speak, and strictly adhered to their rule: "A revolutionary must never admit anything in court."

Despite the fact that members of the German Communist League were at that moment on trial in Germany, those at Communist headquarters in London did not cease to send agents throughout all of Germany, who swiftly attempted to repair the damage that had been done to the League.

However, above all, the leaders Marx and Engels tried to influence, in any way they could, the course of the trial of the German leaders of the League in Cologne. Thus, during the trial, I discovered a secret correspondence between Cologne and London whose purpose it was to procure false witnesses and evidence favorable to the accused and to influence public opinion in their favor. From London there emanated the rumor that all the evidence against the accused had been forged by me and other Germans in authority, and thus represented nothing but lies and deception.

I was tireless in my efforts to trace these secret influences, and, in particular, the aforementioned correspondence; and I not only succeeded in this attempt, but also, in the process, discovered a completely new branch of the Communist League in Cologne that had in fact first come into being during the long investigation of its imprisoned leaders. Besides their slanderous attacks against me, the principal concern of the central office in London was the elimination of their former emissary Haupt, who had betrayed them by revealing to the court the most important links between the Cologne conspirators and headquarters in London. This star witness was ceaselessly threatened with death, and finally the London Communists succeeded in frightening him so badly that he fled to America shortly before the trial began in Cologne, so that he was unable to testify in court.

I intercepted in Cologne all the secret correspondence that the Communist League had sent there from London, and, upon reading the confiscated material, I was struck by the repeated statement that the letters would be sent by the "courier" along with money and clothing. At first, I believed that this statement referred to the express ship called the *Courier* that regularly travelled between Bremen and London. But then, I began to suspect the royal Prussian courier, a man samed Feise, who travelled between London and Berlin. Thus I intercepted Feise on his next return-trip from London and actually found letters from the Communist headquarters in London in his luggage. Feise had undertaken to pass on these letters, of whose significance he was completely unaware, at the instigation of a London Communist who had befriended him expressly in order to get him to do so. He immediately lost his post as courier for the Prussian cabinet.

My tireless labors were acknowledged when in January, 1853, I was made director of the "Security Division" at Berlin police headquarters, and King Friedrich Wilhelm IV commissioned me to record all the experiences I had undergone during my pursuit of the conspirators in England, France and Germany. This account, which comprised two volumes, was then printed by the royal printing house in Berlin under the title, *The Communist Conspiracies of the Nineteenth Century.*

At the conclusion of my book, I had expressed my realization that the soil that nourished all efforts to overthrow governments was the poverty that was so widespread among the people, and that thus the only really effective weapon against subversion was the abolition of this poverty, which could be achieved only through better education and better pay for workers. This, in his view, overly liberal declaration earned me the hostility of Simons, the Prussian Royal Minister of Justice, later causing me considerable trouble. Simons felt nothing but contempt for revolutionaries. In his view, all the reasons they gave to explain their actions were nothing but excuses. He considered them no different from common criminals, on an equal footing with ordinary murderers, burglars and swindlers, who twisted the law to suit their own purposes and whose criminal misdeeds deserved to be punished.

I, on the other hand, believed that we had to try to continually improve our people's standard of living, thereby immunizing them against the insinuations of revolutionaries. To be sure, we ought to suppress conspiracies and attempts to overthrow the government, but we ought not, to the degree that they were rational and just, suppress the ideas underlying them. On the contrary, we ought to attempt to implement these ideas within the framework of justice and law, for such an approach would make us far more effective than our enemies, who sought to enforce change by means of violence and lawlessness.

Soon all the German princes applied for my assistance and asked me for suggestions as to how to unmask members of secret societies in their realms. Drawing on the evidence and documents I had amassed, I not only supplied the authorities of all the German states with personal data relating to conspirators who had been living in their territories undetected, and briefed them as to the activities of these conspirators, but also informed them about men who had emigrated from Germany to Paris or London and who continued to exert influence on their homeland from these distant cities and to support secret associations.

Thus, I soon came to be regarded as living proof—to the few people left who might still be in ignorance—of the network that the secret Communist leagues had already spun throughout the world, and was able to convince them of the degree to which these leagues had already hollowed out the earth that they imagined so secure beneath their feet.

I also investigated the counterfeiters of fraudulent Prussian treasury bills and coins, as well as counterfeiters of French and English money, who were alarmingly active all over Germany, France, England and America. Extremely convincing replicas of paper money and coins were being manufactured, and refined methods were used to make the money appear old and worn, making its spurious nature more difficult to detect. Obviously the counterfeiters were masters of their trade, for their counterfeit had always passed through many hands before being removed from circulation.

I had begun to investigate this matter because it seemed to me entirely possible that counterfeiting on such a comprehensive scale might well reflect revolutionary aims, namely the confusion and destruction of trade in countries whose governments were destined to be overthrown.

By means of a painstaking comparison of all the raw materials used by the counterfeiters, which actually turned out to be completely identical in all the counterfeit money examined, and a tireless examination of maps to locate all the places where counterfeit had been discovered, I arrived at the conclusion that it must originate in the Rhineland and Westphalia, and therefore I suspected that it was there the counterfeiters were at work.

I travelled there, although I had no other clue to guide me in my investigations. Up to that point, the Rhenish and Westphalian police had not detected a single person thought to be in contact with the counterfeiters and with those who circulated the counterfeit money.

With the assistance of a few Rhenish constables who had been assigned to my command, I began to look for the counterfeiters. Among these constables was a man named Schild who had a remarkably ready tongue. One evening, Schild, dressed in civilian clothes, was crossing a bridge, when suddenly someone tapped him on the shoulder and said, "Cortegas, how did you get here, the cops are here!"

Schild, who immediately suspected that the stranger thought he was one of the counterfeiters, took advantage of the mix-up to get into a conversation with the deluded man. In the course of the conversation he confirmed that he bore an astonishing resemblance to one of the principal counterfeiters.

Then the constable invited the man with whom he was talking to follow him to his lodgings, and the man agreed. The constable did not have to think twice before deciding to take the suspect to my lodgings, and I arrested him there at once. He struggled like a madman, using both his hands and feet, so that in the end Schild and I barely managed to subdue him by our combined efforts.

Thanks to the resemblance between my constable and one of the principal counterfeiters, I soon succeeded in arresting close to one hundred people who had been engaged in the manufacture and distribution of counterfeit money, as well as in shutting down a great number of their workshops. I got my first prisoner to betray all his cronies by promising him that I should release him as soon as I had verified his testimony, and I kept my promise. For it always seemed to me better to let one criminal go free, provided that his testimony enabled us to apprehend all the others, than the other way around.

It could not be proved that the counterfeiters had had any connection with secret revolutionaries and conspirators, but several indications confirmed this suspicion.

In the autumn of 1854, it was noted at the Berlin stock exchange that a simple bank official who had been hired only temporarily and who had been completely without means, suddenly began to come to the stock exchange every day, purchasing large quantities of foreign government securities that always increased in value immediately after the speculator had purchased them.

At first, my initially discreet surveillance of the bank official revealed nothing but the fact that the speculator's younger brother, who was only twenty-two, came to the stock exchange at the start of every day's trade, spoke briefly with the speculator, and then departed. Continued surveillance of the younger brother led me to discover that every day, shortly before the beginning of trade, he met a telegraph operator in a pub near the main telegraph office, and that the telegraph operator always slipped something into his hand.

Thereupon I arrested the speculator's brother as he was hurrying to the stock exchange after a meeting with the telegraph operator. In his pocket I found a piece of paper on which the telegraph operator had written the names of several foreign government securities. Then I arrested the telegraph operator and the speculator. At first, they denied everything, but then they confessed that they had been working together and also gave me the name of a banker who had supplied them with the considerable sums of money they needed to carry out their secret speculations.

The transactions I uncovered were quite simple: The telegraph operator read incoming telegrams addressed to large Berlin banking houses and made note of orders to purchase certain securities, especially foreign government securities. Then he transferred the note to the speculator in the manner I have described, meanwhile taking care that the telegrams were somewhat delayed in arriving at their destination. Thus, the speculator had a head-start of around half an hour, which he used to purchase the government securities named in the telegrams. When the telegrams had reached their recipients and the latter were complying with the purchase orders they contained, he sold the securities to them at a great profit.

In the course of my investigations, I arrested a second telegraph operator and two more bankers whom I suspected of having participated in this swindle involving the disclosure of telegrams. However, the only men to be convicted were the first telegraph operator, his two accomplices, whom I had arrested first, and the aforementioned banker, who had supplied them with funds.

I had chosen to investigate this case because such a betrayal of the contents of telegrams, which could take place at any time, could easily lead to the betrayal of state secrets.

Subsequently, I was occupied with an ostensible attempt to assassinate King Friedrich Wilhelm IV. My painstaking investigations uncovered a truly diabolical plot, which, however, was directed not against the King, but against the men who had supposedly tried to assassinate him:

In the spring of 1857, the security police in Berlin received two letters from the state of Minnesota in America. The letters were signed "G. Langner" and "W. Harter." They accused a certain Menthe, a man of independent means who lived in Berlin, and a master carpenter named Sprung, also a citizen of Berlin and the son-in-law of Mrs. Menthe, of being agents of an American conspiracy who were planning to poison the King of Prussia. The letters stated that Menthe and Sprung intended to engage in a treasonous correspondence, written in code, with the leader of the conspiracy in America. They also supplied the key to this code and indicated that in the next three days, three letters containing poison destined for the King would be sent to Menthe from America.

Finally, this letter of denunciation advised me, as director of the police, to arrest Sprung and an apprentice shopkeeper named Hove, who was related to Menthe's wife, and who was also privy to the murder plot, and to immediately confiscate all letters addressed to Menthe that arrived from America.

Although I suspected from the very beginning that this denunciation might be some kind of trick, I could not rule out the possibility that it contained an element of truth, and I immediately ordered a thorough investigation.

However, a meticulous surveillance of Menthe, Sprung and the apprentice Hove did nothing to confirm the accusations against them. Indeed, Menthe and Hove proved to be completely harmless people who had never shown an interest in politics. Moreover, Menthe was a sickly man lacking in energy, and not only did he have no contact with Sprung, but he and Sprung were actually enemies.

Nevertheless, I ordered the confiscation of all Menthe's incoming mail from America. By these measures, I succeeded in acquiring two letters postmarked New York and St. Paul, Minnesota, and when I opened them I found that they contained the same thing: a white, unscented powder wrapped in thin paper, accompanied by a note on which eight lines were written in code.

When these eight lines were decoded with the aid of the key contained in the aforementioned letter of denunciation, they read: "Here is the means to silence the devourer of men! The brothers of the league." Chemical analysis revealed that the white powder found in the letters was pure strychnine, one of the most lethal of all poisons.

In order to clarify this puzzling state of affairs and gain some clue as to the guilt or innocence of the addressee of these letters, I had recourse to a stratagem: Such exact copies were made of the two letters sent to Menthe and of their envelopes that no one could tell the difference between the copies and the originals. However, instead of the dangerous poison, a harmless white powder was placed inside them. Then a police officer dressed in a mailman's uniform delivered the two letters to Menthe; the second letter was not delivered until the following day.

Menthe accepted the first letter, postmarked in New York, without hesitation, but when the second letter, with the St. Paul postmark, was delivered a few days later, he refused to accept it and behaved in such an obviously unsuspecting way toward the police officer, disguised as a mailman, who had brought him the two letters, that no one could harbor the slightest doubt of his innocence.

He told the postman that a few days before he had received a letter from New York that contained a note covered with incomprehensible writing, as well as some white powder. He could not, he claimed, explain this mysterious missive, and said that he had shown the letter to his doctor, but that his doctor could not unriddle its contents either. After tasting it, the doctor had turned the powder over to a nearby apothecary shop.

At the same time, Menthe expressed to the postman his suspicion that the letters might have come from a minister named Krause, a relative of his wife who lived in America and was an enemy of his. Upon receiving this information, the pseudo-postman took his leave without taking any further measures against Menthe.

The mere mention of Krause, the clergyman who lived in

America, sufficed to dispel the mist that had hitherto veiled this mysterious affair. Krause, as it happened, was a swindler well known at Berlin police headquarters. He had made a profession out of ensnaring the authorities with illusory evidence of political conspiracies. Formerly, the seat of his activities had been Berlin, but even after his flight to America he used to denounce people falsely to the authorities and to people in high positions, and swindled them out of money by promising to get information for them. As a swindler, Krause had developed a skill surpassing the skill of similar swindlers who had cost the Prussian government so much in the years before I came to office.

A comparison of the handwriting in the two letters addressed to Menthe and Sprung with the handwriting used by the clergyman Krause in his earlier denunciations, revealed that they were identical. I then had the property of Menthe and Sprung searched and interrogated them myself; the results showed that they were both completely innocent.

However, while the houses of Menthe and Sprung were being searched, I discovered some correspondence that Menthe had exchanged with Krause. This correspondence revealed that the clergyman Krause was the brother-in-law of Mr. and Mrs. Menthe, and that Menthe had placed his dead brother's daughter, a girl named Sophia, in the care of Krause in America. Later, two other children, Berthold and his sister Maria, who were Mrs. Menthe's children by a previous marriage, were sent to join Sophia. However, Krause used Menthe's trust in him to conduct an unscrupulous swindle. He wrote Menthe that he had purchased land for his three wards in America and asked, ostensibly on behalf of the children, that Menthe send him the purchase price of the land— five thousand talers—as soon as possible.

Menthe, who was not himself in a position to pay out such a large sum of money, borrowed it at an exorbitant rate of interest. However, the children, whom he had given into Krause's care when he sent them to America, wrote him that their supposedly God-fearing uncle, Pastor Krause, was perpetrating a fraud. Thereupon, Menthe relieved him of his guardianship and told the three wards to return to him. This deprived Krause of his source of revenue, the money that Menthe regularly sent for the children's support.

Driven by the desire to revenge himself against the Menthe family and by the fear that Menthe might turn him over to the authorities, Krause dreamed up his truly diabolical plan to accuse Menthe of attempting to assassinate the King of Prussia and to send him poison to verify his accusations.

Although, in response to this piece of villainy, I urged in my report to the King that Krause should be prosecuted through foreign diplomatic channels, unfortunately my urgings were not heeded, and I discovered that Krause continued to live in America for many years, unmolested by the American authorities.

In the year 1858, I succeeded, through decisive action, in being of service to Prince Carl, the brother of King Friedrich Wilhelm IV, in connection with another infamous affair. This affair concerned Privy Councillor Horst Wedeke, who, during their childhood, had been a playmate of Prince Carl and who enjoyed the Prince's friendship for years, until he vilely abused it. For Wedeke attempted to extort a large sum of money from Prince Carl by threatening to publish some compromising letters that he claimed to have received from him.

I feared that if he were subjected to a public investigation and trial, the blackmailer would abandon all reserve and repeat to all the world his filthy insinuations about the prince. Thus, at first, I proceeded in secret to conduct the most painstaking investigation, which very soon brought the following facts to light:

Prince Carl and Wedeke had been raised together as boys, and at the age of puberty, when they were twelve and thirteen years old, had written each other extravagant letters; but these letters contained no evidence that, when he became an adult, the Prince was guilty of any compromising and culpable inclination. Moreover, the blackmailer overlooked the fact that the Prince had kept similar letters from him and that all the letters had been written when their authors were boys, still under age. Thus he exaggerated their importance and believed that, as long as he possessed the Prince's letters, he was completely secure and that no one would dare to take action against him.

Thus I was astonished that when he learned, despite the secrecy in which they were being held, of my investigations—he must have learned of them at once, how, I have never been able to discover—he fled to Switzerland. Then, I went to Freiburg in Breisgau and from there—once I had learned where he was living, and ostensibly on behalf of the Prince—began to exchange letters with Wedeke. In my letters, I suggested that we could settle the affair amicably and invited him to come to Freiburg and discuss the matter with me in person.

Wedeke, believing that no legal steps could be taken against him in Baden, allowed himself to be lured to Freiburg, where I immediately arrested him. However, he did not bring along the letters which he had used to threaten Prince Carl. He had left them in Switzerland in the keeping of his secretary.

Thereupon, I reflected that if his employer did not return as he expected, Wedeke's companion would be afraid that some accident had befallen him or that Wedeke intended to leave him in the lurch. I believed that the secretary would soon follow Wedeke to Freiburg in order to find out what was going on.

I sent a courier to the secretary, who had stayed behind in Switzerland, with a fraudulent letter of dismissal from Wedeke, whom I had arrested and forced to write this letter in his own handwriting. I forced him to do this by threatening to arrest his companion too unless he complied.

And the young dandy did in fact come to Freiburg, carrying the papers Wedeke had left behind in his luggage. One reason for his coming was that without the money Wedeke had been giving him, he was left completely penniless.

When he arrived in Freiburg and learned of his master's arrest, he tried to escape, whereupon I arrested him and, despite his violent resistance, took the letters away from him. In the process, a piquant fact came to light: the blackmailer Wedeke's supposed secretary and travelling companion was actually a woman, an extremely young actress dressed in man's clothing for reasons that I had no cause to investigate.

A short time later, the Swiss newspapers circulated rumors that Wedeke had had papers which compromised the Prussian King Friedrich Wilhelm IV himself and that the King had offered a large sum of money for their return.

On behalf of the King, I sent the newspapers vigorous corrections of their stories and issued the following threat: "The stories released in the Swiss press are untrue, as can be proved at any time, and the King of Prussia will take legal measures through diplomatic channels to prevent their circulation if you do not retract and amend them at once!"

However, the truth could not be confirmed by the courts because during the proceedings, while he was still in custody, Wedeke died.

A short time later, King Friedrich Wilhelm IV sent me an urgent summons to his private chambers, where I encountered Dr. Lepsius, a professor at the University of Berlin and a member of the Berlin Academy of Science.

His Majesty, who was very excited, told me that a man named Simonides, who claimed to be a scholar from Athens, Greece and who was now living in Leipzig, had offered to sell to the Berlin Academy of Science an ancient Greek manuscript of inestimable value and had asked that he be given an immediate reply, since otherwise he intended to sell it to the University of Leipzig. The Academy reported this offer to the King, who at once declared that in order to procure the precious manuscript for his country, he was prepared to purchase it for five thousand talers from his private purse. Thereupon, the five thousand talers were paid to Simonides through a courier, and in return, Simonides handed over the old manuscript.

But then, after a painstaking examination of the ostensibly ancient manuscript (it consisted of papers and documents in several ancient languages: Syrian, Egyptian, Chaldean, etc., and it took Professor Lepsius eight days just to get them in order), Professor Lepsius was forced to conclude that it was a skillful forgery, and that Simonides, the man who had sold it and who had posed as a Greek scholar, was without doubt a swindler of the rankest sort.

At stake was the sum of five thousand talers that the King had so willingly paid for the manuscript, and thus we had to arrest Simonides as quickly as possible in order to convict him of forgery and fraud and recover the King's money.

Thus, accompanied by Professor Lepsius, I swiftly travelled to Leipzig, where I arranged for the authorities to arrest Simonides at once. However, Simonides did not have the King's money on him, nor was he prepared to reveal where he had hidden it.

My subsequent investigations soon revealed that Simonides had copied all of the supposedly ancient codex in his own hand and that he was a professional forger. Thus I experienced no difficulty in having the Greek swindler extradited from Saxony to Berlin.

When I saw Simonides on the following morning, I discovered that he spoke nothing but modern Greek and that at the moment there was no one in Berlin capable of translating this language; thus, no one was able to exchange a syllable with the swindler. I tried in every way I could think of to find someone who could speak his language so that I could proceed to the interrogation, which I deemed so urgent.

After I had unsuccessfully approached scholars, professors, physicians and others, I finally found an interpreter in a circus that was then performing in Berlin, in the person of a magician and fire-eater named Ben Ali, who was almost eighty years old and who had been married to a Greek woman, from whom he had learned her language, for fifty years. Like many old people, this otherwise vigorous old man was hard of hearing and scarcely understood half of what the accused and I discussed. Thus, both the swindler and I were forced to write down everything we said and then to hold our words close to the short-sighted, blinking eyes of our half-deaf interpreter.

After Simonides had been in custody for several weeks, the Municipal Court of Berlin declared that it was not competent to bring charges against him because his act of fraud had been committed abroad (in Saxony). Moreover, the court in Leipzig was not able to bring charges against this foreigner because, according to Leipzig law, he would have to be sentenced in Saxony, and no such sentence had been proposed. Thus, it appeared that I should actually have to release this swindler who was as slippery as an eel.

However, as soon as the prisoner realized that he could not be punished for his despicable fraud, he impudently addressed to police headquarters and the Municipal Court the demand that he be released forthwith and that he be allowed to keep the five thousand talers which had been given him, on the grounds that the charge of forgery could not be legally proved and that thus the contract entered into by himself and the King of Prussia was completely binding.

This swindler was sufficiently imprudent as to threaten, at the conclusion of this demand, that if I did not comply with its terms, he would appeal to the press and to the public and attract as much attention as possible to his cause by denouncing my supposed "breach of the law." I was concerned with avoiding publicity at all costs, in compliance with the wishes of the King, who wanted, in this uncertain age, to avoid any unseasonable scandal concerning the use of his private financial resources.

Therefore, I informed the prisoner that I could continue to hold him in custody for the crime of coercion and blackmail, which he had committed against me, and had him placed in a pitch-black dungeon that was completely isolated from the light of day. Then I allowed this brazen swindler to stew in his cell for three days. I did not deprive him of food or water, even though he refused the food he was offered and indeed, threw it at the guard's feet.

On the third day of his confinement in the dark hole I once again summoned my Greek interpreter and between us we arranged to act out the following scene: With a casual air and taking care to make a lot of noise, we paused outside Simonides' cell, where, while I prudently kept still, the interpreter loudly cried in the swindler's native tongue:

"So he's a prisoner in there, that capital swindler? Good! Do I want to see him? No! For as soon as we receive the records of the frauds he committed in my country, Greece, this scoundrel will be sent back to his own country! Until that happens we'll keep him here safe in his cell!"

During this loud monologue, which I had carefully taught my valiant interpreter from the circus, I, as I said, remained silent, but made a lot of noise when I walked and occasionally cleared my throat or muttered in a tone of approbation.

The next morning, I had the swindler brought to me again and, with the aid of the interpreter, informed him that on the previous evening a high-ranking police officer and his assistant had arrived from Greece and had asked to see the door of the dungeon where his fellow-countryman was imprisoned. The officer, I said, intended to take him back to Greece as soon as we had received the police records of the crimes he, Simonides, had committed there.

While I was speaking, I fixed the swindler with a grim stare, whereupon he immediately began to reveal how successful my stratagem had been. For the Greek grew pale and started to tremble like a leaf before the wind. Then he fell to his knees and begged me to release him at once so that he would not fall into the hands of his vengeful countrymen. Their accusations against him were, to be sure, nothing but malicious lies, but he could not prove that they were untrue once he had fallen into the clutches of the cruel Greek police.

Thus my initially vague and unfounded suspicion that the unscrupulous Simonides had committed fraud in his own country and that he feared nothing so much as extradition to Greece, was confirmed. In the presence of the interpreter (whose voice the frightened Simonides had not recognized as that of the Greek "police officer" who had uttered the threats of the night before) I allowed him to fidget for a while and then finally remarked graciously that I would think the matter over again. Then the swindler, who was almost out of his mind with fear and impatience, was led back to his dark hole again, and I did not summon him for another interview until the following day.

With the aid of my inexhaustible interpreter, I explained to him that I could comply with his request only under the condition that he immediately return the talers of which he had unjustly gained possession and that he sign a full confession of his forgery.

Simonides immediately signed the confession I had prepared for him, and just as swiftly told me where he had buried the King's money: in a plot of disused, uncultivated land behind the house in which he had last had his lodgings.

The police officers whom I forthwith dispatched to the scene did, in fact, find the entire sum buried in a shallow hole. Simonides swore to me by all that was holy that after his release he would never, to the end of his days, set foot in Prussia again, and on my orders, he was taken across the Prussian border in that very hour.

When I told the King of the happy and discreet outcome of my delicate mission, and in particular when I described the stratagem by which I had outtricked the trickster, he laughed out loud. Then he freely expressed his gratitude that my cleverness had restored to him his five thousand talers.

Because of my successful solution of cases involving King Friedrich Wilhelm IV and his family, the sovereign adopted towards me an attitude of trust which afforded me an influence extending far beyond that which derived from my official function.

I made the following statement about this influence in a report

to the Minister of the Interior, Count von Schwerin: "Purely for-
tuitous events created a very intimate relationship between the
sovereign and the police, namely myself."

In reality, I was promoted to the post of personal adviser to
the King, and this role was evidenced by the fact that I was summoned to his presence increasingly often in order to undertake
private missions that demanded particularly discreet handling.

Thus, in compliance with the personal wishes of the King, I
quietly took over management of the famous Kroll Café in Berlin,
so that, in effect, I played the role of innkeeper. This old family
business, which had been hallowed by tradition and represented
all that was best in the city, had, although few people were aware
of this fact, been built on the King's property in the Tiergarten
quarter of Berlin, and only the building itself was privately
owned. Not until after the death of the proprietor, Kroll, did the
King learn that the establishment was deeply in debt, and that the
countless creditors wanted it to be sold at auction. Because the
King wanted to keep the restaurant, which was famous well beyond the confines of Berlin, in the family of the man who had
founded it, I advised him to make an official declaration that after
the auction, the establishment, which stood on land belonging to
the royal family, could no longer be used.

Thus, the creditors were compelled to settle with the Kroll
family out of court, after which the restaurant continued to earn
profits for them, and the King was asked to turn over management
of the place to someone he trusted. Thereupon, the King appointed me manager of the Kroll establishment, and I managed
this venerable Berlin restaurant for one and a half years. During
this time, I was able to reorganize its finances so effectively that
Kroll's children were able to take over the business themselves
and in a short time managed to extricate it permanently from all
its difficulties.

During this interlude as an innkeeper, I received a visit from
the famous tragic actress at the Royal Theater in Berlin, Charlotte
von Hagen. She was unhappily married to a certain Mr. von Oven
and wanted to get a divorce, but she lacked evidence, necessary if
she were to obtain a divorce, that her husband was responsible for
the failure of the marriage.

In her distress, Charlotte von Hagen turned to me, asking me
to investigate the conduct of her husband, from whom she was
already separated, and to see if I could procure evidence that

would enable her to sue successfully for a divorce. Although such a commission on behalf of this artist, who was celebrated throughout Berlin, did not by any means lie within the competence of a police officer (to be sure, I was asked to detect the crime of adultery, but I was not being asked to do so with a view to instituting criminal proceedings against the adulterer, but only with a view to having him pronounced guilty in a divorce case), I undertook, after brief hesitation, to accept it. For I hoped that in this way, I might find some clues to the dissolute behavior of the upper classes in Berlin, which at that time went so far beyond the boundaries of what was lawful that I, as head of the Berlin police, could no longer watch what was going on without taking some action.

My assumption was completely correct. I soon discovered that Mr. von Oven spent a great deal of time with a Mrs. von T., a woman whose respectability was, as I learned, beyond question, although she was not herself of noble family and had only married into the nobility. Very young girls met every evening in her richly furnished home, and, as a rule, did not leave until very late at night. The possibility existed that something illegal took place at these meetings, which Mr. von Oven attended, and I abruptly decided to find out for certain what was going on.

I chose an evening when, as I had learned, a large number of married men of high rank were planning to attend a party with several very young girls of low origin. After my police officers, dressed in plain clothes, had surrounded the house and ascertained that all the guests were already inside, I rang the bell. Humming cheerfully, the unsuspecting Mrs. von T., dressed in a kimono which did not conceal the fact that underneath it she was completely naked, opened the door, holding a burning candle in her hand. Obviously, she thought that she was welcoming a belated guest, but suddenly, she saw before her the feared myrmidons of the law. Carrying her light, she recoiled in horror, as if she had caught a glimpse of poisonous snakes, but then, mute with terror, she was forced to lead her remorseless visitors, who would not tolerate any delay, into her home.

Here, absorbed in the most shameless games and "dressed" only in black masks which they wore over their faces, several of our highest city officials were sitting and lying in the embrace of equally naked girls. Screaming aloud, they all scattered when the forces of distraint suddenly crossed the threshold that until then had afforded them secrecy and sanctuary.

When they saw that all the doors were being guarded by police officers, two of the gentlemen rushed to the ground-floor windows and jumped down stark naked onto the street outside, where they found more officers waiting for them. This extremely delicate situation became all the more painful when my officers, trying to avoid any unnecessary scandal, behaving with exquisite politeness and completely ignoring the awkwardness of the circumstances, asked everyone present to produce identification. Naturally, this made the sweat of fear start from everyone's forehead.

After I had promised all the men who had been caught in the act that I should not arrest them if they immediately showed me valid identification, the laments began to die down and the celebrants hurried to their clothes, which they had cast off in disorderly heaps. But while all this was going on, the doorbell rang again. I opened the door, and behold, there was Mr. von Oven, the husband of the revered actress, Charlotte von Hagen. At once, he understood what was going on, and obstinately refused to supply any information about himself, mistakenly hoping that I had not recognized him, which, given the situation, naturally could not be the case.

Finally, I left, explaining that it was my duty to take Mrs. von T. (or Tilly, as her guests called her) with me to criminal court. The result was a general wailing and lament, mingled with the screeching of a parrot that happened to be in the room, while the freewheeling hostess, after she had gotten dressed, climbed into my cab to travel to the fearful place where her interrogation was to be held.

I made sure that the names of those who had attended the party were not revealed to the public, but I also made sure that the tale of the action I had taken was immediately published and received the widest possible circulation in the newspapers, so that it would breed a wholesome fear.

At that time, I was unaware that the action I had taken against the hospitable house of Mrs. von T. would not only enable my revered principal Charlotte von Hagen to obtain an immediate divorce, but would also serve as a guide to my future activities. For this experience deeply impressed upon me the fact that there were, in this city of Berlin where the King and his court resided, an increasing number of women belonging to the upper classes who had hitherto enjoyed spotless reputations, whose homes were frequented at certain nocturnal hours by young women who came here to engage in immoral encounters with men of all ages. Moreover, the men in question were generally of high, even of the highest rank, and their positions did not permit them to visit brothels or to accost prostitutes in the streets.

One element that substantially contributed to their conduct was the trend of the times, for at this time, men were increasingly dissatisfied with the kind of erotic pleasure they could experience in a brothel and were learning to prefer more refined, but also secret and completely confidential experiences with cultivated partners.

These "high-class" prostitutes—for such they were—in their new, ever more sumptuously furnished rooms, dealt with "clients" who demanded as much as they dared from the girls and women with whom they associated. At the same time, if these "servants of love" wished to be successful in their trade, they had to guarantee the most complete discretion. Thus, all the prostitutes one met were extremely refined and concealed their profession with such skill that an outsider had to possess a penetrating eye and a great deal of experience to fathom its nature.

Most of them hid their true intentions by means of a strange contrivance. When the guest entered the rooms in question, he did not see the girls but only their portraits, which were often painted by excellent artists, were of the finest quality and adorned walls covered with expensive wall paper. Each of these works of art bore a hidden number, and upon citing this number, the guest would see the beauty he desired appear, as if by chance.

Moreover, the proprietresses of many houses engaged in actual procuring, arranging to send young girls to men's homes on order; and, indeed, a few such proprietresses had comprehensive lists printed which contained involved allusions to the special physical attributes of each of their "society ladies," and distributed them to interested parties.

Within the course of a few days, a thousand or more of these frivolous "catalogues of pleasure" would be printed, and many of the industrious madams even found the courage, born of poor taste, to honor the birthdays of all the members, both living and dead, of the ruling family of Prussia, by means of special "memorial presentations" performed by their women. In these entertainments, the ladies, more or less scantily clad and adopting provocative poses, presented "pantomimes" and "panoramas" based on scenes from the lives of the royal family, to regale the greedy eyes of their male public.

The proprietresses of such secret houses of prostitution always observed with painstaking care the rule that they themselves were never to receive gifts of money from their well-to-do guests, but that the money was to be given as a "tip" to a simple servant or lady's maid. And indeed, in order to avoid legal inquiry and possible detection by the police, they maintained the fiction that the rendezvous which took place in their homes had happened quite by accident and that they did not profit from them materially in any way. Thus, the police did not have the legal evidence they needed to take active steps against those who came there, for they always swore by all that was holy that they were only good friends who dropped by for an occasional visit.

The principal vice I discovered in all the prostitutes was an abnormal love of finery. For one thing, their profession demanded that they dress as expensively as possible; also, the satisfaction of vanity and the maintenance of a distinguished appearance were the only pleasures that their sad trade permitted them to enjoy. All these women were downright extravagant and wore great quantities of the most expensive jewelry!

Often their desires outstripped their means, and thus there lay everywhere in wait usurious female moneylenders, who made their living by lending the prostitutes the largest possible sums at a murderous rate of interest—up to two hundred per cent. They "rented" goods to these girls who were greedy for pomp and circumstance; and not only supplied them with dresses and jewelry, but also elegant furniture, charging between two and three times as much as the articles were worth; and these things did not become the girls' property until they had paid the full purchase price.

It was the hope of eventually owning these goods that drove the prostitutes, who were actually being cheated, to sign the usurious contracts, whose terms they usually could not fulfill later, because their incomes fluctuated too drastically. If a woman fell the least bit behind in her payments, the true owner of the goods she was renting would immediately reclaim her property, even if it was almost completely paid for; and woe to the renter of the goods if, confident because they were almost paid for, she had sold them to someone else: for the usurer immediately reported her to the criminal court, and she was bound to be punished for her misappropriation of someone else's property.

Thus, although they earned large sums of money, many of these prostitutes could call nothing their own but their bodies. Even if one or another of them actually acquired some possessions, usually all she had to do to lose everything again was to get sick once or to spend a little time in jail. I found that pawntickets were these women's only possession, and thus their secret unchastity created, by twisted paths, a reliable source of income for our royal pawnshop.

I learned that our law, which protected underage girls until they were twenty-one, was a source of considerable vexation for the hostesses of secret brothels because it placed the youngest, and therefore most sought-after, girls beyond their reach. They found a deceitful way to get around this ordinance and by its means, even very young girls were distributed among the profit-hungry madams. If a madam wanted in her business a girl who was still under age, she procured for her a copy of a baptismal certificate belonging to a girl who had already reached her majority and fraudulently lent her youngest novice the older girl's name. I discovered that, unfortunately, our churches would give copies of baptismal certificates to anyone who asked for them, provided he paid the necessary fee, and that they did not ask to see any identification.

After such deceptions had been perpetrated, children were often offered as "choice items" in the brothels, and the hostess and her visitors did not have to fear that they would be punished for breaking the law that protected underage girls. Indeed, there existed usurious moneylenders who earned a lucrative income by procuring this kind of fraudulent identification for underage girls who had secretly become prostitutes.

In general, I could scarcely credit how great was the number of fees extorted from these unprotected prostitutes, and how great was the quantity of the vampires who sucked their blood and lived riotously from their labors.

However, I soon determined that almost all the men who sought to vent their passion in these secret houses of procurement belonged to the highest social strata, for no one else was able to defray the expenses involved. The majority were high-ranking officers and officials, and it was not unusual for one of them to choose this locale in which to throw a party or a banquet for his friends—a party of a sort that he would never have dared to throw in his own plain home. The guests were in disguise when they arrived, but they had no clothes on underneath their coats or capes. After dining sumptuously they would begin to dance, at which time the lights were extinguished and the coats and capes fell to the ground. Then in the darkness they celebrated the most shameless orgies with their female partners.

To my amazement, I discovered that among the prostitutes who frequented these brothels, there were actually many who had acquired a certain amount of education through their constant association with their highly-placed visitors, so that they could recite lines by Virgil and Horace and often commanded an entire catalogue of legal and military concepts; and to my horror, I found among them women who appeared to have been predestined to become spies. As yet, they fulfilled only the initial requirements for those who would participate in this profession so dangerous to the State, for although, without actually choosing to know things, they were initiated into the public and private secrets of the men who visited them, they did not, for the time being, take advantage of what they knew to blackmail these men.

However, some of them had already made a regular business out of enticing intimate, compromising information out of married men in the highest reaches of society and then extorting large sums of money from them by threatening to reveal these secrets to their wives; then, they passed some of the money on to their friends and acquaintances.

I grew dizzy when I thought about the possibility, which might occur to anyone at any time, that one day one of the men who visited the brothels might, instead of money, betray to his blackmailer some well-guarded secret relating to his high office, thus converting a potential danger to the State into an actual danger.

I want to emphasize a remarkable trait which existed in these prostitutes: Almost all of them, even the youngest, had a "sweetheart," and towards him she demonstrated a wealth of passion and self-sacrifice of which one would not have deemed so low a person to be capable.

It was as if, in the relationship between the prostitute and her sweetheart, love exacted compensation for the outrage which was continually inflicted upon it by the act of prostitution. However, the prostitutes' sweethearts were always a bad lot; for a man must be unfeeling, if not degenerate, to live off the earnings of a woman whom he has to share with every other man who happens to come along.

It seemed to me quite logical that these men were guilty of the most appalling abuse and brutality towards the girls, whom they secretly despised. Nevertheless, the girls were not scared off and shared even the ultimate degradation with their tormentors; the slightest ray of hope that her "sweetheart" might one day make her his wife, thus liberating her from her bleak existence, was apparently so tempting to a girl that she willingly plunged deeply into debt simply in order to gratify the extravagant desires of the man who was exploiting her.

It was no wonder that when the girls who supported them landed in jail, the idlers who lived off them and hated work, did everything they could to get them released as soon as possible. In the name of the girl's mother, brother or employer (naturally she did not really have an employer), the sweetheart would immediately barrage the authorities with petitions for her release and often hired the most expensive attorney to help them obtain it.

However, it seemed to me that the greatest danger to the public lay in the fact that when prostitutes were prevented by illness from continuing to exercise their trade, almost all of them chose to support themselves through all sorts of misdemeanors and crimes, which they either committed alone or with the aid of their dubious companions. All this drove the crime rate up to many times what it would have been otherwise and contributed to the general insecurity.

Thereupon, I dared to do something that no police chief had ever dared to do or even thought of doing: Whereas the citizens of Prussia wanted to continue living in ignorance and did not want to know anything about the existence of prostitution in their country, I openly endeavored to analyze and throw light on the phenomenon, according to the principles of criminology and also those of humanity. I had recognized that we could no longer respond to the moral problems of a growing capital by simply dispatching the police to punish offenders.

To King Friedrich Wilhelm IV, I submitted a petition expressing my conviction that the methods by which the police had supervised prostitution in Prussia in the past were now antiquated and in no way met the needs of the situation. I recommended the establishment, for the first time, of a "Prostitutes' Recovery Fund," which the King then actually approved in the following words: "A welfare fund of this kind will be established and administered by the police, a fund to which each of the women who live by prostitution will make a monthly contribution, and from which each of the contributors will, when she falls ill, draw funds for her support, her food and hospital care until she gets well."

The establishment of the "Prostitutes' Recovery Fund," which I had recommended, and which was financed by monthly contributions from women and girls who practiced what was probably the world's oldest profession, produced such wonderful results, literally overnight, that no one who did not observe them for himself can really comprehend them. For not only did the countless sick practitioners of this "profession" spontaneously cease to resort to crime because now, when they were not earning any money themselves, money was provided for their support, but in addition, venereal disease, the scourge of the "trade," could now be tracked down and combatted. The identities of unsupervised prostitutes were discovered, and, if they were ill, they were taken out of circulation. Moreover, the fund acquainted the police with secret brothels that, if they were spreading venereal disease, could be abolished and thus would cease to do harm. Every year from then on, the incidence of venereal disease was drastically reduced. Indeed, the happy effects of my simple notion of making provisions for the care of prostitutes who could not earn a living, spread from Prussia to neighboring states. The authorities in Mecklenburg, Hanover and Saxony, imitating the tactics of the Prussians, found out the hiding-places of prostitutes and brothels that were spreading venereal disease in their own territories. The authorities in all these states enthusiastically thanked me, and police headquarters in Berlin were soon filled with fat files full of letters singing our praises.

Besides the prostitutes' fund, we experienced another phenomenon which was novel in the annals of police work. From then on, I and the police officers who served under me, could rely on the prostitutes and their friends, who seemed to be grateful for the fund, to supply us with frequently invaluable information relating to capital crimes, for now that the prostitutes and their "sweethearts" no longer felt "threatened" by the police, they wanted to make it as clear as possible how radically they differed from those who committed such crimes. Very quickly, criminals of all kinds ceased to be able to escape police pursuit by hiding in a different brothel every night, and soon, Berlin enjoyed a security it had never known before that proved to be constant and lasting.

Likewise, as a token of "gratitude," my police from then on afforded prostitutes the same protection as they did to all other citizens, and a man who raped or stole from a prostitute or harmed her in some other way was punished by the police, so that the unfortunate principle of Roman law, *struorum non coittitur cum meritrice*, was no longer binding in the land of Prussia.

On the one hand, the *filles de joie* soon became the best of agents and spies in the service of my police officers and contributed to their hunt for evildoers of all sorts; but on the other hand— and this was the other side of the coin I forged by the unusual measure I had taken—from that time on, they felt much freer and more powerful, whereas in the past they had always felt outlawed and abandoned. Indeed, they formed, as it were, a state within a state, which is clearly evident in this petition written by a woebegone clergyman whose church and parish were located in a quarter of the city much frequented by prostitutes:

A baptism or a wedding in my church is a really hellish celebration. The procurers and prostitutes appear in public with the most gleaming coaches, the richest costumes, the most numerous retinue, all of which they can afford because they possess the abundant wages of sin. Groups of procurers and mercenary prostitutes, with their lady's maids, surround the clergyman as he performs the ceremony and smile at his reverent mien. The organ and the hymns resound, the chandeliers and the wax tapers burn, the church and the altars are adorned with the costliest pomp, the most beautiful flowers, but what should a pastor preach to such a congregation? The noisy populace gapes outside the church, for crowds of them are lured thither by the lascivious spectacle, and thus the holy act is performed amid lewd cries and shameless display.

At this point, I might also mention the case of the P. family, which earned an historic reputation in the annals of the police and which consisted of a father, a mother and eleven children. Both parents were confirmed thieves and for this reason served long terms in prison; moreover, all the sons were criminals and all the daughters were famous whores. During the wars of liberation the progenitors of this clan had played a role as card-cheats and camp-followers, and the most famous of the daughters was the eldest, whose beauty was causing quite a stir in Berlin.

And now she actually had on the hook an aged but genuine baron who was descended from an old and famous family and who was at this time almost eighty years old; formerly he had even served as an officer, but frivolity, drink and unhappy inclinations had brought him down in the world. In return for her "princely" gift of five thousand talers, a new wardrobe and a giant pike (the old Baron adored eating pike), he actually agreed to marry this prostitute and thus elevate her to the rank of a baroness.

This recent and splendid marriage of one of their own had caused a sensation among the prostitutes of Berlin and their hangers-on, and two of them, out of sheer envy, went so far as to spit into the beautifully decorated wedding coach of their colleague as she travelled to church with her baron.

At that time, a barrel of ignition mechanisms was stolen from a railroad car that was transporting goods belonging to the Sömmerda Armaments Factory, in Erfurt, while the car was in a railroad station in Düsseldorf, where it had spent the night. Private persons could have no interest in stealing such mechanisms, as they could not be put to use unless one also had the weapons they belonged to, and so it was suspected that the theft was the result of espionage activities on the part of Russia, which hoped to replace its antiquated weaponry, which had proved inadequate during the Crimean War, with modern weapons, once it had penetrated the strictly guarded secret of the construction of the newest Prussian armaments.

In the last war between Russia and the nations of the West, Russian weapon supplies were inadequate. Thus, Russia maintained a large number of foreign agents who bought up weapons of all kinds or who had weapons manufactured and then sent them to Russia. In particular, large quantities of weapons were manufactured for the Russians in Belgium and England. However, it was difficult to transport these weapons. At sea, the ships were threatened by the English cruiser, and transport through the German customs union was forbidden because the weapons were regarded as contraband of war.

Thus, the Russians maintained countless middlemen in the German customs union to whom they sent these weapons transports, described as "iron ingots," and who claimed that the "ingots" were destined for their own use. The Russian General Benkendorff directed these transports from his headquarters in Berlin. The English and French ambassadors, in their turn, maintained spies to keep watch on the transports, and towards the end of the war revealed their existence, thus forcing the Prussian government to officially intervene. As a result of these revelations, I myself was forced to confiscate several thousand weapons at the Moreau-Valette royal shipping agency in Berlin.

Although the war had, meanwhile, come to an end, bitter experience in that war caused Russia to take steps to improve its weapons stores, and especially to procure weapons from Germany, for this kind of direct purchase did not violate international treaties; the only thing that violated the treaties was the transport of foreign weapons through Germany.

Disguised as a railroad worker, I conducted an unobtrusive investigation in Düsseldorf that proved that the cargo had been stolen by common thieves who, encouraged by the fact that railway stations are not properly guarded, had thought they could make use of the barrel of ignition mechanisms. If spies had stolen these devices, they could only have done it with a view to subjecting them to chemical analysis, but to achieve this they would only have needed to take one. One can steal a single specimen relatively easily and without attracting attention to what one is doing, as one would if one stole an entire barrel. Certainly, given its relations with the Prussian state, Russia did not need to risk committing such an obvious crime merely in order to procure a single ignition mechanism, which every soldier carries with his cartridges.

Although my investigations revealed that the disappearance of the barrel of ignition mechanisms was not of such a sensational character as had first been supposed, they put me on the trail of a mysterious foreigner (whose features suggested that he was Oriental) who had come to Berlin from Düsseldorf, where he had turned up first, and who introduced himself as Prince Leo of Armenia, a title which gave him undisputed entrée to the best society.

The ostensible Prince had, with a patronizing air, suggested to a middle-class banker that they found an armaments factory together that would manufacture armaments for Russia, and the banker, feeling highly honored, passed on the suggestion to his stockholders. However, to their deep regret, they had to reject the Prince's offer because of lack of funds.

The mysterious foreigner made this proposal with monetary, rather than political, ends in view; however, I concluded that he had intended to deceive the credulous Rhenish bankers. In any case, the alleged Prince intended to impress his ingenuous Rhenish would-be associates by exaggerating his prestige, and to do this he engaged in the pretense, quite irrelevant to his true purpose, that he was engaged in diplomatic missions; he thereby caused quite a sensation. Thus, his correspondence consisted solely of lengthy dispatches; he claimed to receive the visits of couriers, and he displayed documents which, he boasted, had been signed by His Highness the Tsar of Russia.

After failing to involve the Rhenish business community in his projects, the shady Armenian Prince had repeated the same proposals to Prussian merchants in Berlin. I took note of this fact, although, in itself, it provided no pretext for the intervention of the police. The Prince arrogantly claimed that he had been introduced to the King of Prussia in a letter from the Queen of Georgia. Moreover, he spread the rumor that the Tsar of Russia had forcibly dispossessed him of land worth many millions and had paid him a compensation of "only" one million. The ostensible Prince also wore a gleaming star-shaped decoration on his coat. This, he claimed, was the Royal Order of Armenia which every Armenian prince received while he was still in the cradle.

However, what attracted my attention to him and caused me to order a police investigation was the fact that he had denounced his landlord to the police, accusing him of having opened a letter addressed to himself. The supposed Prince said that the letter was a dispatch from his aide-de-camp Amur Khan in London.

However, my investigation of this denunciation revealed that the Prince's complaint was unfounded, because the address on the envelope was almost illegible and the landlord had opened it by mistake. Moreover, the envelope did not contain a dispatch but a bill from the Hoveneder Toiletries Firm in London in which the Prince was addressed as "Amur Khan" and was bluntly ordered to pay for ten jars of hair pomade which he had had delivered to him in London; if he did not pay, the letter said, he would be sued.

This episode convinced me that the Prince was an impostor and that he had staged the denunciation solely in order to be addressed as "Prince" in the police reports relating to the case, thus, as it were, procuring official verification of the validity of his fraudulent princely title. I investigated further and discovered that not only had the "Prince" not submitted a letter of introduction from the Queen of Georgia to the King of Prussia, but that there was no Queen of Georgia; moreover, his claim that the Russian Tsar had seized his property was utter nonsense, and the alleged "Royal Order of Armenia" which the "Prince" wore on his breast was merely a worthless stage prop that the swindler had probably purchased in a junk shop.

Among the papers that I then confiscated from his lodgings, was a letter that had been "sealed" with the side of the Prussian taler bearing the coat of arms and, to judge by the words inscribed on it in French, was a "secret dispatch" from Prince Petrosbey to His Royal Highness the Prince of Armenia; it was addressed to Italy. However, the envelope contained nothing but a blank sheet of paper and an old, worn passport made out in the name of Amur Khan, which, I learned, was the name the impostor had gone by in London. This was the passport with which he had crossed the Prussian border. I also discovered that the "Prince" had written to the editors of the *Almanach de Gotha* under the name "Adjutant Prince Petrosbey," which he had invented, in order to ensure that the almanac would list him as a prince.

Further investigation revealed that several years before, the impostor had spent some time in Berlin under the name of "Prince Koriocz," and that he had been arrested for running up substantial debts. After his arrest, von Puttkamer, who was then Chief of Police, had had him deported. In addition, it was discovered that the supposed Prince had been sentenced to twelve months' imprisonment for fraud in Brussels and to eight months' imprisonment in Paris.

On the other hand, despite all my efforts, I was unable to discover the impostor's true name and where he came from, nor were we able to prove that he had committed any crime during the brief time he had spent in Berlin in the guise of the "Prince." He himself refused to give us any information about his family, his past life or the source of his income, and when my officers and I asked him why he refused to answer, he always replied that even here the police were bribed by the Russian Tsar and that they would steal the "treasure of his nation" if he showed it to us.

All these revelations convinced me that the fraudulent Prince was only a petty rogue who wanted to make himself seem important. It would not have been worthwhile to have brought charges against him for having claimed a fraudulent title, dignities and orders, for in order to procure the necessary evidence it would have been necessary to make more extensive investigations in Paris, Brussels and London, costing too much of the funds set aside for the administration of the law. And after all, the end result would only have been a short prison sentence.

Police Chief von Hinkeldey did not share my opinion. Instead, he assumed that the impostor was a political agent sent to Berlin by the Russian government. Therefore, since he could not keep him in the city jail for longer than a few days, he had him placed in the workhouse as a "homeless vagabond," rather than forcing him to leave the country. By so doing, he hoped that over the course of time, he could compel the prisoner to reveal the truth about himself and the reason he had come to Berlin.

Secretly, I learned that considerations of a delicate nature had moved Police Chief von Hinkeldey to frame this harsh resolution. When we were examining the impostor's papers, von Hinkeldey had shown an interest in a passionate love letter from an aristocratic French lady; he immediately appropriated the letter, and it was not restored to the documents belonging to the "Prince." This lady was no other than Princess Napoleon-Wyse, the cousin of Emperor Louis Napoleon, who had banished her from Paris after she had served there as von Hinkeldey's private agent. The man who claimed to be the Prince of Armenia actually seemed, on the evidence of her letter, to have had a love affair with this lady of exalted station.

The day after the Prince had been turned over to the workhouse, von Hinkeldey subjected him to a rigorous interrogation in his study. During the interrogation the prisoner showed no respect for the Police Chief and scornfully refused to give him any information about himself and his reason for being here, so that finally von Hinkeldey became so enraged at his prisoner's recalcitrance that he summoned the director of the workhouse and expressed his disapproval that the impostor had not been forced to wear the uniform of the workhouse but instead had been permitted to wear his own clothes. (Presumably, the officials at the workhouse had been impressed by the impostor's false air of distinction, and thus had granted him this favor.) The Police Chief gruffly ordered the head of the workhouse not to show the impudent impostor the slightest consideration in the future.

For three months, the pseudo-Prince languished in the workhouse, during which time von Hinkeldey had ordered that he be treated as harshly as possible; however, he stubbornly continued to refuse to give any information about himself.

Then von Hinkeldey finally had the obdurate fellow released and conducted across the Prussian border.

The false Prince had scarcely set foot on foreign soil before he began to write to countless newspapers inside and outside Germany, complaining of his "illegal rape by the Prussian police," who without any legal grounds had kept him prisoner for months. The newspapers were happy to publish these complaints and accusations.

As a result, King Friedrich Wilhelm IV asked me to give him a detailed report of the results of the police investigation of the "Prince," to be sent to the same newspapers so that they could correct their stories.

While all this was going on, I learned that the swindler had been imprisoned for fraud in Vienna and that the Austrian police had finally succeeded in discovering the truth about him.

It appeared that he was a Montenegran by birth and that he had travelled to Paris in his youth, where he acquired an education that was just barely adequate for an Oriental prince and where he later hit on the idea of posing as an Armenian prince. After he had successfully played this role in Paris, London and Brussels, he went to Berlin and then to Vienna.

The Austrian police turned the swindler over to the government of Montenegro, for he had committed countless acts of fraud in Montenegro, too. He was finally rendered incapable of doing further harm when he was sentenced to twelve years in prison in his native land. (Then, in the year 1875, in the newspaper *Die Neuzeit*, Gustav Rasch described his encounter with this adventurer in the Montenegro state prison, which he inspected during a trip to the Black Mountains. The "Prince" was treated fairly well there and made himself useful by teaching languages in the prison school.)

The following letter, which I received soon thereafter and which King Friedrich Wilhelm IV wrote with his own hand, proved to me how carefully the King studied most of the German-language newspapers:

"The attached *Allgemeine-Augsburger-Zeitung* contains some information from Berlin; I want to know where it came from and what its purpose is. I order you to inquire into this matter and also to direct your attention to those responsible for reports which regularly appear in the *Bremer-Weser-Zeitung*, which represent special communications from Berlin and which appear at a time when no one could know about them without the occurrence of a security breach. I order you to be as accurate as possible in your investigations and look forward to hearing your report very soon. Friedrich Wilhelm."

Shortly after receiving this letter I was told by Mrs. von T. (the same woman whose brothel I visited as I have described, but had not subsequently closed or reported) that, after having drunk several bottles of champagne, a man who had visited one of her society ladies had boasted that he knew more state secrets than the King of Prussia himself, and that members of the press went down on their knees before him to beg for information; but he did not betray anything of what he knew until he had been richly rewarded.

Thereupon, I had an interview with the girl in question, a fairly well-educated person of twenty-two, who confirmed the information given me by her employer, told me that her lover was a certain Lieutenant Wagner, and added that he visited her often and threw a lot of money around.

Wagner was secretly placed under police surveillance until we had learned enough to take some action, and our investigations revealed some quite astonishing facts.

Wagner, a tall, handsome, twenty-five-year-old officer in the royal palace guard, who came from an old family of Prussian officers, had fallen prey to wine, women and, above all, games of chance. The latter were chiefly responsible for the fact that he had fallen hopelessly into debt.

Then he became acquainted with a number of writers and newspaper editors to whom he complained about his lack of funds and who said that they knew a way to help him.

The remedy they suggested to Wagner was simple enough: Did he not serve in the King's palace, did he not have access to most of its chambers, and did not those who governed the nation, above all, the King himself, repeatedly discuss legislation and other governmental measures in these chambers and consign them to paper at a time when no other mortal yet knew anything about them? And did he not also have access to documents and reports about political and military questions that arrived at the palace from outside: memoranda, petitions and plans of the most secret and confidential nature—to everything, in fact, that couriers brought to and carried away from the King's residence?

Wagner had only to gain access to these informative conversations and documents and to copy them or take notes on them, or have someone else do this for him, and then to turn over what he had heard and read to the scribblers of the press—in return for a generous reward.

Wagner reached out with both hands for this rope, which promised to rescue him from the sea of debts that was threatening to drown him, and immediately took possession, in the royal palace, of papers belonging to General von Gerlach and his cabinet adviser Niebuhr, including some top secret reports by Count Meinhövel, the Prussian military plenipotentiary in St. Petersburg, containing notes written in the King's own hand. Wagner gave copies of these papers to the press and was immediately paid so well that he became even more daring.

In return for the abundant wages of sin, he now succeeded in approaching an employee of the King. Wagner induced this *valet de chambre* to steal any papers he could from the King's private chambers and to turn them over to him so that he could copy them. In some cases, this servant whom Wagner had bribed even went so far as to copy the papers himself. Among the tragicomic facts that I uncovered was that he did not always deal honorably with Wagner but more than once simply invented, i.e., forged, the material that he claimed he had copied and then gave it to Wagner in return for a generous fee.

However, what really made me angry was the discovery that another servant, whom Wagner had also bribed, was crouching inside a cabinet and listening to me while I was closeted with the King, giving His Majesty a confidential report about the adjudication of offenses committed by members of the press without employing a normal jury (restriction of the freedom of the press).

Wagner immediately sold to the newspapers the information he had gleaned from this interview, which caused a great hue and cry.

The importance ascribed to him and to the material he had revealed went to Lieutenant Wagner's head. The last copies of secret and private documents that he obtained from the royal palace contained information about Prussia's current military situation and led Wagner to believe that they might be of the greatest interest to the French government. Thereupon, Wagner wrote, under a false name, to Rothan, Secretary of the Legation at the French embassy in Berlin, saying that he possessed important secret information, that he wished to offer France his services as a spy, and that he wished to meet with him. If the French ambassadorial staff agreed with his proposals, they were to insert in the Berlin *Vossische Zeitung* a recognition signal that was to read: "Test on July 24 at 4:00 P.M. in the theater union."

In return for the information he had stolen, Wagner immediately received a thousand francs, a greater sum than any he had received from members of the press. He was also told to go to the Rhineland and to discover for the French what was going on there while the King of Prussia was there. However, Wagner, who had grown careless, lied to the Secretary of the French Legation, claiming that he had gone to the Rhineland but that because so many police officers were present, he had not been able to learn anything.

In reality, he had not gone to the Rhineland but had travelled to Nice with his sweetheart, the girl who worked for Mrs. von T., where he had spent most of the thousand francs in riotous living.

The large sums of money he was earning in his new capacity led the insatiable Wagner to offer his services to the Russian embassy as well. In order to increase his income he went so far as to inform the staff at the Russian embassy that he was a secret agent working for the French embassy, and he offered to reveal to the Russian embassy any orders he received from the French embassy.

The Russian embassy in Berlin actually agreed to Wagner's proposal, and thus he simultaneously served as a secret agent for both powers, France and Russia. In his role as a double agent, he was forced to deal more honorably with the Russians than with the French because the Russians did not confide in him but confined themselves to receiving information he had procured from the French embassy.

The discovery of all these facts entitled me to place Wagner under immediate arrest and to search his home. I found what I was looking for: almost eight hundred pages of copies of letters, documents and reports of all descriptions. I also found skeleton-keys to a large number of cabinets in the King's private chambers. Wagner confessed that he had had these keys made with the aid of the King's servants so that he could periodically search the cabinets for private papers that might have been deposited there.

Everything had gone so smoothly for Wagner in the past that he had become careless and, instead of copying stolen documents himself, turned over the job to a professional copyist. I immediately went to the copyist's place of business, and after a brief introductory speech about censorship and the security measures it involved, turned the conversation to the subject of the copyist's employer, the aforesaid Lieutenant Wagner.

"You mean the King's private secretary?" asked the copyist, who clearly did not suspect that anything was amiss. "I didn't know that his name was Wagner. But don't worry, there's nothing for you to be concerned about: I handle these personal commissions from the King very discreetly."

"Commissions from the King?" I asked. "What sort of documents are involved?"

The copyist hesitated, but then his features lost their furrowed look. "There is certainly nothing wrong in my showing it to the police," he said. "I just happen to be working on some copies now."

A few seconds later, filled with horror, I was holding in my hand the top-secret originals of documents that had been removed from the King's desk. Thereupon, I immediately took the copyist and his documents to police headquarters. However, I soon discovered that the forlorn copyist had not believed that he was doing anything wrong but had merely thought that he was performing a service for the King's secretary.

That same day, I held a conference in the royal palace. It was attended by members of the cabinet, court officials and even the King himself.

The monarch had not suspected anything and did not want to believe what I told him until I gave him irrefutable proof, namely the copies Wagner had had made of the King's secret papers.

Meanwhile, additional documents and copies were found in Wagner's elegant apartment, which was decorated with a number of portraits of beautiful ladies, and while my officers were still searching, a courier from the Russian embassy arrived with a large sum of money, the ultimate proof of Wagner's guilt.

Wagner was calm and almost cheerful while I interrogated him in the King's presence. The only thing he cared about was that he had been able to pay all his debts with the money he had earned through his forbidden trade. At his trial, he behaved irreproachably and frequently cursed his former frivolous lifestyle, which had gotten him into debt and thus forced him into the commission of his crimes.

After a brief hearing in closed chambers, he was sentenced to expulsion from the army and ten years at hard labor. His accomplice, the King's servant, who was already sixty years old, received seven years at hard labor.

But then, His Majesty the King decided that Wagner's link with a large number of newspapers inside and outside Prussia, coupled with the fact that the delinquent now had nothing to lose and therefore would not bother to keep his mouth shut, would result in widespread publicity about the sentence which Wagner had received. Thus, the King judged it expedient to buy the silence of Wagner and his confederate by releasing them and giving them a suspended sentence.

Thus, I arranged for the condemned men to be quietly released "with a view to maintaining the greatest possible discretion." This was done out of concern for the current political situation in Prussia, which made it inadvisable to permit any public discussion that might have disturbed the peace.

A second measure the King took in response to this case and that affected the police, led to misinterpretations on the part of the public and, in fact, also led to a dubious exceeding of their authority on the part of the police.

According to the King's well-meant decree, in future cases of "morally hazardous indebtedness," the police, as a precaution, were to work to arrange a settlement between the creditor and the debtor, even though no legal pretext existed for their intervention. The actual result of this directive was that from then on, lazy people who happened to be in debt would call on the police to aid them against their creditors and to enable them to procure some relaxation in the terms of payment.

For the officer assigned to act as mediator began his efforts to achieve a settlement by "looking up," i.e., tracking down the creditor; and of course he was wearing his uniform. If the creditor who was thus tracked down (and whose reputation was jeopardized by a visit from the police) agreed immediately to accept the settlement he was offered, the uniformed officer graciously departed and noted in his duty book: "The party declared that he was satisfied with the arrangement." On the other hand, if the creditor remained obstinate and refused to agree, the officer escorted him to the police station so that there he could formally sign a statement saying that he did not agree to the settlement.

Obviously, these types of "settlements," which were achieved through the power of the police to intimidate people, were not truly just, and everyone came to believe the rumor that police officers often received substantial gifts from debtors for engaging in "arbitration" favorable to themselves.

King Friedrich IV had ordered the police to engage in this activity which was so alien to their profession primarily in order to quietly effect the regulation of the enormous debts of his officers, who fell into the clutches of usurious moneylenders and signed disastrous "promissory notes" that they could not honor. There was a crime involved—usury—but the police were not to treat it as a crime. They were merely supposed to make use of the fact that it was a crime in order to get the moneylenders to waive their claims, and to keep in the army those indebted officers who would lose their positions if it became known that they had broken their word of honor.

Actually the King's decree resulted from a desire to relieve distress, for at that time, half of all the younger officers in the King's army were in the power of unscrupulous moneylenders; indeed, the moneylenders had had forms printed up that the officers were to use for their "declarations of their intention to pay, on their word of honor," and there also existed a horde of "agents" whose duty it was to press loans on young officers who had had no business experience.

Interest of up to one thousand percent was charged for these loans. In many cases, the officers did not even receive money in exchange for the promissory notes they signed so thoughtlessly, yet they were compelled to pay money back if they did not want to lose their posts. As a result, the debtors sometimes committed suicide or murdered their creditors, and at times, the indebted officers were blackmailed by shady customers into performing all sorts of dubious services.

Moreover, it was precisely the most efficient and capable officers in the army who became entangled in debt, and thus, finally, the King decreed that it was illegal for anyone to accept promissory notes from an officer; he also ordered the police to take energetic steps to prevent the usurious moneylenders from doing so.

On this account, I was summoned to my sovereign and received from his own mouth the strictest instructions about how to proceed. He also gave me money from the privy purse to be used when neither the indebted officers nor their families could pay back immediately all the monies that had been lent to them. At the same time, the King conferred on every single one of my officers the express authority to "noiselessly" cancel debts in this manner.

The regulations were enforced by the police, who confiscated all the bills and promissory notes of the indebted officers. The usurers were, to be sure, to be repaid, along with the interest to which they were entitled by law, but not the interest they had originally demanded, greatly exceeding that to which they were legally entitled.

The police would avoid arresting a usurer only if a settlement could be achieved smoothly. If the usurer refused to agree to the settlement, according to the universal laws of the land, he was to get back nothing and instead would be reported and arrested for practicing usury. It is no wonder that the usurers drew in their horns as a result of this police pressure.

Until the year 1857, I was kept busy eradicating debts by these admittedly coercive means and did not suspect that the good intentions of the King, in causing these debts to be wiped out, was destined to cost one of his most capable police officers his life.

When the police arrived to close down a gambling club for officers which, despite the law forbidding such clubs, was being run by wealthy usurers in the distinguished Tiergarten quarter of Berlin, Police Chief von Hinkeldey darted into the gaming room ahead of all his officers in order to seize the money and gambling paraphernalia before they could be disposed of, and thus to procure evidence of the fact that unlawful gambling had, in fact, been going on there.

There he came to grips with Mr. von Rochow-Plessow, who was in charge of the bank. Von Rochow-Plessow called von Hinkeldey an informer and a thief, whereupon, von Hinkeldey, greatly agitated, stated that von Rochow-Plessow had committed a crime against the State because he had violated the King's prohibition, which was expressly designed to prevent his irreplaceable officers from continuing to get into debt.

Thereupon, von Rochow-Plessow challenged Police Chief von Hinkeldey to a duel with pistols, and von Hinkeldey immediately chose me, the head of the Berlin police force, to act as an "impartial judge," which I resolutely refused to do. However, von Hinkeldey pointed out that my professional honor forbade me to refuse without a sound reason.

Thereupon, I asked von Hinkeldey to bear in mind that von Rochow-Plessow was a crack shot, and pointed out to the Police Chief that von Rochow-Plessow had challenged him because he was doing his duty, and that therefore, according to the same code of honor, he was entitled to refuse.

But the inflexible von Hinkeldey was foaming with rage at the "ignorant Junkers," who, as he expressed it, needed to be taught a lesson, and doom took its course!

The battle arena chosen by von Rochow-Plessow, who was the owner of an estate, lay, as seemed quite sensible, in the old Berlin cemetery, and when our two-horse carriage, occupied by von Hinkeldey, his second and me, came to a halt there early in the morning, the first ghostly light of dawn was falling on the gravestones, both those that were still erect and those that had already fallen over, and at that same instant, startled night-birds rose into the air and fluttered soundlessly around our heads.

The sight of something living above the field of death would certainly have sent a shudder through souls more sensitive than ours, but I noticed that von Hinkeldey did not spare a glance for this uncanny sight and merely spat with an air of contempt.

Then the seconds, with pedantic accuracy, made von Hinkeldey and von Rochow-Plessow pace off the proper distance through the wet grass, whereupon the duellists assumed their positions and took off their overcoats so that their white shirts glowed in the morning light. Then the two seconds walked over to the principals and handed them their weapons. (Von Rochow-Plessow used a fearfully long-barrelled, large-caliber cavalryman's pistol, whereas von Hinkeldey relied on his police weapon.)

Thereupon, von Hinkeldey gestured to me. Leaving my place a little off to the side I walked over to him, and he gave me a small key, quickly explaining that it belonged to a box in his desk whose contents I was to destroy in case . . . ! The imploring tone in which he spoke, without looking at me and without fully expressing his thought, cut me to the quick.

Then we heard the piercing, commanding voice of von Rochow-Plessow echo across the field, asking whether von Hinkeldey did not want to take back the insults with which he had sullied his honor. But von Hinkeldey replied in an equally audible voice that he had only done his duty as a police officer and that there was no way he could withdraw now.

Thereupon, von Rochow-Plessow, who as the insulted party was entitled to fire the first shot, stretched out the arm with which he held his weapon, took calm and careful aim at von Hinkeldey, who was standing erect not far away, and pulled the trigger.

A streak of fire shot from the long barrel of his weapon, and as the shot thundered forth, abruptly breaking the stillness of the morning, hundreds of startled crows rose up from the tall trees of the cemetery as a discordant croaking and screeching, like the sounds of a hellish inferno, issued from countless throats.

When I opened my eyes I saw von Rochow-Plessow standing erect in his place, but von Hinkeldey had disappeared.

But then I saw the doctor and the seconds running over to the place where he had been standing, and by the time I got there, von Hinkeldey was lying dead in the grass with his eyes wide open.

Just before leaving to fight the duel, von Hinkeldey had written a letter to King Friedrich Wilhelm IV in which he asked his employer to forgive him for having accepted the challenge without having first sought to gain His Majesty's consent. This letter did not reach the King, who at that time was residing in Charlottenburg, until after the duel had been fought, and soon after it arrived von Münchhausen, von Hinkeldey's second, appeared at the door to bring the King the shocking news of von Hinkeldey's death.

At the same time I had resorted to von Hinkeldey's study, now abandoned, at police headquarters and locked the door from the inside, preparatory to opening the dead man's strongbox with the key he had given me in the last minute of his life.

To my surprise, in addition to some private notes concerning the most exalted representatives of the government, the locked box that stood on von Hinkeldey's worktable contained a bundle of letters tied together with a silk ribbon. I soon saw that these were love letters of the most passionate kind, written to von Hinkeldey by the woman, whom I have already mentioned, whom I had assumed to be the lover of the swindler, the false "Prince of Armenia."

However, on top of the bundle of letters lay another letter in the same handwriting, but this time addressed to Amur Khan and bearing a recent date. It was the love letter that this lady had sent to the spurious "Prince of Armenia," that von Hinkeldey had found in the "Prince's" lodgings and had kept for himself instead of returning it to the files, and that had moved him to take charge of the entire case and to behave severely toward the recipient of the letter by sending him into the workhouse instead of doing as I had suggested, regarding him as a petty swindler, and forcing him to cross the Prussian border.

I quickly gathered up all the letters and notes in von Hinkeldey's box, concealing them in the pocket of my coat, and had scarcely finished when someone knocked at the locked door. A courier, who had searched for me for a long time before being told my whereabouts, brought me the news that the King wanted to pay his respects to the dead man, who would be lying in state at police headquarters, that very day, but that his advisers were concerned that the Molkenmarkt, which was located in front of police headquarters, might be very crowded and that the crowds might endanger the King. His Majesty wanted to hear my opinion before he proceeded.

I replied to the courier, without delay, that I was convinced that the King need not hesitate to come to police headquarters; and that I should guarantee that he would not be subjected to any outrageous behavior during his journey from the palace and across the Molkenmarkt.

That same day, the King did indeed travel to the house of mourning in his town carriage, drawn by two horses, through a vast and mute crowd of people extending from the palace to the Molkenmarkt, and nothing untoward occurred. After the obsequies the monarch returned to the Charlottenburg Palace in a subdued frame of mind and withdrew for the evening to think about that high-ranking officer who had fallen in a duel.

Later, the King admitted to me that the mute mourning and sympathy of his people, whose reaction I had so correctly predicted, had moved him most deeply. I kept silent, and through my mind there flashed a picture of that box of letters whose contents I had seized a short time ago in compliance with the dead man's instructions.

Although my relationship with von Hinkeldey had been a purely professional one, I now did everything I could for his bereaved family. The King ordered me to give him a detailed report of the matter and to propose the sum necessary for the generous support of the widow and her children. However, the members of the Ministry, who had not been kindly disposed towards von Hinkeldey, allowed the matter to drag on for weeks without taking any action. I complained to the King about this "shameful delay" and brought this sad affair to a swift and, for von Hinkeldey's family, happy conclusion.

Then something unexpected occurred. King Friedrich Wilhelm IV became incurably ill with a brain tumor in 1857, and that same year, because he himself had no children, turned over the reins of government to his younger, "liberal"-minded brother Wilhelm. As a result, men of "liberal" sympathies took over many government posts that had previously been held by men who were "reactionary" in their thought and actions.

The public hoped for the most favorable results from this change of policy. They hoped that the changes taking place would bring an end to the "coercive rule" of the police, which, in actual practice, continued to exist, and would finally bring about the application and materialization of the more liberal laws that had already been agreed upon in 1848 and 1849.

A speech by the new Prince Regent, expressing broad-minded views and attracting a great deal of notice, appeared to justify these hopes, for in it he stated that "reforms should be introduced in areas characterized by obsolescence and by phenomena opposed to the needs of a new age."

However, for the time being, Simons, the Minister of Justice, and Schwarck, his much-feared Attorney General, neither of whom could be immediately replaced, were allowed to retain their posts even under the new, more liberal régime. They now took pains to cultivate as conspicuous a "proliberal" attitude as possible and offered spectacular proofs of the same. In order to prevent any discussion of their former activities, which had been anything but liberal, they eagerly looked around for scapegoats to whom they could shift all the blame for their past actions.

I, who continued to hold my former post as head of the Berlin police force, must have seemed to them a perfect scapegoat, and they were prepared to sacrifice me if it would help them to save their own skins.

However, what they appeared to have forgotten was that an attempt to shift the blame to me might bring about their own destruction, for I, as their subordinate, compelled to carry out their wishes, had been forced to obey their written orders and had, moreover, kept these orders in a place accessible only to me.

But, perhaps, they did suspect that I might have kept their orders, for they quite unexpectedly (at least they believed that it was unexpectedly; in reality, I had foreseen their tactics) sent a group of police officers to my private residence to search for records and documents that might be incriminating to them.

This search took place on the evening of April 13, 1860. Four horse-drawn carriages came to a halt outside my house on the Alexanderstrasse in Berlin. Rain was pouring down and a large number of police officers wrapped in inconspicuous cloaks of a type worn by civilians knocked at my door. I opened the door, holding a sharp knife in my hand, for I was in the middle of my evening meal. The men greeted me and their leader said sympathetically, "I'm sorry, Director, but we have orders to search your house."

I looked calmly at the officers, all of whom I knew well, and then I just said curtly, "Do your duty."

Hereupon, the plainclothes policemen hurried into my home as if an entire band of robbers were hiding there. Indeed, some of them even watched me suspiciously as I made my way to the lavatory, thus ensuring that I could not conceal anything in this secluded place.

All my books and clothes were ripped out of the cabinets, and the officers even confiscated a half-completed note that was lying on my desk, in which I requested my housekeeper to mend some holes in my laundry.

However, because I had, as I have stated, safely concealed in another place what the officers were seeking, they had to accept the fact that they had failed and had to be satisfied to take possession of my person. They led me, walking in their midst, to the Berlin city jail, attracting great attention from passers-by.

Like wildfire, the word had soon spread throughout Berlin: Something incredible, something unprecedented has happened; the head of the Berlin police has been arrested, has himself become a prisoner of the police!

Now I crouched on a musty sack filled with straw, gazing gloomily at a jar of water, in one of those dimly-lit cells in which, in carrying out my past duties, I had so often confined criminals of the most varied description, and which, besides a hard bed and a stinking toilet bucket, contained nothing but cockroaches and mice.

My thoughts became even gloomier because of the fact that the news of my arrest was spreading like a high wind through the jail, as well as outside it, and that I was welcomed with a ghastly howl of scorn from the neighboring dungeon, in which several rogues were apparently confined. The mocking sounds continued until I cried in a sharp tone: "Just wait—as soon as I get out, I'll take care of you rascals personally!" Instantly, there was silence.

I finally controlled my anger at the machinations of my adversaries, who had so unscrupulously thrown me into prison, with the reflection that they had not wanted to attack me personally so much as to save their own skin, which was being threatened. As a result of this insight my thoughts grew calm and clarity was restored!

The next day I was visited by Attorney General Schwarck, who seemed to me all the more dangerous because of the extreme friendliness which he displayed from the outset! I knew only too well, from the interrogations of criminals that we had often conducted together, what he had in mind. I felt like a butterfly that has finally been captured and which its malicious captor is about to impale on a pin so that he can add it to his collection.

"It really distresses me to see such an important man in such unfortunate circumstances," the hypocrite mocked, and then, instead of inquiring into any crime I was supposed to have committed, asked me about something quite different:

"Director, where do you keep your official records?" he asked with something bordering on curiosity. When I merely replied that the officers under his command could not have been searching my house to find records, the Attorney General made a desperate attempt to pin me down. He accused me of having had a false passport, which had been found in my house.

However, because he could not present me with the evidence (because it did not exist) and could offer no sound reason for having arrested me, I turned the tables on him and protested violently against his behavior, whereupon Schwarck left without a word.

From then on, I feverishly sought an opportunity to escape my unlawful imprisonment, and finally found it the following morning, when religious services were held.

After all the prisoners had taken their places in the prison church, the minister began to preach. While he was preaching, I slipped through an opening in the side of the organ and, before the organist began to play, loosened one of the little pipes. When the organist pulled out all the stops and began his chorale, its solemn tones were disrupted by the hideously discordant sound coming from the loosened pipe.

The effect was all I could have wished for: The organist stopped playing and appeared to be on the point of swearing out loud. His organ seemed to be defective, and no one could repair it except me; for I boldly claimed that in my youth I had studied the craft of organ-building.

In their distress those in charge were ready to believe my thumping lie and sent me, with a guard, to the prison workshop, to look for the proper tools.

Although my repairs were completed as soon as I had put the organ pipe back in place, I created such confusion around the organ that my guard lost sight of me.

And as I finally left the scene where I had pretended to work so busily, I was concealing two sharp sawblades against my naked breast; and the following night, when the guards had barely completed their rounds, began to saw away at the bars of my window. I was careful to dribble water from my jar onto the bars in order to conceal the sound of the saw, which might have betrayed me.

After working zealously for two nights I succeeded in cutting away the grate, lifted it out, and swung myself through the empty hole onto the roof lying opposite. In total darkness, I made my way across the ridge of the roof to the adjacent wall that surrounded the prison, jumped down onto its broad summit, and thence to freedom. No one saw or stopped me.

At once, I hurried away from the prison which was, alas, so familiar, and hastened through the dark night to the place where I had hidden the documents that proved that I was absolutely innocent. Carrying this precious burden in my arms, I then moved through the dark streets of Berlin to the house of Mrs. von T., whose discreet establishment I had once, in my role as a police officer, preserved from scandal, which act of generosity was now to prove my salvation.

Mrs. von T. had already read about my bad luck in the newspapers and, without asking any questions, quartered me and my burden in a room belonging to her lady's maid, that could be reached only from her bedroom, through a concealed door.

She showed her gratitude, not only by providing me with this secret sanctuary, but also by giving me some of the sumptuous fare which was daily served up from her kitchen, so that I soon felt as snug as a bug in a rug.

In this hidden sanctuary, where—as I believed—none of my adversaries would ever come to look for me, I now established my secret "command headquarters," to which Mrs. von T. every day brought the most up-to-date newspapers. From these, I finally learned what I was accused of.

The charge against me was nothing less than "unlawful deprivation of freedom and abuse of his authority as head of the Berlin police force," and at the beginning of the story was written in the largest letters the typesetter could find: "Director escapes from prison! Police conducting a search! Warning: Stieber is armed!"

Not only was the latter statement an impudent lie (for I never carried a weapon), but so were the misrepresentations, falsifications and slander that from then on flooded my hiding place from the daily newspapers.

One "witness for the prosecution" had sworn that he had several times heard me "praise the reactionary conditions" which had existed, and another swore that I had subjected his wife (arrested for theft) to "unethical threats." When it appeared that these unproven claims provided insufficient grounds to bring any action against me, they were quickly supplemented by another charge, "suspicion of having stolen official records."

To achieve their purposes, my enemies searched the house of an artist whom I had commissioned to paint my portrait some years before, and when this search produced no results, they subjected my housekeeper, in violation of the law, to a highly embarrassing interrogation, at the same time, threatening to arrest her if she did not reveal my whereabouts (the wretched woman did not have the slightest idea where I was).

All this made it clear to me that my adversaries had absolutely no evidence against me. After weeks of investigation they were back where they had started. And because they had had nothing to begin with, I was left to puzzle over the question of what they would accuse me of next; but I could find no answer.

Unexpectedly, after midnight, at an hour at which, as I knew all too well, it was customary to engage in such enterprises, a troop of police officers surrounded the peacefully-sleeping house of Mrs. von T. and demanded admittance. After opening the door my hostess barely had time to throw a woolen shawl around her neck and jump into my bed, concealing me beneath the feather coverlet. To prevent the searchers from coming too close, she claimed that she was sick and had a fever.

As I lay completely still against the soft, warm limbs of Mrs. von T., none of the intruders, who were turning everything upside down, dared to approach our bed, either out of consideration for the "sick" woman or because they were afraid of catching something.

My head pressed to her swelling breast like that of a helpless child, and my arms wrapped around her body, which was trembling with fear, like those of a drowning man, I awaited, still as stone, the end of the "persecution." But when I was also forced to hear my protectress, with a courage born of despair, explain that the bump in the coverlet made by my concealed body was caused by her hot-water bottle, despite the danger, I was almost sent into a paroxysm of laughter.

Finally the searchers took their leave, leaving chaos behind them, and the door had barely shut when, half suffocated, I threw back the covers and tried to catch my breath.

Before arriving at the house of Mrs. von T., I had promised myself to avoid making any advances to my hostess for fear of placing myself too completely in her power, but now I was forced to break this oath in the presence of her charming body, which she offered to me unveiled and triumphant. Given my situation, what would have become of me if I had wounded her with my reserve or even made an enemy of her!

Thus I threw discretion to the winds, and the certainty that together we had successfully survived our danger united us in grateful rapture!

Later I learned from Mrs. von T. that my worst enemy, Simons, the Minister of Justice, was among her most aristocratic visitors, and that she was expecting him here this week as usual. The very next evening, a delectable thing happened: Not suspecting that I was present, the Prussian Minister of Justice visited my charming hostess, while I crouched behind the concealed door and heard every word he said.

Mrs. von T. and I had agreed that when her exalted guest arrived she would, as if by chance, steer the conversation around to my spectacular fall from grace, and she did this, exercising her powers of womanly dissimulation so convincingly that even I believed she was being completely straightforward. Then I heard the Minister's voice, roughened with tobacco smoke, clearly reply that the Attorney General had demanded that I be placed under arrest, whereas he, the Minister of Justice, had been against it because he could not find any solid evidence against me. None of the evidence that had so far been discovered had stood up to close scrutiny.

While I tried to rejoice in this confession from the leader of the opposition, my satisfaction was embittered again by the sounds that revealed that the carefree visitor was making advances to my hostess, and that now penetrated through the concealed door with the same clarity as the words he had spoken.

The following morning the Berlin press published something that really represented the straw that broke the camel's back. Because my adversary, Attorney General Schwarck, wanted at all costs to resolve the proceedings against me in a way that would be favorable to himself, he published a "general invitation" in all the newspapers of our capital, asking anyone who had any complaints against the fallen head of the Berlin police force to report to him immediately.

Gnashing my teeth, I was forced to read in the gazettes that the criminals of Berlin were apparently having a field-day at my expense. In order to bring charges against me it had to be proved that I had broken the law or at least done something irregular, and now testimony of the most dubious sort was wrung out of people who had been convicted of several crimes and even those who had been convicted of perjury—all of whom I had once punished for their crimes.

When a scoundrel námed Luger *(nomen est omen!)*° turned up and, lying through his teeth, reported that during his interrogation, I had not only carried a horsewhip, but had also put it to effective use (I did not own a whip), this fictitious "testimony" pleased my accuser so much that, drunk with victory, he boldly proclaimed, in words that were likewise quoted in the newspapers: "This revelation will scare Stieber out of his wits! The accused is done for, and we have him just where we want him!"

But now, I saw that the time had arrived for me to take action. Relying on the irrefutable records and documents that recorded

---

° The name Luger closely resembles the German *Lügner,* or "liar."—Tr.

the history of my service as a police officer, I composed, while remaining in my hiding place, a passionate written defense to which I gave the title, "Forced to Defend Myself," and in which I not only established my complete innocence, but charged my accusers with all the crimes of which they had accused me. I mailed this revelatory text to all the newspapers, without giving them my present address.

I had done something that no Prussian official had ever dared to do before: I called on public opinion to aid me against my superiors. I revealed, irrefutably and on the basis of my official records, that all the illegal acts my former superiors and present accusers charged me with having committed on my own authority were really committed under express written orders from them, and that frequently I, also in writing, had expressed my opposition to these orders. Thus, they were lying when they swore today that they had not had the slightest notion of what I was doing!

I took care to be precise and noted the numbers and descriptions of the documents, so that anyone could have found the corresponding duplicates in my office (provided, of course, that they had not been removed).

The Berlin press published my far-from-tactful apologia as greedily as they had formerly printed the boasts of my accusers. Thus, the "case of Stieber, head of the Berlin police" turned into an unprecedented "duel in the press," and my name actually became a byword all over Prussia!

At the beginning of the letter, I had made no less a claim than that the liberal constitution which King Friedrich Wilhelm IV had, with the best intentions, imposed on the nation in 1848, had distorted and falsified my activities as head of the Berlin police force because from the time it first began to take effect, the constitution itself had been *forged!*

The same year "fraudulent elections" were held in Prussia; their results were falsified so that the reactionary forces in the land once again became the majority and regained political control.

The King resisted their pressure to restore the old order, based on class distinction, and did not want to take away the liberal constitution that he had just finished granting; but it was changed, at the instigation of the conservatives, so that a "powerful ruling body could govern."

The result was the forged constitutional charter of 1850, that simply suppressed many of the liberal laws that had just been enacted, eliminating them from the text.

Nevertheless, the King approved the text, disfigured as it was, and merely expressed the "personal wish" that it would be administered in a way suitable to the "new conditions of modern life."

Minister of Justice Simons, after securing his position, did everything in his power to twist the meaning of the King's modest wish and attempted, one by one, to curtail and abolish the remaining innovations.

Thus, the magisterial power of the police was quietly restored, and "political" trials continued to be held without benefit of a jury. However, the liberal reformation of criminal procedure and the resultant limitations on the power of the police were the "red flags" that really aroused the wrath of the incorrigible Simons, the Minister of Justice, and Attorney General Schwarck, who was as like him as if they were two peas in a pod.

In the past, the police had had the right to hold suspects in custody until their innocence or guilt had been determined, but the new, more liberal laws forbade them to do so and did not permit an arrest until after offenses had been investigated.

The new laws were so closely bound to the text of the new constitution that to have openly suppressed them would have been tantamount to violating the constitution. Even the reactionaries could not bring themselves to take such a radical step, for they feared that if they did so, they might reawaken the wrath of the people.

Therefore, they acknowledged the troublesome new laws as a matter of form, but in practice, and in secret, they ignored and broke them.

Thus, in accordance with written orders, that I quoted, from Simons and Schwarck, prisoners were arrested and held in custody for weeks or months, although the new law expressly ordered that within twenty-four hours they should be taken before a judge so that he could determine whether they should be released or should remain under arrest.

In my combined apologia and indictment I offered proof of countless cases in which, in accordance with express orders, signed by the Minister of Justice and the Attorney General, "politically suspect persons" were illegally held in the custody of the Berlin police for periods of up to a year and nine months. Their cases were not heard by a judge, and no judge was called in to determine whether they should remain under arrest.

I also revealed the fact that both the Minister of Justice and the Attorney General had secretly sanctioned the practice, on the part of influential people, of using the police for purposes that were not only alien, but actually opposed to the administration of public justice. These people could have persons they did not like arrested, and no duly appointed court would learn about it; they could also conceal and suppress all traces of offenses they had committed themselves.

In addition, I quoted, in a way that could not be refuted, records that the Minister of Justice and the Attorney General intervened in cases involving disputes between family members, and other cases that had nothing to do with criminal law, employing coercive measures as they saw fit; they repeatedly employed the services of my police officers to carry out their private wishes and conduct their private business, in a way that made it impossible for me to take steps to prevent them from doing so. My tyrannical superiors ordered houses searched and property confiscated whenever they chose and without any legal justification, and Attorney General Schwarck even went so far as to evince his open contempt for the sentences of judges by secretly arresting again people who had been released by the courts!

My superiors were fully aware that they were breaking the law and abusing their power and felt completely secure in doing so. In 1852, they held a secret conference with officers subordinate to them (I was among them), at which they took counsel with them as to how one could, in practice but "without incurring any risk," get around the new liberal law guaranteeing personal liberty contained in the 1850 constitution.

When Attorney General Schwarck openly confessed that if he continued to obey the new laws, he would no longer guarantee that he could maintain order in the capital, his superior, Minister of Justice Simons, expressly agreed that in order to maintain security in Berlin we were "permitted to cast off all the new laws which fettered the police."

Along with the other records, I also had in my possession the word-for-word minutes of this secret conference and did not hesitate to allude to them when I wrote my exposé. I also alluded to the fact that Attorney General Schwarck had put the crowning touch on all his illegal acts by sending me written orders to the effect that in future, my police should "have no scruples in setting an example" by taking energetic action, a statement which in effect encouraged us beforehand to twist the laws to suit our own purposes.

The relentless letter of indictment that circumstances had forced me to write and every point of which I had, as I have already stated, verified by a reference to the appropriate document, was enormously successful! In a hearing held immediately, I was acquitted because my "innocence had been established" of the charges brought against me, which all proved to be unsupported. At the hearing, the court cited all the arguments and incidents that I had brought forward.

However, my greatest triumph was the fact that, as a result of my vindication, my two accusers, Minister of Justice Simons and Attorney General Schwarck, were removed from office, if for no other reason than because the irrefutable evidence I had presented proved they had been lying when they claimed they had known nothing about the breaches of the law that had occurred.

To make my victory complete, I now dedicated myself to taking revenge against those criminals in Berlin who had been so willing to blacken my reputation with their base lies. I was all the more eager to punish them because such punishment would, at the same time, serve the common good.

I knew that, like all criminals, the scoundrels of Berlin could make a living from their "trade" only if they could sell their booty at a profit.

Thus, if I were to secretly set up a fictitious establishment, staffed by my officers, for the receiving of stolen goods, I should not only capture the criminals who unsuspectingly came there to sell their booty, but could also set in motion a wave of arrests that would decimate the Berlin underworld.

Later, I could not remember exactly how I had hit on the plan, but it had scarcely taken shape in my mind before I began to carry it out. It was my intention that police officers who had been selected and trained especially for this purpose would be released from regular duty and set up as "fences." If they were not to betray their true identity they would have to act and speak exactly like their underworld clientèle.

The three officers I selected for this dangerous task were the son of an impoverished baron, who had been a police officer for years and had proved his worth, a former wrestler who had also served me faithfully for years, and an ex-actor who, of all my officers, was the most successful at tracking down criminals.

Whereas the powerful wrestler was to serve as the doorman in my nest of fences and to protect it from encroachments of any sort, the clever nobleman played the proprietor of my fictitious firm, while the actor, his sharp eyes hidden behind a pair of (non-prescription) spectacles and his straight body padded so that he looked flabby and fat, posed as the bookkeeper.

I had a go-between rent an empty warehouse that would be run by my factitious fences, in a location that would attract criminals because they could reach it without being seen. Additional officers would be concealed there to observe the business dealings between my officers and members of the underworld and to identify wanted criminals so that they could be arrested later; thanks to the solid evidence we gathered, these criminals could be tried and sentenced quickly.

I supervised my officers as they studied their roles inside the closed warehouse, almost as if we were in a theater. After they had their roles down pat, my three officers, all in disguise, assumed their new duties as fences in an area where these criminals were most active. In front of the warehouse waited a truck I had also rented, bearing the inscription "Lehmann & Co., Shippers." Lehmann was actually the name of one of my police officers, while I, in a melancholy mood, related the "& Co." to the police force.

Armed police officers hidden inside the truck observed through concealed openings all the customers who entered my fictitious fences' headquarters. In other respects, too, I had thought of everything: "Transport orders" sealed with genuine seals arrived in the mail every day, although they contained nothing but blank paper and were fabricated by the police, as were the many crates, bales and bundles in my spacious storeroom containing nothing but rags and tow.

I commissioned secret police-agents to get busy and spread the word in the Berlin underworld about the new buyer who paid extremely high prices for goods of all kinds; thus I laid out the bait. And my methods were effective: Soon scoundrels from all over the city were streaming, with their loot, to the new fence whom they had heard so much about, as moths are attracted to a flame; and because my industrious officers, taking care not to betray themselves by a word or a gesture, promptly forked over top dollar for their goods, soon every criminal in town knew where he could quickly and profitably turn "hot" goods into cash.

Night after night, my officers-in-disguise loaded onto the truck all the stolen goods they had ransomed and stored in my warehouse, and secretly drove it to police headquarters by a roundabout route. There I had my "harvest" recorded and conducted an investigation to find out which of the goods had been recently stolen, so that I could return them to their owners.

Within a short time, my tireless police force had raked in mountains of stolen goods, and I was forced to bring their expensive traffic to a halt, for the man who had financed my private campaign of vengeance, a banker friend of mine, could not advance me any more money against my far-from-luxurious salary.

The list of scoundrels, whose identities we had not known but who now constantly frequented my fencing establishment, grew longer and longer and finally became so long that I decided the time had come for me to strike. For a long time now, I had had more than enough circumstantial evidence to justify arresting most of my zealous suppliers.

Thus, at cockcrow when, as I knew by experience, most criminals were still enjoying undeserved slumbers, my officers took to the streets and in one single surprise attack arrested around thirty of the most infamous criminals, whom up to this point we had sought in vain, and who had revealed to my fictitious fences where they were hiding. They were all so surprised that they did not try to resist when my officers grabbed them and immediately locked them up behind bars.

More criminals were captured on this occasion than the Berlin police had ever captured before in a single raid, and the bills of indictment that the judges quickly drew up ensured swift adjudication. All the men I had caught in the act were convicted; some were sentenced to a few months in prison, most to a number of years.

This event dealt a severe blow to the underworld in the Prussian capital, but it brought me a great deal of satisfaction. My act of revenge against the criminals of Berlin had been a resounding success, as much a success as the letter I had written to defend myself against the men who had accused me falsely. But I had been counting my chickens before they were hatched: Despite the undisputed success of my latest coup as a policeman, I was suddenly, out of a clear blue sky, placed on "temporary reserve," i.e., given a leave of absence from my post as head of the Berlin police.

This painful and completely unexpected blow was dealt me by the new Prince Regent, Wilhelm himself, who suspected that people would no longer regard the "highest-ranking crimefighter" in his capital with the proper respect after this crimefighter—rightly or wrongly—had publicly quarrelled with his superiors in the press. He feared that, at least in the near future, neither his subordinates nor wrongdoers would "obey" such a man! Thus, against my will I became a private citizen, reduced to living on the small salary accorded an officer who was not on active duty. But just as no cat every really leaves off chasing mice, so I too continued to keep my ear to the ground, and soon I learned such a terrible piece of news that the detective in me was immediately reactivated, indeed galvanized into action: Through a foreigner I had formerly used as a go-between, I discovered nothing less than that unknown persons were planning to assassinate the newly appointed Premier of Prussia, Otto von Bismarck.

PART THREE

The assassination attempt was only a rumor, but I realized at once that it would take too long to check out the facts, and that, instead, the probable victim should be warned as soon as possible.

Although I had no time left to investigate the matter, I did have time to find out something about the intended victim. A short time later, through a former police detective, I had gathered informative but alarming data about the man.

According to this data, the man whom the Regent had recently appointed to guide Prussian politics had not only pleaded passionately for the restoration of all class privileges and attacked all opponents of such a restoration as "envious men without property," but at the same time—and here, certainly, was the key to the terrible fate that had been planned for him—had advocated that "Prussia engage in a struggle with Austria to determine which nation should hold the ascendancy in this world."

When a liberal Member of Parliament attacked the speaker as "Germany's prodigal son," Bismarck fervently replied, "Prussia is my fatherland, and when it summons me to its banners, I always harken to its call."

These sharp words provoked an equally sharp echo among Prussian liberals, as well as among our ever-suspicious critics abroad. In fact, even the King of Prussia found fault with his new Premier's maiden address, saying, "He would experience nothing but pleasure when the bayonet holds unbounded sway!"

There was universal fear of a Prussia "ruled by the sabre," and the Austrian press even warned, "Let us beware that firebrand, for he really intends to practice what he preaches!"

Thus, I considered it possible that the enemies of such an outlaw, so grimly swimming against the current of our age, might be planning his "timely" downfall, and I decided to speak to him as soon as possible.

Prussia's new Premier, Otto von Bismarck, was a tall and powerful-looking man, but he also captivated me with his charm and thus turned out to be completely different from what his public conduct had led me to believe he would be like. He even looked different from pictures I had been shown of him, for his eyes had a soft, almost dreamy look. However, his powers as a speaker were evident even in conversation, and I had to confess that I was fascinated by the man.

After introducing myself, I spent more than an hour with

Bismarck, not concealing the fact that I had been given a leave of absence and was now a "reserve" officer. (He appeared to know what had happened, at least in its main outlines.) Without trying to spare his feelings, I told him about my fears for his safety, although I did not tell him what I thought was the cause of the threat, for it was not for me to criticize the words and deeds of the Premier of Prussia!

Bismarck answered skeptically, and as if the idea amused him, "You're imagining things . . . Now if I wore a crown! Where did you dig up this horror story?"

I answered in a tone of entreaty, "A detective hears more than other people do, and finds things out in time to do something about them!"

Then Bismarck stood up, offered me his right hand and laughed, "All right then, I'll do whatever you say. What do you, as a policeman, plan to do to protect me?"

Feeling relieved, I explained the plan I had devised some time ago, which had to do with the route the Premier invariably took when he went to his office.

I ordered that, rather than travelling this same route all the time, my charge should, for a while, cease to use his coach, which was familiar to everyone, and travel in hired carriages, a different one each time, and should always go by a different route.

Moreover, instead of wearing his hat, which everyone knew well, I advised the Premier to wear some other kind of hat or to wear none at all. Indeed, I should have preferred that he change the way he wore his hair and the appearance of his beard as well.

Again, I urgently entreated this man who, as I believed, was being careless, for his own sake, to obey my instructions. "If you do, it could save your life," I admonished him with heartfelt urgency. Bismarck continued to be skeptical, but he was impressed by my persistent and genuine concern and finally gave me a free hand to take whatever measures I chose.

The first thing I did was to pay an extremely surprised tailor a healthy sum for a life-sized dummy which, painted with the features of a distinguished gentleman and dressed in the latest fashions, was adorning the showcase window. After I had dressed the dummy in Bismarck's hat and coat, I tied it with invisible ropes inside the Prussian Premier's coach, leaning back in the corner in the posture in which Bismarck usually sat.

I had this equipage, carrying the dummy, continue to travel its usual route at the accustomed hour, while an inconspicuous hired carriage carried the Premier to his destination by a circuitous route.

It was not long before we learned how right I had been to take these precautions. A few days later, when the Prussian Premier's coach, containing the dummy, was halfway to the ministry, an individual at the edge of the street, who until that time had behaved quite unobtrusively, suddenly drew a pistol and shot through the coach window, hitting my dummy in the forehead so that, as I later learned, to my fury, the bullet emerged from the back of its head and flew through the window opposite into the open air.

The insidious unknown sharpshooter was immediately overwhelmed by the police who, at my command, had been patrolling the route travelled by Bismarck's coach, and turned out to be a disciple of the professional Russian revolutionary Bakunin.

This strangest of all revolutionaries, who was of noble birth, had studied philosophy in Berlin and had composed an opera that was never performed, and then began to dream of a society of free men without laws, state or any executive authority. In 1849, he took part in the riots in Dresden, was deported to Austria, then from Austria to Russia, and from there to Siberia, whence he returned to Europe by way of Japan, and since then had spent his time hiring murderers for liquidation squads in accordance with his motto: "Revolution hallows bullet, dagger, rope and poison!"

As soon as I had introduced this marksman, as a piece of living evidence, to Premier Bismarck, the revolutionary stated coldly that he had recognized that the coach contained a dummy, that he had aimed his pistol at it just to have a bit of fun, and that the gun had gone off by accident.

No one could prove that he was lying, and since he was an Austrian by birth, and thus a foreigner, Bismarck, who did not want any publicity, ordered that the would-be assassin be quietly forced across the border for having endangered the public.

And yet the epilogue to this attempted assassination was destined to change my entire life.

Soon after dismissing me with his warmest thanks, the Prussian Premier Bismarck summoned me back and asked me whether, despite the fact that I had been dismissed from office, I still "kept in touch with people abroad."

I gave an evasive reply (for before saying anything definite I wanted to find out what he had in mind), saying that I had not taken any steps to dissolve my relationships with people outside Prussia. Bismarck laughed and said, "And do such relationships fall within the purview of a director of the Berlin police force?"

"They make it easier for him to carry out his duties," I replied, still unable to see where he was heading.

Then Bismarck came straight out and told me that he had a task for me that was far more important than any I had performed in the past. He said that the fact that I had been officially suspended from duty would even work in my favor because it would deceive the enemy.

"What enemy?" I asked in amazement.

Then the Prussian Premier asked me to tell him straight out whether I could "observe matters" in Austria as I had previously done in Prussia.

"What should I have to observe there?" I asked, still very surprised.

"Everything," Bismarck remarked carelessly, as if the whole thing were self-evident. "Conditions in the country, such as what plans the Austrians have in case of war!"

"But Austria is not our enemy!" I ejaculated.

"But it isn't our friend either!" said Bismarck, laughing again. As long, he told me, as no clairvoyant came along to tell him what was being planned at army headquarters and in the chambers of government within our neighbor's borders, he was reduced to simple guesswork in his task of representing the interests of Prussia. Therefore, he considered it essential to engage in a "prophylactic investigation of our dear brother," and indeed, in future, such precautionary measures would determine the entire course of his politics.

"I have always considered it my duty," I hastened to assure him, "to serve not only my fatherland, but above all its sovereign," and therefore, I continued, I should consider myself very fortunate if I could contribute to the plans of my sovereign's Premier.

I was given ten days' time, at the end of which I was able to submit my plans for the establishment of a secret observation service in Austria. The essential part of my report read as follows:

"The type of isolated observation, involving only a few spies, which has traditionally been employed to spy on other nations, has produced very limited results. For an individual pays attention only to what he thinks is important, whereas things he considers inconsequential are, when viewed in terms of the total picture, highly significant.

"Thus, in the first place, instead of employing a few isolated spies as has been done in the past, my observation service will employ as many as possible. Unlike isolated spies, a whole 'army' of tireless observers do not have to be satisfied with a few pieces of information, which moreover are dangerous to obtain and, being out of context, can easily be misinterpreted.

"The reports streaming in from my mass of agents, who like hungry dogs will sniff around even in lavatories and out-of-the-way corners, will not be filtered until they have all flowed together, and the concentrate extracted from the stream will make its possessors truly omniscient.

"Such a multiplicity of spies will enable us to penetrate to the best-protected secrets more often and more easily than a single spy or only a few spies. Moreover, the importance and accuracy of each piece of information collected by an army of agents can be more carefully analyzed in terms of the other pieces of information which verify or contradict it and which continue to arrive in a steady stream. Thus one always quite naturally acquires an accurate picture of conditions and intentions in the country under observation.

"The agents of the past, who worked alone, were in more danger because they had to rely on themselves. The longer they observed, the more numerous were the traps which were set for them, and the threat of these traps distressed them and caused them to make mistakes, and finally they were unmasked. The danger also existed that those who had unmasked them would conceal from them the fact that they had been unmasked, and would then feed them and their homeland false and misleading information.

"When hundreds or even thousands of spies are active at the same time, it takes more police to keep them under surveillance and moreover would necessitate that these police officers spend all their time in such surveillance, which naturally is impossible—and therefore my army of agents can never be stopped.

"If one of them gets caught, it is no great tragedy, for the individuals in this mass of agents know almost nothing about each other! They are like a system of watertight bulkheads: each one scarcely knows his neighbor; thus even if several are unmasked or tracked down, there is little they can reveal.

"The responsibility for sifting through and taking advantage of all the facts which flow in will devolve upon a 'central headquarters' in our homeland which will select an excerpt from this data, always keeping it up-to-date, to present to their political and military employers, thus enabling them to take correct and effective countermeasures as quickly as possible.

"Whereas the isolated spies of the past were like fish lost in the sea who had to wait until they came across their prey, I shall spread a dense network throughout the country under observation, a network made up of 'home bases' and those attached to them. In each place we shall need only one 'resident spy,' who will not spy himself but will organize his district so as to force it to yield as much information as possible. It is also his duty to track down and recruit efficient 'assistants' (informers).

"Foreigners would attract attention, and thus all the spies should be natives and preferably should live in the area where they do their spying, and should pursue the same professions they always have. Each home base comprises only a small area, for this will be advantageous to the spies located there, who thus are spared the necessity of taking trips and going on errands which might attract attention.

"The efficiency of my network lies in the fact that things worth knowing will repeatedly occur at each of the home bases, things which we should never have found out about in any other way and which, in the context of information derived from the other home bases, will often lead to the most important discoveries. When we stumble across really important information we can assign special agents to investigate it. These agents will find it easier to achieve their goal than would have been the case if they had had to rely on themselves alone from the very beginning; for the 'foot soldiers' of the home base at each location will make all the necessary preparations—preparations which, if they had had to make them themselves like the spies of the past, might have proved their undoing and thus prevented them from getting started on their true job.

"However, to construct my new network of resident spies I should like to make use of the equally new and growing power of the press! This modern institution, with its investigators who are eternally hungry for news, will alone make it possible for us to press our inquiries everywhere and to obtain the information we need.

"Because members of the press have a right, which is everywhere acknowledged, to ask questions, and are not regarded with suspicion when they do so, they are the ideal staff of a secret observation service, especially because they possess the ability to depict facts in a comprehensible way and to distinguish facts from mere rumors. Members of the press can find out even the most strictly guarded economic and military secrets; indeed, often they are on such friendly terms with high-ranking politicians and soldiers that in their presence these people do not even attempt to conceal what they know.

"A great boon to our efforts is the vanity of many persons in authority, who like to see their words and their knowledge come to the attention of the public. Often an arms-supplier or a general chatters so much when he is in the public eye that he reveals more than ten zealous spies could have found out on their own, and one can glean a great deal of information from the public lectures and speeches they give on the most varied occasions, as well as from reference works, trade journals and the like, which are always available to members of the press.

"Therefore I advise that, if they are not themselves newsmen, my resident spies should at least recruit newsmen to their cause, but without informing them as to what use the news they gather is put. Instead they should simply be told that their cooperation as journalists is required, and considering the fact that most newswriters suffer from a chronic lack of funds, the promise of fees as generous as we can make them should act as irresistible bait.

"To sum up, one can create no more convincing mask for a secret investigatory service than a system of what purport to be newspaper reporters which extends across an entire country. For even the humblest of these men has special privileges, and the title 'newspaper reporter' serves as a genuine 'Open Sesame' and affords them entrée to places to which an ordinary mortal would never be admitted. A reporter is admitted, introduced, taken along everywhere, and thus the press functions as a hiding-place in which one attracts less suspicion than in any other, and from which, even in peacetime, we can investigate a country more thoroughly and will always be fully informed about its intentions and plans the moment they leave the heads of those who devise them."

When Bismarck, the Premier of Prussia, had attentively scanned my proposals, he smiled in amusement: "So you want a press bureau? You can have it! Chance has come to your aid." And he explained to me that the King had just expressed his wish that energetic steps be taken to prevent the spread of London's "Reuter's Telegraph Company" to cities on the continent. Press agencies played an important role in the shaping of public opinion, and thus, instead of relying on Reuter's, the King wanted control turned over to a Prussian organization, and the government was already in touch with the "telegraph bureau" of a certain Dr. Wolff in Berlin and intended to turn it into a government agency.

Shortly thereafter, Bismarck authorized me to set up my secret observation service in Austria under cover of press activities, and the only person who protested against the plan was the Crown Prince, who insisted on repeating his old warning against engaging in a "fraternal war between Germans," i.e., a war between Prussia and Austria. However, Field Marshal von Moltke advocated that a spy service be secretly set up in peacetime on the grounds that this "was in our best military interests," and to prove his point quoted a remark of Napoleon I, "A spy who keeps his eyes open at the right time and in the right place is worth a whole corps of soldiers!"

A short time later, the Englishman Reuter asked permission to establish branches of his news agency in Berlin and Frankfurt-am-Main, but was refused because foreign news services offered no guarantee that material they supplied the newspapers would be in the best interests of Prussia. Then Reuter attempted to get around this prohibition by trying to open what purported to be a German news agency in the name of former Prussian Privy Councillor Albert (who was for years head of the Prussian embassy in London). However, I immediately discovered this dissimulation, and the factitious firm was closed down before it could begin work.

Bismarck's authorization permitted me to spread my spy network across Austria; but the question of how it was to be financed had not been decided. I had told my patron that, especially at the beginning, such a large intelligence system would cost a great deal of money, and had received the answer that the King would probably be unwilling to consent to such an enormous expenditure, which was increased by my desire to establish my own press bureau, to be used as a façade behind which to recruit an army of spies in Austria.

The Premier did not, in fact, approach the King about this matter at first, but sought a source of funds that would be less easily exhausted.

"Didn't you arrest some skilled counterfeiters while you were head of the Berlin police force?" he asked me. When I replied that I had, Bismarck suggested that we finance our secret intelligence operations in Austria with "imitation" Austrian money. Thus, in a short time, I had released from the Prussian prisons an illustrious group of "experts": engravers, etchers, printers—among them counterfeiters of world-wide reputation.

We went to work immediately, and the first excellent counterfeits of Austrian currency were ready. We made our first test in the financial stronghold of Vienna, and it revealed that even experienced native bankers could not tell the difference between our counterfeit money and the genuine money we had mixed in with it.

Then, the printing presses in Berlin began working at full steam, and we ended by fabricating millions in counterfeit Austrian money—too little to undermine Austrian currency, but too much to circulate without its attracting attention; for I did not recruit enough resident spies, agents and informers to pay with all this money, and my enterprise literally threatened to drown in money.

However, in a short time I succeeded in spreading my system of "press bases," which initially were quite large but gradually grew smaller and smaller, all over Austria. With the aid of princely fees drawn from my inexhaustible fund of counterfeit currency, everything began, from the very beginning, to function as I had predicted it would, and from the very beginning, it began to verify the following facts for the Prussian government:

1. The fact that Austrians desired a united Germany and wished to replace the obsolete constitution of the German Confederation. Indeed, they wanted to satisfy the longing of all Germans for unity by means of a "federation of states with Austria at

their head," that would permit the individual states to retain their sovereignty. In fact, people were busily planning for this future in the ministerial offices of Austria, and those who were working toward it most busily were not native Austrians but Germans from the southern states. As Catholics, they were all strictly opposed to granting supremacy to Protestant Prussia, and the most influential of their number, Baron von Biegeleben, a native Hessian from Darmstadt (whose pen had produced most of the diplomatic missives written to Berlin by the Viennese court) preached that the salvation of all Germans did not lie in a single state; but in the union of all previously existing states beneath the sceptre of the Austrian Emperor.

2. Apparently these peaceful plans were the source of the incredible air of frivolity one saw everywhere. For example, military provisions, and even more the lack of military provisions, led one to conclude that the highest authorities in Vienna did not fear that any war was in the offing. Thus, our spies had noted, with as much amazement as gratitude, that even military installations were not adequately guarded, and, indeed, were scarcely guarded at all. Thus, they were virtually able to walk in and out whenever they chose. The Viennese War Ministry had too few "observers" at its disposal, and the same thing was true of the Ministry of the Interior; moreover, the two ministries had been crippled by years of bitter rivalry, the principal ill afflicting many of Austria's outmoded institutions. Vienna had turned over the task of hunting down spies to retired police officers who almost never caught one and who created confusion with false denunciations, which they often made purely in order to prove that they were on the job.

3. To sum up: Believing itself protected by a glorious but antiquated army, Austria and its rulers demonstrated a carelessness that could only be explained by their complete lack of any warlike intentions, and that should in fact have proved to us that no such intentions existed. All the Austrian people seemed opposed to war, and the city councils of Austria sent their Emperor birthday addresses in which they adjured him to keep the peace. Thus, in military matters Austria was not nearly so advanced as Prussia, which also possessed a superiority with respect to armaments (the needle gun). Barely one-fourth of Austrian military maneuvers were offensive maneuvers; three-quarters were purely defensive maneuvers, and the weakness of Austria lay in the time it would

take the country to mobilize its military forces—at least two weeks longer than it would take Prussia. (Indeed, any change in the military situation might have plunged Austria into the dilemma faced by all peaceful states: Whether to finally arm itself, and thus be suspected of contemplating an offensive move, or to remain as it was, and run the risk of being overwhelmed by a surprise attack.)

I had expected that the news of the supremely peaceful intentions of Austria would encourage my employer, the Prussian Premier Otto von Bismarck, to adopt an attitude of gratitude and peacefulness, but I was wrong!

After he had summoned me for an interview and had asked me once again to verify the accuracy of this "inviting idyll," he explained that, although it was repugnant to him to take advantage of these "apparent sins of omission" committed by the Austrian politicians, he could not, despite his sympathy for them as members of the same race, forebear to do so! Every peacetime success on the part of Austria was, he claimed, a defeat for him, for the Austrian Emperor Franz Joseph wanted to reduce Prussia to a powerless petty state, and thus, coexistence between the two countries was an impossibility.

Later, he assigned me no less a task than the "stirring up of our competitor" by spreading false news reports to all the newspapers. It became my specialty and the specialty of my agents to invent news that might lure peaceful Austria into taking measures to disown its present policy, measures it would not have taken otherwise that would justify Prussia in taking steps against it.

Above all, these false reports were designed to disrupt the relationship that had existed in the past between Austria's rulers and their subjects. We did this by inventing or exaggerating acts of despotism committed by the authorities, and alarmed people by broadcasting incidents in which the police had exceeded their authority, and reporting illegal arrests and cases of hair-raising corruption, and other things of this nature. It was the task of my press bureau to send these news reports to as many Prussian and foreign newspapers as possible, where they were always printed because of their sensational character; these tactics succeeded brilliantly in creating the desired effect. One of these "harassments" (as Bismarck called them) was the false report that Italy planned to disrupt the peace by undertaking an invasion of Austria, whereupon the startled Viennese took "precautionary measures" against Italy that immediately provoked trouble between the two nations.

Furthermore, Bismarck now expected my agents to incite revolution among all the nationalities of this country made up of many peoples: the Hungarians, Slavs, Czechs . . . all the demons of 1848 were to awaken again! I employed a great deal of (counterfeit) money in this enterprise and soon was supporting, for this purpose, eight hundred generously-paid agitators and troublemakers, who skillfully lit a fire under the hundreds of thousands of hotheads who belonged to the Czech and Slovakian minorities, and incited them, in case of war, to start fighting in Hungary, Dalmatia and Slovenia. Indeed, acting on Bismarck's orders I had a flood of posters released overnight all over Prague; the posters bore a passionate "proclamation to all the citizens of the Kingdom of Bohemia and Moravia," which promised them that their "desires for national liberation" would soon be fulfilled.

An even more provocative plan was the establishment, by means of floods of counterfeit Austrian money, of a "Hungarian Freedom Legion" made up of deserters from the Austrian army. A certain Klapka, a passionate Hungarian patriot, was named "Supreme Commander" of the Legion, and his aim was nothing less than to separate an "independent kingdom of Hungary" from Austria. Thus, in the end, even before war broke out, I had almost succeeded in paving the way for a revolution in Austria.

Meanwhile, I learned that Bismarck, too, was secretly making preparations for war. As early as 1864, the firm of Friedrich Krupp in Essen, Prussia's most important arms manufacturer, pointing out that the liberal majority in Parliament had refused to allocate funds for armaments, had secretly offered credit in the amount of two million talers. Now Bismarck was taking advantage of the offer, as he did of an offer, likewise secret, from the steel industrialist Stumm. At the same time, Bismarck sold railroad stock belonging to the Prussian government for the sum of thirteen million talers, and, in additon, issued government bonds in the sum of forty million talers, without bothering to get approval from Parliament first as prescribed by law.

While war with Austria loomed nearer and nearer, an attempt was made to assassinate Bismarck in May, 1866. As the Premier was leaving the King's palace in Berlin, a young fellow whose face was twisted with hatred fired a pistol at him on Unter den Linden Avenue.

This time, too, I was informed of the threatened assassination days ahead of time, and the warning that I immediately conveyed to Bismarck bore fruit; for before going out, Bismarck donned a bullet-proof vest of the type worn by arms manufacturers when testing their products. All three shots fired by the murderous marksman bounced off the vest without doing any harm.

The would-be assassin turned out to be a German student named Cohen-Blind, the stepson of Carl Blind, a revolutionary who had been active in 1848, who was well-known to the police, and who was living in exile in London. Immediately after the assassination attempt Cohen was arrested and committed suicide during his first night in prison. I gave his suicide note to Prussian Premier Bismarck, who only skimmed through it and then calmly tore it up. The note had said: "I wanted to protect the German people from a war with their brothers by killing the merciless man who is instigating this war."

Seeing the bullets of the would-be assassin bounce off Bismarck without doing any harm, an elegantly dressed gentleman walking along the street exclaimed loudly and angrily, "What miserable revolvers we have in Germany!" The man was immediately arrested and turned out to be the university professor and renowned physiologist Emil Reimond; but Bismarck did not draw any conclusions from this. Only four years later, the same professor enthusiastically proclaimed in the great hall of the University of Berlin, "We professors of Berlin regard ourselves as the intellectual bodyguards of the glorious Otto von Bismarck" *(Tempora mutantur et nos mutamur in illis).*°

Now, Bismarck needed only to find a reason to attack; he also needed a halfway favorable reaction from the people. However, he met with bitter opposition from the Prussian Parliament. Bismarck's response was to deliberately provoke its members. For the first time, he declared publicly:

"The problem of our strained relations with Austria can be solved only by a war. We can find cause for such a war at any time, if necessary, the cause of victory!"

The members of Parliament (led by Twesten and Simson) re-

°"Times change and we change with them."

sponded by raising an uproar and declared their passionate opposition to "shooting at fellow-Germans," whereupon Bismarck replied, "If I must wage a war, I will wage it, even without your approval!"

It was now Bismarck's task to talk the King out of feeling any similar pangs of conscience. The King believed passionately in the unity of all German-speaking peoples and thus abhorred the idea of "any fraternal bloodshed" between Prussians and Austrians, but the Premier suggested to his King that war between the two countries was inevitable. Therefore, war should be waged while it could be won, and in my presence, he alluded to the fact that Austria was ill-prepared for a war, a fact that my observers throughout Austria had verified.

Thereupon, the King withdrew into the next room, and from where I was standing I could see the exalted gentleman in a gilded mirror on the wall as he knelt down there and prayed for around three minutes. He came back into the room, looking pale, and said almost tonelessly, "I have decided in favor of your proposal!"

Later, Bismarck influenced King Wilhelm I to such a point that the King, fully conscious that he telling an untruth, swore to the Austrian Emperor Franz Joseph by his honor as a king that Prussia was not planning any warlike measures against Austria. Bismarck confided to me with great satisfaction, "That is my doing, and I'm proud of it!"

During these days of secret tension, a last attempt was made to prevent war. The Austrian Governor-General, Ludwig von Gablenz, assigned his brother Anton, a Prussian citizen and a member of the Prussian Parliament, no less a task than to save the peace, thus sparing the two peoples to whom they belonged from going through a bloody war. Thus, with the consent of his brother, Ludwig, an Austrian; the Prussian, Anton, made a truly desperate attempt to mediate between Berlin and Vienna. He engaged in zealous negotiations in both capitals, but whereas in Vienna he encountered nothing but indecisiveness and confusion, he was profoundly discouraged by Bismarck's grim determination to fight.

Shortly thereafter, the Prussian Premier ordered me, "for the time being," to close down the activities of my intelligence service in Austria. He wanted this done so that the country that was soon to become our adversary would find no clues to the fact that even in peacetime, we had conducted extensive spying activities there. Thus, projects that had barely begun had to be broken off and secret contacts disrupted, so that soon, to my sorrow, the uninterrupted stream of information that had been flowing in from Austria through me or rather through my organization, dried up. However, I had to obey Bismarck's orders.

Nevertheless, I did make a concluding report to the Prussian Premier Otto von Bismarck at my headquarters in Berlin, a gloomy house at the Gendarmenmarkt that had seen a lot of history. In my report, I noted that of the more than twenty thousand reports by observers that had been gathered from all over Austria since the beginning of my work there, more than two thousand contained important information and four hundred contained information of very great importance. Moreover, my agents had stolen around two hundred informative articles from civilian and army offices in Austria that were carelessly guarded or not guarded at all, and—as my spies later discovered—no one ever noticed that these objects were missing. No fewer than five hundred and thirty high-ranking Austrians, all men who occupied posts of honor, had been recruited by my "resident agents" to commit treason in the interests of Prussia. Probably not even the Austrians themselves knew the moods and habits of their people better than the leading observers of my secret service in Berlin ultimately came to know them. In the end, they even knew that:

• Since revolutionary plots had begun to agitate his country, the Austrian Emperor Franz Joseph had employed a double who resembled him to a remarkable degree and who, without anyone's knowledge, represented him on public occasions,

• Two of his closest advisers secretly spied for me and, indeed, were among my most-highly-paid agents (they were paid with counterfeit money),

• Some members of society at the Emperor's court were hopelessly addicted to opiates,

• The Emperor's consort, the "Empress of Austria," loved a groom who worked in her riding stables and who had just turned eighteen . . .

After that the Prussian Premier Otto von Bismarck publicized the outline of a new "Constitution of the German Confederation" that delivered an ultimatum to Austria, demanding that it withdraw from the German Confederation and allow Prussia to occupy the position of dominance that had formerly been held by Austria. Bismarck also issued another ultimatum, demanding the unconditional acceptance of this compact by all the other German lands, and threatened that they would be invaded by Prussian battalions if they refused.

Thereby, he provoked Austria to such an extent that it demanded that the confederation of German states, of which it had hitherto been the leader, immediately mobilize all its troops against "insubordinate Prussia." Thus, the Austrians had initiated hostilities, just as Bismarck had wanted them to do. Now Prussia could wage the war for which he had carefully paved the way, while maintaining the status of the victim that had been attacked and was "forced to defend itself"!

On the evening of June 15, 1866, I was with the Prussian Premier in the garden of the Foreign Office on the Wilhelmstrasse in Berlin, and with us was the English ambassador Lord Loftus. When it struck midnight Bismarck rose from his chair and solemnly proclaimed, "The war has begun! At this hour Prussian troops are marching into Hanover, Saxony and the Electorate of Hesse—long live the King!" Without batting an eyelash, the English ambassador said that Europe would never tolerate such an invasion, whereupon I heard Bismarck reply, "Who is Europe?"

The inconceivable—the fraternal warfare of Germans against Germans on German soil, a war for supremacy between Prussia and Austria—had become a reality, and when the King of Prussia travelled to the theater of operations, I was given the delicate mission of arranging for his personal protection. At dawn, I repaired to the place where the royal battalion was being drawn up. Despite the earliness of the hour, I found everyone engaged in lively activity: Great numbers of relatives and friends, and especially women friends of the departing soldiers, had arrived to say touching farewells and to shower their soldiers with flowers, liquor and good things to eat. The cries of some of the troops, who wanted to prove their enthusiasm and fighting spirit by singing war songs, set up a strange counterpoint to the scenes of farewell. The troops were composed almost exclusively of artisans, travelling journeymen and impoverished paid substitutes. There were very few one-year volunteers, for everyone who could afford to pay for a substitute had done so; during the past few weeks, this "trade in human flesh" had reached alarming proportions. And yet, the people here were in good spirits and appeared as happy as if they were going on an outing instead of to war. The battalion leader read the Commander-in-Chief's orders for the day in the splendid hall at the railroad station, which was built in Gothic style, and was so moved by what he read that he could hardly utter the final words. Everyone cheered the King, and, accompanied by cries of rejoicing and the waving of handkerchiefs, the long, endless train rolled off into the grey morning.

The German states of Saxony, Hanover, Bavaria, Württemberg, Baden, the Electorate of Hesse, Nassau, Frankfurt and several German principalities fought on the side of Austria, whereas Prussia's only allies were a couple of petty states of Thuringia and northern Germany. The German states allied with Austria were able to drum up around one hundred and twenty thousand soldiers, and Austria's main army in Bohemia consisted of another two hundred and eighty thousand soldiers at its disposal. Moreover, in the hour of need, Austria, which had hitherto appeared so "flabby," now showed unexpected resolution, a resolution that made itself felt in various ways, among them, in the fact that the revolutionary legion that Prussia had initiated in Hungary, broke down at the outset, disappointing the hopes Prussia had placed in it. For from the first day of the war, the citizens of Hungary demonstrated no desire to be freed from "the yoke of Hapsburg tyranny." Not only did they fail to take the side of the Legion in its uprising, but Hungarians everywhere helped the Austrian soldiers to disperse its members.

But from the very beginning, the states of middle and southern Germany were half-hearted in their attempts to defend themselves against their Prussian brothers, and also lacked adequate means to do so. Their kings had scarcely started marching at the head of their troops before the Prussian soldiers, with lightning swiftness, had occupied Saxony and the Electorate of Hesse; the Elector of Hesse was taken prisoner and his army fled to Bavaria. The leaders of the Bavarian army could not decide on the proper tactics by which to aid their allies, the troops of Hanover, against the Prussians. They simply did not know where the Prussians would break through, whether they would appear near Eisenach or would cross through the Thuringian forest and turn up at Gotha. Not one single courier arrived from the Hanoverians, the Bavarian couriers were captured, and thus, the Bavarian troops were hurled endlessly back and forth, marching for days and placed under an incredible strain until they were completely exhausted. The King of Hanover, George V, on the other hand, had no trouble making up his mind; he had the stubbornness typical of the Guelphs and was determined, cost what it might, to remain loyal to Austria and to defend Austria's German Confederation. He led all his soldiers to the southern part of his kingdom, but at Langensalza, he encountered the Prussians, who had been moving forward by forced marches, and, surrounded on all sides, was forced to lay down his arms and flee to England.

Only a few days later, on July 3, 1866, Prussia launched its major assault against Austria, its real adversary. The attack was led by three wedges of Prussian troops who marched forward concentrically and were supposed to reunite at Königgrätz. The Austrian Commander-in-Chief, Lieutenant Field Marshal von Benedek, regarded the situation of his troops as so hopeless that before the battle began, he recommended that Austria make an immediate peace offer to Prussia, but his Emperor, Franz Joseph, stubbornly demanded that the Austrians "fearlessly engage in this decisive battle," for his sense of dynastic and military honor could not endure a "shameful peace based on renunciation." The result was a grievous armed conflict in which many lives were lost, and in which the fate of the Prussians depended on whether the Crown Prince's army would arrive on time. It arrived with Prussian punctuality and the victory was complete. On the afternoon of the day the battle was ending, Field Marshal von Moltke was able to congratulate the King of Prussia, saying "Your Majesty has not only won the battle, you have won the war!" The military reforms instituted by Wilhelm I, who lived only for his army, had borne fruit in the improved training and the better discipline that reigned among Prussian soldiers, in the swifter and more accurate strategy of their leaders, and above all, in the absolute technological superiority of the newest Prussian weapon, the destructive "needle gun." This replaced the musketloader and the thrust tactics of the bayonet attack with a steady stream of lightning-fast salvos.

I, with the adjutants and aides who had been assigned to me, travelled in the train of vehicles that conducted the King, Bismarck and Prussian supreme headquarters to the theater of operations, and it was my responsibility, as a sort of combined policeman and chief quartermaster, to ensure its safety and unimpeded progress. In the evening, we were quartered among the impoverished inhabitants of a remote mountain valley, where I found lodgings in the house of the parson. I retired early and had scarcely gone to bed when I was awakened by the sound of voices loudly singing a hymn; it was the minister and his servants, singing in the kitchen. The hymn echoed solemnly through the still moonlit night. But the hymn was promptly followed by a prayer which closed with the equally audible words, "Oh Lord, punish the Prussian intruders!" At this point, I hastily closed my window.

Next morning, I had a great deal of trouble with our vehicles. I wanted to have them fitted with drags for their trip through the mountainous terrain, but the Prussian troops had carried off all the tools and iron implements and the blacksmith did not want to help the Prussian army, not even for the generous sum of money that I was prepared to pay him. Then I lost patience and had him taken prisoner, threatening to take him along with us, using him as a living drag. But not until I made it clear that I was about to summon some soldiers did he draw in his horns and agree to make the brakes we needed so desperately for mountain travel. After we had received word of our victory in the battle that decided the outcome of the war, we moved our headquarters to Horitz. Endless columns of wagons filled with wounded men streamed toward us pulled by endless processions of horses, so that we were forced to reduce our speed to a walk as we moved along the narrow, extremely bumpy road. Toward evening, we finally arrived in Horitz, where the King, Prince Karl and Bismarck found uncomfortable beds in the old palace. Meanwhile, Prussian soldiers bivouacked in the fields all around us, taking shelter from the ceaseless rain beneath piles of branches. General Steinmetz was still busy pursuing fleeing Austrians and occasionally we heard a distant cannon. Horitz was a dismal sight. All its citizens had abandoned it days before, and it looked as lifeless as Pompeii and Herculaneum. Before we arrived, one hundred thousand Austrian soldiers had camped here and then had been succeeded by an almost equal number of Prussians, so that now there was nothing left to eat but dirty water.

After travelling for many hours, we got nothing to eat, for our chow wagon had been left behind somewhere, and so we began to break into houses. The first place I broke into had been an inn, but I found nothing inside but some coffee and made a pot on the billiard table because everything else was covered with dirt. Just then, the Duke of Ujest walked in complaining that he had not eaten since yesterday. No sooner had I expressed my sympathy that I could offer him, the wealthiest man in the country, nothing but thin coffee, than he gratefully swallowed it in thirsty gulps.

Immediately afterward, army doctors forced their way into our inn and began filling it with wounded men. Amputations were performed on six officers, including two Prussians and two Austrians, at the place where I had just finished brewing my coffee; they were all young people of good family! Both legs were taken from an Austrian cadet with a complexion of cream and roses, and we, who had completely lost our appetites, heard the doctors complain that half of their patients would die because they had none of the supplies they needed, especially the most important thing, ice. I broke into another house and tried to sleep on a bed there, but in a short time I was again knee-deep in wounded men to whom I could offer nothing because I had nothing myself. I fled to a third house, but I was confronted there by a filthy Bohemian woman who scolded me furiously, and decided to leave.

Finally, our chow wagon arrived, and we all ate as if we were starving: The King, the princes and Bismarck were all surrounded by soldiers, and afterwards I drove a wagon, drawn by a single horse, out onto the battlefield, where thousands of dead and wounded men were still lying everywhere in the open fields, in the underbrush, and piled in heaps in the mud of streams—a veritable apocalypse! As I turned away, shuddering, Prince Karl came riding up, shook hands with me with tears in his eyes and told me all about the battle: "To the right, to the left, nearby, far away—everywhere we heard the crashing sound of the Austrian regimental bands with their sparkling horns and jingling Johnnies; they were all playing the Radetzky March. But another kind of music was emerging from the Prussian ranks to greet them, a hellish music—the ceaseless patter of salvos being fired from rapid-fire weapons. But the Austrians flung themselves at us with a courage that showed their disdain of death, advancing in splendor with their officers, covered with gold braid, in the lead, and when the officers fell, others sprang to take their places. But they could not withstand our deadly and persistent fire, and so they wavered and were forced to retreat. We too suffered fearful losses, especially among the Guards. One battalion lost all its officers so that a sergeant had to lead them . . ." As he was telling the story the Prince turned away and openly wept, not trying to hide his tears.

Bismarck, the Prussian Premier, was also horrified by the atrocities that had been committed. "War is hell, and the man who starts a war with the flick of his pen is a devil!" he declared, despite the fact that he himself had labored tirelessly to help bring about this war. Our generals, and especially His Majesty King Wilhelm I, urged that we follow up their victory by marching into Vienna. Bismarck alone opposed this plan, exclaiming, "The struggle has been decided, now we must work to bring about friendship!" It is no wonder that everyone disagreed with him! His stubborn resistance to the plan that the army should advance deeper into Austria led to such a loud dispute that it could be heard all over the camp. The King, his Premier and the generals all shouted at once, and King Wilhelm demanded that he be allowed to exercise the victor's right to take anything he chose from the vanquished—demanded, in fact, the "punishment of all our defeated enemies." Why, he asked, should we not take any of Bohemia, the Sudetenland and the Egerland away from Austria and the old Hohenzollern lands of Ansbach and Bayreuth from Bavaria? Bismarck, on the contrary, warned that to do so would earn us the enmity of Austria and the other nations of Europe. "Every additional step we take towards the south will stir up their jealousy!" he cried, and said that there was nothing he feared more than the possibility that all these nations might join together to take action against Prussia.

Then we saw him tear out of the room, his face bright red, and he seemed to be on the point of slamming the doors as he left, the King and his generals behind him. But the Crown Prince followed him, grabbed him by his coat, and cried in a voice audible to us all (we were just standing there rigid with horror at the harsh words that these exalted gentlemen had exchanged after their victory), "I was against your war—but now, if you want peace, I'll try to change my father's mind!" Then he hurried back inside, looking troubled; but when, after a long time had passed, he returned, he laughed joyfully and said, "It was terribly difficult, but my father agrees!" However, at the meal that followed, King Wilhelm complained, "A Premier who knuckles under to the enemy and a son who is in league with him have forced me, after such a brilliant victory, to bring my armies to a shameful halt!" His headquarters moved to Nikolsburg, a town located in glorious surroundings resembling the Alps and crowned by the Dietrichstein Palace, which Napoleon I had occupied and which now belonged to that same Count von Mensdorff, the Austrian Foreign Secretary, who had so carelessly declared war on Prussia. Bismarck had hastened there ahead of us, and when the rest of us arrived, he was already enthroned in the palace with a heap of papers and plans and listening to a report. Meanwhile his King, the Crown Prince and Prince Friedrich were promenading in the palace courtyard with their victorious generals and commanders-in-chief; they were there when two dusty hired coaches and a genuine Viennese cab bearing the number 382 drove up with the Austrian negotiators: Count Degenfeld, the War Minister himself; Austria's ambassador to Berlin, Count Karolyi; and the estimable Councillors of the Legation, von Brönner and Kufstein. As the "highest-ranking police officer in the field," I led the gentlemen to Bismarck. This was an historic moment because the emissaries of the proud house of Lorraine, of the Emperor of Austria, had arrived on the doorstep of their former vassal, the Baron of Nuremberg, to plead that their country be spared—the same country in whose capital, Vienna, the Hohenzollern counts had once performed duties at the court of their mighty Emperor—all the more so because this was taking place in the palace, now conquered by the Prussians, of a genuine imperial minister.

The peace negotiations dragged on slowly at first, and several times it appeared that they were about to be broken off, although (or because) the Austrians at once arrogantly declared that in any case, they wanted to secede from Germany, whether that was one of the conditions demanded or not. Indeed, after their most recent experience with their former confederate, Prussia, they would regard it as a stroke of luck for Austria to be able to do so! But then, Bismarck held an intimate conference with the Austrian ambassador, Count Karolyi, over a tankard of beer (which a Prussian orderly hastened to bring), and after that things went more smoothly! For despite all the harshness with which he had conducted the war against Austria, Bismarck now wanted exactly the same thing the Austrians were pleading for: the stability of their country. The reason for Bismarck's attitude was his far-seeing view that it was not in the interests of Prussia to make an enemy of Austria. This was the thinking of a true statesman, that can never be clouded, no matter how alluring the temptations of the moment! Peace was concluded after a mere two hours of bargaining, and—in view of the devastating defeat it had suffered—Austria actually received very generous terms. It had to pay a financial penalty of only twenty million talers, and in land it lost Venetia and its portion of Schleswig, which it had, to all practical purposes, given up some time ago. But it had taken Prussia only six weeks of war to remove its all-powerful rival from the German throne and to assume that throne itself, and at noon of that memorable day, the Austrian supplicants and their conquerors, the King of Prussia and his ministers, celebrated the peace by eating together a meal in celebration of the peace—a sure sign that they had reached an agreement!

Here is another note on the character of King Wilhelm I. When a greedy Austrian wine dealer asked whether champagne would be wanted, the King had von Krosigk, commander of his headquarters, dismiss the man by saying rudely, "Not a drop! Because it is not seemly for us to carouse where so many men died!" The King showed equal severity when he ordered me, his police officer in the field, to have all Prussian thieves who had stolen things from the battlefields shot without mercy. Indeed, he showed a painstaking concern that Prussian sutlers' wagons not be used for smuggling home stolen goods, and ordered that they be thoroughly searched at the Prussian border on their homeward journey. On the other hand, as the spoils of the victorious war with Austria, Prussia acquired Schleswig-Holstein, the kingdom of Hanover, the Electorate of Hesse, Nassau and the free city of Frankfurt-am-Main—no fewer than five formerly independent states that had belonged to the "German Confederation" ruled by Austria. King Wilhelm wanted Saxony, too, but Austria protested vehemently against this idea, probably because Saxony was the only state that had followed it wholeheartedly into the war against Prussia. So Saxony was spared! Nevertheless, Prussia had now expanded to embrace such an immense block of land (from the border of Holland in the west to the border of Poland in the east) that the non-Prussian territory submerged in this mass (Hamburg, Bremen, Lübeck and the petty states of Thuringia, Lippe and Saxony, as well as Oldenburg, Brunswick and Mecklenburg) disappeared in it like drops in the ocean. There was no doubt: Bismarck's "fraternal war" had raised Prussia to the rank of the ruler of Germany, and Austria would never hold that position again!

In token of his gratitude, the King conferred on Bismarck the title of count, as well as four hundred thousand talers to be used in purchasing an estate in Pomerania suitable to his rank. I was rewarded too. Although, up until now, I had kept secret the pride I felt at Prussia's swift victory (after all, it was due to my labors that the Prussian leaders had learned their opponent's weaknesses before the battle, so that they could formulate plans), my service was now acknowledged publicly when King Wilhelm I appointed me a "Privy Councillor." And yet I was not happy about this honor when I thought about the revolutionary troop I had set up in Hungary at Bismarck's instigation. Not only had the Austrians destroyed the troop at the very beginning of the war and captured the agitators among them, they expressed their intention to treat them as collaborators and execute them in front of a firing squad. Bismarck attempted to save them by threatening that if they were shot, he would shoot ten citizens of the Austrian town of Trautenau who had been imprisoned at the beginning of the war because they had fired on Prussian troops. This meant that I was about to become responsible for their deaths, too! Thank God, literally at the last moment, a "general amnesty" was proclaimed for all prisoners, and finally I could be completely happy!

After that, Bismarck had to take a leave of absence and retire to his new estate because of illness, for the ceaseless labor and tension had undermined even his iron constitution; and when I came to see him there, his worried wife warned me that he did not want to hear a single word about politics and wanted to spend the day in his easy chair. The convalescent did not return home to Berlin for months and when he did, he immediately devoted himself to the new labors attendant on his "North German Confederation." With the formation of this confederation, he resurrected Austria's "German Confederation," which he had just destroyed; but now, the confederation was under Prussian leadership and existed only in the north. Primarily, it was composed of Oldenburg, Brunswick, Anhalt, Mecklenburg, Darmstadt, Meiningen and (against its will!) Saxony—a total of more than twenty previously independent German states, comprising thirty million inhabitants, all now subject to the King of Prussia. Bismarck offered the King the office of "President" that was hereditary in his house, the house of Hohenzollern, along with the supreme command of all troops, as well as the right to appoint a "Federal Chancellor of Germany" who would guide the political destinies of all the states in the confederation. For the peace treaty with Austria gave Prussia supremacy only in the north, whereas southern Germany, everything located south of the Main River, was expressly exempt from this supremacy (this defeated Austria's last hope to maintain influence there). The states south of the Main River maintained the right to form an independent confederation, but before they were able to do so, Bismarck forced them all to accept a "protective treaty" with mighty Prussia that frustrated their hopes of independence by placing their troops at the disposal of the King of Prussia in case of war. Bismarck threatened that the victorious Prussians would occupy their countries, too, if they did not consent. Thus, by means of this military and political strategy, Prussia took over power in southern Germany, as well, and the lands of the south, having succumbed to a surprise attack, preserved their independence only with respect to their laws, schools and churches. They were allowed to retain this degree of independence in order to pacify their impotent sovereigns, who had been shocked that the advancing Prussians had driven away the King of Hanover and imprisoned the Elector of Hesse.

But when elections were held in Prussia to elect members to the Provincial Diet, everyone was so impressed by all these brilliant achievements that the Conservative Party won a resounding victory (increasing the number of seats it held from a mere thirty-eight to one hundred and twenty-three) and now demanded the retroactive sanction of the war expenses, which Bismarck had paid out without being granted the approval of Parliament. However, King Wilhelm, who possessed great pride of sovereignty, was so displeased by the fact that the government had "bent its knee before the people" that even Bismarck, with all his skill as a speaker, could only partially appease his wrath. For in his subsequent address to Parliament, the wounded monarch attacked his more moderate Premier from the rear, saying rudely that as the King of Prussia, he had won his victory without the blessings of Parliament; and that if it were necessary, he would do the same thing all over again. Bismarck had feared that such language would cause an uproar in Parliament, but instead, it had just the opposite effect, for all the expenses that had been under debate were approved by an overwhelming majority, amid cries of "Bravo!" and much applause! The only one of the defeated states forced to do penance was the city of Frankfurt-am-Main, which had previously been a free city. No one was surprised that it lost its independence and was reduced to a Prussian provincial city, but everyone was amazed at the draconian punishment it received. Although it had not taken the slightest belligerent action in the war, and the Federal Diet located within its walls had merely voted against Prussia before the war began, it was fined six million talers, and after it had forked over this sum with many groans, it was fined another twenty-five million. Bismarck himself ordered this severe punishment for the revolutionary city he hated, on the same day when he struggled in Nikolsburg to obtain generous terms for Austria; indeed, for every day Frankfurt failed to pay, he threatened to impose an additional fine of one million talers, and if this did not bring about the desired results, he threatened to bring all traffic, business dealings and mail delivery in Frankfurt to a halt, in other words, to starve it out! The news that such pressures were being brought to bear against a city occupied by Prussia reached countries abroad, and their newspapers denounced Prussia's behavior as a piece of "vengefulness reminiscent of the Old Testament," whereupon Augusta, the Queen of Prussia, implored her consort King Wilhelm to treat more generously a defeated city of which he was the sovereign. Nothing helped. The citizens of Frankfurt had to bleed, whereupon their mayor, who had been driven to despair, hanged himself!

George V, the King of Hanover, whom Prussia had driven into exile, possessed a large cash fortune that Bismarck now appropriated with the same severity he had shown toward Frankfurt. A "progressive" deputy in the new Prussian Provincial Diet, Rudolf von Virchow, a famous physician and professor, protested this appropriation. (I later learned that the escaped monarch, who had been Virchow's patient, was still deeply in debt to him.) Bismarck defended himself by saying that (I had discovered this fact, too) the fugitive was still agitating against Prussia from his seat abroad, whereupon Bismarck called him a poisonous reptile and claimed that he had to smoke him out with the help of his own money (which people called "reptile's money" from that time on!). In reality, Bismarck used the money to expand and render more efficient my secret service, which was maintained in both peace and war. Something new had happened that caused him to take this action:

The Foreign Office in Berlin had received a top-secret letter from America, from von Gerold, Prussia's Consul-General in Washington, in which he delivered an urgent warning. According to information he had received from New Orleans, von Gerold claimed, men faithful to the King of Hanover who had fled to New Orleans, had formed a conspiracy to take the lives of King

Wilhelm I of Prussia and his aide Otto von Bismarck. Several assassins were to be sent to Prussia to kill them. Thereupon, while remaining in Berlin, I immediately had searched all ships leaving America and setting sail for Germany, and my agents in Hamburg and Berlin kept strangers who arrived from overseas under such close surveillance, both day and night, that they could not take a step without being observed. And yet, no clue was found that suggested that the dual assassination we had heard about was to take place. However, more or less as a byproduct of the search for the assassins, we found evidence of a secret anti-Prussian conspiracy operating in the former kingdom of Hanover that had already reached rather extensive proportions. In order to enable me to take swift measures against it, on May 17, 1867, Count Bismarck conferred on me the comprehensive "General Security Commission" placing in my hands alone the authority I needed to protect Prussia from this threat, as well as from similar threats in the future.

Travelling incognito, I immediately went to Hanover, and the first discovery I made was the curious fact that even citizens belonging to the most exalted and distinguished circles named their dogs and cats "Wilhelm" and "Bismarck"; so that they could continually insult them in public without incurring any punishment, crying out, "Wilhelm, you dog!" or "Bismarck—get out, march!" Indeed, I soon saw that people all over Hanover were dreaming of the restoration of the kingdom, even if it had to be under the crown of England as it had been two hundred years ago. In fact, around thirty thousand signatures had been collected in support of the "union of the kingdom of Hanover with England," which was not a surprising notion to anyone who knew the history of Hanover. Since the Elector Ludwig of Hanover ascended the English throne as George I and proceeded to rule Hanover from London, both crowns had remained in the same ruling family, and they had done so even when the Congress of Vienna raised Hanover to the rank of an independent kingdom. For at this point, another Guelph came from the Thames to the Leine: "His Royal Highness" Ernest Augustus, Prince of Great Britain and Ireland, Duke of Cumberland! Thus, I was not particularly surprised when my agents informed me that soldiers were being secretly recruited in Hanover and England and that the recruits swore an oath of loyalty to the King of Hanover. To facilitate this recruitment, a liaison network had been spun between Hanover and other countries, with a recruiting office in London, and a rendezvous in Arnhem, Holland for soldiers in Hanover who had been bribed into deserting the Prussian military service. Thereupon, I arrested one of the secret recruiters, a man named Winning, and found that he was carrying a number of papers, dispatches, and orders written by the former sovereign George V himself, unequivocally convicting this sovereign of engaging in treasonous agitation. At the same time, this evidence established that close ties existed between the Hanoverian nobility and their fugitive King and if, as they hoped, war should break out between Prussia and France, they would give France a battle-ready Hanoverian "Guelph legion."

The principal result of my investigations was the arrest of the leader of these subversive conspirators, Count Platen-Hallermund, who had been the Premier of the King of Hanover. We found, in his possession, an inflammatory "patriotic appeal" stating that the King of Hanover would hold fast his right to the throne and that he would never yield to Prussian "rapacity." This appeal claimed that the division of the tribes of Germany into separate states was the result of a "natural growth" and was the only healthy route for Germany to take; the union Prussia had forced on Germany by violence was a disease that would continually give rise to new wars. Only one medicine could cure this disease: the annihilation of the source of the infection, Prussia, which the Hanoverians, with the aid of France, would hurl back across the Elbe and even farther, as Napoleon I had done, and so forth.

A more important discovery was made by my agents when they accidentally came across a depot filled with new weapons and ammunition in the woods. This discovery enabled me to capture, at one blow, many go-betweens and aides working for the Guelphic cause and thus to prevent other people from joining them. Among the men arrested was a certain Baron von L. (out of consideration for living persons I have changed even the initial), who seemed to be the most deeply embroiled in these plans. I had him brought to me for interrogation, and the following conversation took place between the suspect and myself:

"The investigations of my officers have shown that you are engaging in military activities here!" I began by saying point-blank.

"I am an officer, a liaison officer!" von L. replied calmly.

"A liaison officer?" I asked in perplexity. "With whom or what are you a liaison?"

"With those inside this country and abroad who are opposed to the occupation of my fatherland!"

"I understand!" I said quietly. "Who are these people, and do you approve of their actions up to now?"

"Are you trying to intimate that I have broken the law?" von L. asked aggressively.

That was, in fact, what I had been trying to intimate, but I took care not to say so, for none of my officers had brought me any evidence.

I answered merely, "I should like to recommend, as a precaution, that you respect the Prussian laws that are now binding here, Baron!"

"Major—if you don't mind!"

"According to your papers, you have not served as a Hanoverian officer for some time," I demurred.

"May I point out that the Hanoverian army is not the only army in the world?" von L. said with a mocking smile. He showed me a commission stating that he held the rank of an English major, signed by the Commander-in-Chief of the British army. This struck a nerve, so that I answered, more rudely than I had intended, "You can never possess such a commission!"

"Why not?"

"In the first place, you are not a British subject but a subject of His Majesty the King of Prussia, and second, you are a German officer!"

"I was a German officer!"

"Even if you are no longer an officer of Hanover, you can be returned to active duty at any time if you are ordered to do so by your present employer, the King of Prussia," I declared. "So don't expect me to acknowledge this scrap of paper!"

Von L. calmly took back the commission. "Is that your official view?" he asked me.

"Absolutely!"

"Then you will not object, sir, if I report it to my commander, the commanding general of the British armed forces, as the official Prussian position!"

I hesitated. Probably, for the time being, this Guelph conspiracy consisted of nothing but a bunch of bored officers who had been discharged from the army. However, given the contemporary political situation, anything seemed possible. In the course of time—today no one could know for certain—these same men might become representatives of a lawful institution, and in this case, a certain director of the Berlin police, who had insulted one of them for no reason, would have compromised himself, not to mention what other uses he might have made of his position! Thus I swallowed my wrath and amended what I had said earlier: "It is not the official Prussian position—I simply expressed my personal views!" Von L. immediately saw that I was backing down and mockingly thanked me, "I shall be happy to report to my superior that you did not do anything here to obstruct my activities!"

"Please report to him, as well, that I should be forced to place you under immediate arrest if it were proved that you had broken the law!" I declared emphatically. This was not an empty threat, and yet I grew pale with impotent rage when he left without a word.

"The fellow can't have accomplished much!" said my adjutant (who was disguised as a peddler), trying to console me. "He didn't have any money on him!"

"He doesn't need any!" I sighed. "He finished arming a battalion long ago and thus he already has the weapons he needs. Our duty now is to look for them!" And into my mind there flooded the nightmarish vision of the inexhaustible fortune of the Guelphs that belonged to the fugitive King of Hanover, who was doubtless the employer of this dubious officer who had served in two armies. For centuries, secrets and legends had grown up around the Guelph treasure, and only a few initiates knew where it was hidden. Henry the Lion began to amass it in the twelfth century from the donations of the faithful, for whom he built the Brunswick Cathedral. His successors added to it, piece by piece, until finally it contained thousands of treasures of inestimable value that were covered with gold and precious stones. I learned that their most recent owner was already selling some pieces to pay for his struggle to regain the kingdom he had lost to Prussia.

That same evening my investigations led me to the castle of the Hanoverian Count G. in T.! Before completing the final third of my journey, I left behind the twenty or so armed plainclothes policemen who had been accompanying me. In the courtyard of the castle, the Count, to whom his steward had announced me, came toward me, visibly amazed to see a stranger, and had his secretary, an affable Englishman, inquire what I wanted. He resembled one of the ancient Germanic noblemen from whom he was doubtless descended; he was tall and had a proud, authoritative face. He dismissed my question by saying that he did not know anything about any weapons and refused to reply to the rest of my questions. Then I explained that I had to search his castle and tried hard to reconcile him to the fact that I had to do my duty, saying that we were merely taking preventive measures necessitated by certain anti-Prussian plots abroad in the land. However, the Count refused to let me search the castle, and I said, expressing my regret, that I should have to arrest him. He hurried over to the candle and blew it out, so that it was pitch black in the room. In order to avoid giving the impression that I was threatening anyone, I had not brought any weapons along, and I had ordered my companions, who were following me here, to fire only in case of emergency. Then a shot was fired in the darkness. I found and lit a candle, and the Count's steward and secretary surrendered to me with their arms raised, even though they had me outnumbered; apparently, they did not believe that I had come alone. But the Count had disappeared, and fearing that he was summoning help, I stormed after him with my people, who had meanwhile arrived, and found him in the hall of the castle, lying on the floor in his own blood. He had been shot through the temple and was dead! Had he shot himself or had he been shot by someone else? We never found out, for there had been no witnesses and afterward, nothing stirred in the castle. I sent for a doctor and said a prayer, and as if it had been ordered for the occasion, the moon shining outside poured through the window to shed its soft light over the dead man. After a brief silence, we began to search the castle, and in the cellars, we finally found what we were looking for: a gigantic storehouse containing armaments of all sorts, as well as mountains of ammunition, bayonets, sabres, even daggers—all made in England.

Although it was considered a proven fact that the national treasure that the King of Hanover had taken with him abroad was being used to train and arm the secret "Guelph legion," I went on the assumption that the fugitive sovereign also had credit with Hanoverian bankers. I thoroughly examined the books in all the banking houses and did, in fact, find a private account belonging to the former King in the establishment of a banker named Mayer; it contained forty thousand talers, which I confiscated. I also found and appropriated another twenty thousand talers at the bank of another Hanoverian banker named Simons. This money appeared to belong to a Mr. Busche-Streithorst, but according to a letter I had discovered from the Lord Chamberlain of Hanover, von Malortie, it was intended to "cover the needs of the King."

In July, 1867, Otto von Bismarck, who was now a count and Chancellor of the North German Federation, entrusted me with the task of guarding King Wilhelm I of Prussia and Tsar Alexander II of Russia during their meeting at the world exhibition in Paris. I had no sooner arrived in Paris with my agents and plain-clothes policemen than I received word that an attempt was going to be made to assassinate the Russian Tsar Alexander. I immediately passed on this information to the Russian Councillor of State, von Schultz, and we agreed that for his own protection the Tsar should not travel to the great troop parade along the road that had been officially reserved for this purpose, but should take a detour, which I should arrange to have strictly guarded. No sooner had our host, the French Emperor Napoleon III, been told about this change in plan, than he summoned me to his presence and had me report my fears about the assassination attempt. This hasty and secret meeting took place in the French Emperor's private chamber, decorated in red and gold. The only other person present was the Parisian Prefect of Police, who was officially responsible for the safety of the monarchs Napoleon had invited to the exhibition. The atmosphere was hostile from the outset, for the highest-ranking police officer in the French capital regarded the conference as unnecessary, indeed, as a sheer waste of time, since—as he categorically assured me—the security measures taken by the Parisian police were truly "impregnable." Napoleon listened to me attentively, but then he said that he could not share my concern as long as the highest-ranking police officer in his service denied that there was any danger of an assassination attempt. Indeed, the French Emperor then suggested to his Russian guest that they travel together in an open carriage to attend the parade, and to my horror, the Tsar agreed.

As they were returning from the parade, a Polish nationalist named Berezowski actually fired a pistol at the Russian Tsar, and it was only by an incredible chance that, instead of hitting the unprotected monarch in the chest, the well-aimed bullet struck the tossing head of a horse trotting beside the carriage that happened to shy just at that moment. The marksman disappeared in the crowd of onlookers and a moment later, took advantage of their confusion to wave them away from him with both arms and to shout loudly, "The assassin is running away down in front there, grab him!" But as he was running away, he ran into a tree on the avenue and I caught up with him. We both fell to the ground, and the murderous marksman and I engaged in a violent struggle. I took away his gun, which he was trying to press to my temple, but he bit my right hand, succeeded in freeing himself and ran away like a veritable hound from hell; I opened fire on him, but failed to hit him. Then the fugitive grabbed a young girl who was standing in his way, rigid with terror, and dragged her along with him as a shield, so that neither I nor my officers, who had hurried up, dared to shoot at him again. The assassin disappeared with his victim into a house resembling a palace, and not only my plainclothes officers, but also uniformed Parisian officers immediately appeared and surrounded it, whereupon the beleaguered man opened a window high in the building, directly beneath the roof and threatened that he would throw his deathly pale prisoner out the window if he were not allowed to leave the building unhindered. Even after the entire area had been occupied and barricaded by the police, the assassin continued to dangle his defenseless victim out the window, insulting the assembled policemen, calling them executioners in the service of the bloodthirsty Tsar of Russia, who had stolen from him his defenseless fatherland, Poland.

The shrieking of the man besieged in the house actually continued all night and into the early morning hours, when the raving fellow finally grew exhausted, surrendered and was hauled off to prison, and his young prisoner, who had fainted but was not hurt, was released. After it was all over, the Parisian Prefect of Police, who had remained there with me until the end, anxiously observing the course of events, declared in a tone of relief, "Thank God even the most fanatical assassins get tired!" I did not reply.

The Pole who had fired at the Russian Tsar with the hope of killing him was released from prison again some weeks later because he had helped to put down a prison riot. He beat his mutinous fellow-prisoners with an iron bar, thus rescuing the warden, who had been captured by the rioters. Napoleon himself pardoned him and had him quietly slipped across the French border. Although I was unable to prevent the assassination attempt, Tsar Alexander II of Russia personally awarded me the Order of the Star of Stanislaus in token of his gratitude and appreciation for my timely warning and my vigorous pursuit of the assassin.

After that, our relations with France, which had been good, grew rapidly worse. The French Emperor Napoleon III expressed the disappointment, ill-will and hostility he felt towards Prussia. The reason for this was that, caught up in the fervor he felt about the war with Austria, the Prussian Premier Otto von Bismarck had promised Napoleon German land between the Rhine and the Moselle rivers if France would "loyally refrain from intervening"; the French had also been promised the Grand Duchy of Luxembourg, complete with a Prussian fortress, and had likewise been told that the entire country of Belgium would be divided up to the best interests of France. Now that he was the Chancellor of the North German Confederation, Bismarck neither could nor wished to make good on these promises.

Instead, Count Bismarck gave me a commission with the words, "Despite all the sympathy I feel for the poor Emperor of France because of his dwindling prestige in his own country, I do not believe that we can avoid going to war with him for very long. But I want to use the respite which remains to us in order to give our army a head start so that our opponent cannot catch up with it, and I shall do so by arming it with the most modern weapons in the world!" He hoped, he said, that he could use his political powers to keep France calm until the Prussian army was ready. However, to do so we needed, once again, to have spies everywhere—and, in fact, this need was even more urgent this time than it had been before the war with Austria—to detect the slightest sign that the French were preparing to attack. This time, Bismarck said triumphantly, he had more than enough money, not from the official defense budget (for to have used this would have made it impossible to keep these matters sufficiently secret), but from the millions that had made up the fortune of the King of Hanover whom he had deposed, and that he had carried to safety in defiance of public supervision.

In November, 1869, the Count sent me to Paris, initially to

investigate the newest weapons invented by the French, the French army rifle and the machine gun.

Upon examining the supposedly revolutionary new hand-weapon, the French army rifle, and comparing it with the older Prussian needle gun, I found that both were so-called breech loaders, that both used cartridges containing the charge, the bullet and the detonator, and that, in addition, the latter were, in both cases, ignited by a horizontal striker. Indeed, I learned that basically the two weapons represented one and the same invention, for the Frenchman Chassepot had merely attempted to improve on Dreyse's Prussian needle gun.

But in addition to the Chassepot army rifle, France had strengthened its artillery with the *mitrailleuse* or machine gun, which had the reputation of being a fearful and murderous weapon. The first news of this new invention had been printed in the Paris newspapers when, after the war in 1866, the French Emperor Napoleon III reformed his army and equipped it with new weapons. The newspapers described in mysterious terms the apocalyptic effect exerted by this new gun. However, I soon discovered that this weapon was not new either, for Struwe, the famous former guerrilla leader, declared that he had been familiar with it since 1848. It had, he said, repeatedly been recommended to him for use in revolutionary endeavors, but the price had been too high for him to pay. Indeed, I learned that this French machine gun, which was supposedly so new, had been in existence for a considerably longer time than Struwe was aware:

The first, admittedly still-imperfect model of this gun had been manufactured in 1827 by a certain Fafchamp, who served in the Grande Armée of Napoleon I. In 1859, the American Gatling constructed a similar weapon possessing four gun barrels which rotated as they were fired, and in 1866 Brame, an Englishman, manufactured another "machine gun." But my most incredible discovery was really no discovery at all: the army of the kingdom of Bavaria had possessed and had been using a "machine gun" (based on the precisely similar blueprint of the arms manufacturer Fedle in Augsburg), and so far no one in Prussia had noticed this fact—incredible as that might have sounded to my Prussian employers until they finally convinced themselves that it was true by personal observation!

France's machine gun, which, far from being new, was merely an imitation of the gun which Fafchamp had manufactured in

1827, consisted of thirty-seven rifled steel barrels welded together into a cylinder cast in bronze, which resembled a pipe with thirty-seven bores.

The shot was ignited almost exactly as it was in Prussia's needle gun, namely, by a striker that pierced the cartridges from behind. The *mitrailleuse* was loaded by inserting the ammunition into the thirty-seven holes in an iron plate, between the breech-plate and the barrels. Then a handle was used to rotate the breech-plate so that the striker rapidly pierced the individual cartridges one after another; the cartridges exploded, creating a continuous fire.

I observed that a skilled three-man crew could load the gun ten times a minute, so that in one minute the *mitrailleuse* could fire three hundred and seventy shots, or more than a thousand shots in three minutes; however, only 66 percent of the shots would hit their target at a distance of one thousand paces, and only 36 percent at three thousand paces. In addition, the weapons frequently jammed and the cartridges frequently failed to ignite.

However, the thing that, above all else, made me believe that this machine gun did not represent a valuable field gun was the fact that all the bullets it fired in such rapid succession struck almost the same point, whereas in the field, one's targets move very quickly; thus, the machine gun could not follow their movements as it fired. Therefore, in my opinion, it would be far less effective than the French desired and the Prussians feared.

Besides all this, while I was in the French capital I once again confronted the old questions: How can I recruit the best secret spies, how can they get hold of the most productive information, and finally, how can I get them safely out of the country without letting anyone find out what they have been doing? From the outset the few agents I had brought with me, highly experienced men who had already proved their worth in Austria, were kept on their feet day and night by their tireless attempt to recruit new spies. I divided the prospective spies they discovered into three categories:

1. People belonging to the unpropertied classes who wanted to survive and wished to earn money without going to any trouble, 2. Officers and officials who either needed large sums of money (to pay gambling debts, etc.) or who wanted to revenge themselves for some personal injury done them or wanted revenge for political reasons (for my purposes I have always preferred these indi-

viduals!), 3. All those whom my agents could blackmail into cooperating with us. Later members of this third group always proved to be the worst and least reliable spies, although, at least in the beginning, they could be most quickly recruited.

Thus, first, I had the financial affairs of all the people who seemed as if they might make suitable spies carefully investigated, and if they were in embarrassed circumstances or even slightly in debt, I immediately attempted to recruit them. My agent would promise and grant extremely easy terms of credit to the person in financial difficulties if he would undertake to secretly spy for us. Primarily, I had my agents address these tempting offers to members of the younger generation, who were usually not yet earning a good income, in the military and in public administration.

In my experience, this procedure represented a purely makeshift expedient, for over half the men who were thus urged to committing treason broke away as soon as possible and freed themselves from the pressure that was being exerted on them because they hated it so much.

Thus, for a long time, the most important task of all my new agents in France was the zealous recruitment of new spies; indeed, I virtually issued categorical orders that they were to ceaselessly search their surroundings for suitable individuals. Of course, it was usually very difficult to tell ahead of time which individuals would make suitable spies, but my principal criterion was that they had to be "persons with access to secrets," persons whom their functions afforded access to secrets of all kinds or who could gain access to them without attracting attention.

Soon my central records office in Berlin was flooded with hundreds, nay, thousands of dossiers about French people in more or less elevated positions who, for the reasons I have mentioned, seemed to be good candidates for the spy business, and the officers who served under me also worked hard to keep the records up to date, for they represented the indispensable foundation of all investigation. Working out of my headquarters in Berlin, I formed all types of people—officers and officials at military headquarters and in offices, scientists, engineers, and manufacturers, not to mention their wives, mistresses, relatives and friends, as well as the secretaries, couriers, servants, coachmen, gardeners and houseboys, who only appeared to be insignificant, and, indeed, even the kitchen personnel of both sexes—into a secret, unbroken network of spies spread across all of France. Without the knowledge of the French people, soon the country was wriggling inside it the way an unsuspecting fish wriggles in the nets of its captors.

The hundreds and hundreds of French traitors who betrayed state and military secrets were, I believed, not people who presently held high positions but people who had formerly held them. For, for whatever reasons he had been dismissed, a man who had lost his post always took away with him his knowledge of secrets, if not actual secret records and documents, and he was always prepared to take vengeance for the pain he had suffered when—rightly or wrongly—he was removed from the office he had previously held.

At my Berlin headquarters, tireless agents continually perused the announcements of the most recent promotions in the French military and civil service, used these announcements to draw up lists of all promoted men and then compared these with lists of French officers and officials of whom it could be predicted that they would be promoted.

In these lists they repeatedly found what I was so urgently seeking: This or that man who had long been overdue for promotion had, for some, at first glance, unknown reason, been passed over, often twice or even three times. If, in addition, this neglected man occupied a position that probably gave him access to information, I immediately sent someone to attempt to recruit him as an "observer"—and my agents usually reported that such attempts were successful. A quiet observer of this kind, who secretly passed on to me at once all information he came across in the line of duty, always seemed to be superior to an obvious, flagrant deserter who could betray secret information only once.

F.M., one of my chief agents in Paris, reported that he was close to high-ranking persons opposed to the régime of Napoleon III. He assured me that it would not be difficult to recruit a group of "élite spies" from their number in Paris and from all over France, for these people were prepared at the outset to work for the enemies of the Emperor they hated. According to F.M. we could, with the aid of this *crème de la crème* who were at odds with their régime, quickly come into the possession of extremely valuable information drawn directly from French government sources.

Thereupon, I expressly granted M. a free hand to conspire with such political individuals and groups and left it entirely up to him how he should go about establishing ties with his contacts all over France. After that, I soon discovered how many Frenchmen there were who secretly spied on their own harbors and factories, stole documents, copied the plans of new machinery and weapons, and indeed, how many of the highest-ranking representatives of the French government, officers and officials who bore the sonorous names of ancient noble families were, for political reasons, all too ready to betray to my agents top secret information they had come to possess because of the positions they held.

The costs and expenses of acquiring this invaluable information remained modest in comparison with its value. The reason was that—apart from a few exceptions—none of the informers regarded themselves as traitors, but instead believed that they were liberating their fatherland from the yoke of the hated Emperor and that thus, their treason constituted·a deed of honor; thus they asked for no reward, or only for a very small one.

No doubt, the unsuspecting German public would have been amazed to learn that my network of secret observers, which had, in fact, soon spread throughout France, was only partially made up of Germans and that the French themselves handled the job much better. It filled me with pride that I had at least *one* informer in almost all the important civilian and military bureaus of France and that, so far, not one of them had been uncloaked and removed from office. Indeed, to my pleasure, I saw that my secret investigation of the land of Napoleon III was apparently easier and involved less risk than my earlier investigation of peace-loving Austria.

Something relating to my intelligence activities happened to me while I was in my Paris lodgings, which I had rented, once again, under the fictitious name of a German journalist called Schmidt. An unknown ˙visitor was announced to me there. I judged him to be about fifty years old, and he had the rigid face of a man who, for a long time, has been accustomed to hiding his feelings. When I asked the stranger to sit down, instead of following my suggestion, he crept back to the door again and suddenly flung it open. Only then did he return to me, obviously relieved that no one had been listening to our conversation.

I asked him what he wanted, and he began to speak hesitatingly but in almost flawless German, "Permit me, sir, to offer you an opportunity, to suggest that we reach an agreement, or whatever you like to call it?" When I glanced at the clock, feeling bored, he immediately protested, "I am sure that you will have enough time, my dear sir, as soon as you learn why I have come!" Thereupon I asked him to come to the point.

"My offer is enormously important to your country!" he continued. "I can" (at this point he hesitated, either because he found it difficult to express himself in German or because he was trying to find out what impression his words were making on me) "supply you with the most secret documents of my country." Again he paused significantly, and then continued, "In case you want to know who I am, my name doesn't matter. I shall give you three days to consider my offer, and then I'll return to learn your decision. If you turn it down, you won't see me again, but if you accept it, in a short time I shall turn over to you several of the most secret documents of the French government, and if you are pleased with this first lot, I'll bring you more and more . . . !"

I did my best not to alter my expression, even though my first thought was that my mysterious guest was a lunatic who wanted to impress others by boasting of his exploits. Nevertheless, I agreed that we should meet again in three days, whereupon he implored me to put out all the lights in my lodgings and on the stairs, saying that he did not want to leave until he was protected by total darkness.

I did as he asked, except that I allowed a single candle to remain lit, screening its light with my hand, and when I returned with it to my visitor, he had raised the collar of his coat and pulled his hat down over his eyes. It was already after midnight, and thus I remained standing in the door rather than accompanying him outside.

As he was flitting past me, the man suddenly grabbed my arm and hissed in my ear, "Do you want to know who I am, sir? Well— I am the valet of His Majesty the Emperor of France!" And without noticing my astonishment, he disappeared into the darkness.

This, then, was my first meeting with a man to whom I was subsequently indebted for providing me with the most invaluable information! However, my agent F.M. in Paris achieved an even more brilliant coup, in the course of which he was able to discover, without its being detected, France's secret plan for the deployment of French troops in the event of a war with Germany.

M. simply assumed that—as was the case in armies all over the world—a plan of this type would have been drawn up even in peacetime and that it must have been stored at the headquarters of the War Ministry, which resembled a gigantic labyrinth and moreover was very closely guarded. How could poor M. acquire the slightest clue to where in this maze the plan he desired had been concealed?

When I say that just one week after his arrival in Paris, my agent had not only discovered where a draft of this secret map was kept, but also had already figured out a method by which he could gain access to it, and at the same time, prevent the French from finding out that he had done so, it will be clear how proud I was of him. For an inquiry can be considered perfectly successful only if it leaves no warning traces behind it. One must gain possession of secret data without being detected, for a secret ceases to be a secret once it becomes known that it has been betrayed! The spy accomplishes his purpose only if the original possessor of the secret continues to believe he is its only possessor.

How did F.M. do it, what complicated maneuver afforded him success? The answer is, it was not a complicated maneuver at all! Instead he simply posed as an Alsatian (this explained his German speech) and got acquainted with one of the sentries who stood guard at the gate in front of the War Ministry, claiming that he was a house-painter looking for work.

The well-meaning sentry told him that they always needed painting done in this building and suggested that he ask about it on the following day. F.M.—dressed like a workman and carrying a ladder, a paintbrush and some whitewash—did as he was told and was immediately led to a dilapidated wall inside the Ministry, where he busily began to apply the whitewash. However, no sooner had he been left alone than he boldly shouldered the tools of his craft and began to wander around the building. He did not even hesitate to ask for directions along the way. Even a high dignitary, dressed in the uniform of a French officer and covered with decorations, affably condescended to explain to this "painter who had lost his way" where he should go.

Thus my master spy quite easily arrived at the right door, pressed the doorknob and found that it was not locked . . . In a moment F.M. had entered the room, closed the doors behind him, leaned his ladder against the nearest wall and begun to apply whitewash. He had attained his goal, for before him on an ebony table gleamed the parti-colored map, covered by a glass lid, which showed the deployment of French troops. Of course it was only a rough draft, but it had clearly been sealed with the official brass seal marked "Secret"!

From his perch on the ladder, holding his paintbrush in his hand, F.M. feverishly studied the map, expecting to be interrupted at any moment—but no one followed him into the sacred room! An hour later, after he had memorized every last detail of France's secret plan for deploying French troops in the event of war with Germany, and relying almost exclusively on his excellent memory (he did make a few notes on his sleeve with the paint and the brush and then immediately rolled up the sleeve), my crafty journeyman painter left the "sanctum sanctorum" of the French War Ministry. No one noticed him leave any more than they had seen him enter. Boldly shouldering his equipment, he went to the exit and thence to freedom, quite unmolested, for his friendly patron had meanwhile gone off duty and been replaced by another guard whom he did not know.

The information we extracted from the stream of observations flowing in from my agents in France soon revealed a surprising picture, the picture of a country which—at least for the present—could pose no danger to Prussia and the North German Confederation. We were particularly struck by the following points:

The machinery in France's armaments factories was, for the most part, old-fashioned, neglected and defective, which would mortally cripple France in case of war.

A severe chronic illness prevented France's Emperor Napoleon III from exercising his function as Commander-in-Chief of the army and even, now that there was peace, from running his government. At this very time, he was suffering acute pain, and while it lasted, he could neither walk, eat nor sleep, so that his physician had even recommended that he abdicate on the grounds that he was too ill to reign! My secret agents, several of whom were at the court itself, said that they were truly shocked at the physical and intellectual decay of this monarch, who only appeared to be one of the most powerful men in the world.

For the ruler of France was struggling against the increasing dissatisfaction many people felt with his régime, a régime his ministers were desperately attempting to preserve, at least in its outward form, by turning over more and more of the Emperor's privileges to parliamentary institutions. Secretly, they implored their sovereign to do nothing to prevent the unification of the German state, because, in its weakened condition, his régime would not survive the war that might result and the many sacrifices it would demand.

Finally, the troops of France were not even available to engage in an armed conflict because they were scattered abroad, far from their arsenals and mobilization centers; they were, in fact, busy protecting the Papal States from the Italians in Rome. In order to wage a war, they would first have to undergo the laborious process of going home again, and if this happened, the Pope would immediately lose the territory over which he had temporal rule, which, in the past, Napoleon had always tried to prevent.

This meant that it would take France at least a fortnight to mobilize a mere one hundred thousand men against Germany, an insufficient force to combat the forces that Prussia alone was now prepared to send against it . . .

Apart from thanking me, Count Bismarck did not comment on my painstaking labors except to say that the results represented an "invitation to the German soldier's boot" to march forward—provided that one could find a reason for it which, in the eyes of all nations and in the judgment of history, would make France alone appear responsible.

However, a reason for engaging in such a war turned up of its own accord, and much sooner than we had expected. The "spark that set off the powderkeg" was the possible candidacy of Prince Leopold von Hohenzollern-Sigmaringen to assume the vacant throne of Spain, from which a revolution had displaced the dissolute Queen Isabella, whereupon the Cortes, the Spanish National Assembly, under the leadership of Premier Prim, drew up a constitution that again placed the reins of government in the hands of a monarch, but did not provide the country with a new king. Prim looked around Europe for a Catholic aspirant suitable to assume the throne, and a group of Spaniards led by a man named Salazar suggested the son of Prince Karl Anton von Hohenzollern.

This prince had himself been a sovereign until he abdicated the throne of his tiny principality of Sigmaringen in favor of the Prussian crown, whereupon he became a member of Prussia's royal family.

Since that time, the Protestant King of Prussia had been the head of the princely Catholic Hohenzollern branch of the family and possessed a monarch's right to refuse to allow any member of his family to mount a foreign throne without his express permission.

However, in view of his relationship with Napoleon III, the ambitious old Prince Anton thought that Napoleon must be favorably disposed toward his son (Prince Karl Anton von Hohenzollern-Sigmaringen was married to Josephine, daughter of Grand Duke Karl von Baden and his wife Stephanie, née Beauharnais, Napoleon III's cousin twice removed!)

At first, no one in Europe took very seriously or paid much attention to the Spanish proposal, which was to have such weighty consequences, that a member of Prussia's ruling family be raised up to sit upon the throne of Spain. Only Count Bismarck, immediately and from the very outset, devoted all his energies to bringing about this event, although he always worked behind the scenes.

Rather than placing himself in the public eye, in May, 1869, he sent to Madrid his confidant, Theo von Bernardi, an historian and political economist whom Bismarck and von Moltke had often sent on secret missions that he carried out under the cloak of being nothing but a scholar.

Count Bismarck gave his secret emissary no less than fifty thousand pounds, which he had taken from the confiscated treasure of the Guelphs, to be used for "recruiting" advocates of the candidacy, which he wished to promote, of the Hohenzollern prince for the Spanish throne.

I never found out exactly who in Spain was bribed with this enormous sum, but it was reported to me that before the visit of Bismarck's money-laden emissary, Spain's Premier Prim was deeply in debt, but that after this visit he lived high off the hog.

Immediately after von Bernardi's secret mission had been completed, Count Bismarck delivered a tempting report to King Wilhelm of Prussia, who was opposed to the idea of a Hohenzollern in Spain on the ground that it was "too venturesome," suggesting to him that having a Hohenzollern sovereign in Spain would save him "two army corps" in the event of a war between Prussia and France, and that in peacetime, it would lend his royal house a "world-wide splendor" like that possessed only by the house of Hapsburg.

Despite this alluring prospect, the Prussian King rejected the whole idea, whereupon in March, 1870, Count Bismarck abruptly invited Prince Karl Anton and his son Leo to the royal palace in

Berlin. There he arranged for a magnificent dinner-party, to which I, too, was invited.

Apart from the guests, the Prussian Crown Prince, Count Bismarck, von Schleinitz, the Prussian Secretary of State for Foreign Affairs, Delbrück, who presided over Bismarck's chancellery, von Thile, the Under-Secretary of State for Foreign Affairs, the War Minister General von Roon, and von Moltke, the chief of his general staff, were also present.

All of them—both statesmen and soldiers—were one in their support of the Prince's acceptance of the Spanish throne, for before dinner, they had made an agreement with the Count that they would support it. Not one of them spoke a word about the open question of whether the assumption by a Hohenzollern of the Spanish throne might lead to war with France. In my hearing, only Delbrück whispered to von Moltke, his neighbor at the table, "But if Napoleon takes it amiss, are we ready?"

Whereupon the leader of the Prussian troops breathed back in the same muted tone, "More than ready!" For the King could not be allowed to hear such words. As everyone at the party knew, he would immediately have forbidden the Prince to ever accept the Spanish throne if there were the slightest danger that it might lead to war.

But this move on Bismarck's part also failed to meet with success. The King continued to refuse his permission, a fact which Bismarck, to be sure, did not allow to disturb him. Again he secretly sent a confidant to Spain, this time Lothar von Bucher, carrying a personal letter to General Prim. When King Wilhelm expressed his irritation at the fact that his Chancellor was secretly engaged in political negotiations behind his back, Count Bismarck reassured him completely by telling him that von Bucher's visit was purely a diplomatic courtesy.

However, in reality, through von Bucher's mediation he agreed on "secret tactics" with Spain's Premier Prim, tactics of which the most important element was the stipulation that it was not to be revealed that he—Bismarck—and his Foreign Office had had anything to do with their formulation. And when von Bucher returned to Berlin bearing assurances to this effect from Prim, King Wilhelm, although he did it with "an extremely heavy heart," gave his consent, necessary according to the laws of his royal house, to the candidacy of a Hohenzollern for the throne of Spain.

Up until this point, all Bismarck's activities had been kept completely secret, for Count Bismarck intended to communicate the news of the acceptance of the Hohenzollern Prince to the Spanish Cortes, who were officially responsible for electing their king, at the last minute, thus forcing the voting to be held so swiftly that Europe would be presented with a *fait accompli*. But this surprise attack failed because the Cortes had just adjourned when Bismarck's courier arrived in Madrid bearing the news of Prince Leo's consent, and the secret was revealed soon thereafter. Spain's Premier Prim was forced to tell the whole truth to the French ambassador in Madrid, who immediately demanded information.

The Emperor Napoleon in France was beside himself with rage at this "malicious trick." After all, Spain was France's neighbor to the south, and he believed that to have a Hohenzollern sovereign there would represent the beginning of the encirclement of France, which could strangle his country with a war on two fronts. However, almost more than this, Napoleon feared that his people would despise him and drive him from his throne if he took no steps to counteract this threatening "foreign plot."

There was, in fact, a great stir all over France as soon as it became known what had happened in Spain! Thereupon Napoleon ordered his ambassador Le Sourd to inquire at the Foreign Office in Berlin what part the government of Prussia had played in this "infamous intrigue." But just at that time, everyone in authority was a long distance from Berlin: King Wilhelm was taking the waters at Bad Ems, Benedetti was doing the same thing at Wildbad, and Count Bismarck was on his estate in Pomerania. Thus the ambassador of the furious Napoleon had to be satisfied with von Thile, the Under-Secretary of State, who truthfully but vainly assured him that his government had had nothing to do with the scandalous affair. Napoleon, who had meanwhile learned about the secret correspondence that had been exchanged between Count Bismarck and Spanish Premier Prim and about the conspiracy in which they had engaged, rejected this "impudent lie."

Thereupon, the French Emperor addressed a sharp threat to Prussia in the presence of his Parliament that abruptly informed a startled Europe that it was on the brink of war. "Never," he said, "shall we permit a foreign power to aspire to the throne of Charles V in order to upset the balance of Europe to the detriment of France. To prevent this, we shall, without hesitation, do our duty, which is self-preservation . . . !" At the same time, the profoundly troubled Emperor of France ordered his ambassador Benedetti to travel to Ems immediately to speak with the King of Prussia.

Under these conditions and according to international custom, it was not only Benedetti's right but his duty, as an ambassador, to speak to the Prussian monarch in person. But far from Berlin, Count Bismarck was troubled by this prospect, for he feared that his king might replace his, Bismarck's, policies with his own peace-loving policies. From the very beginning, he had been convinced that only a war could bring about the unity, which he desired, of the German states. More than once he complained to me that "the tribes of Germany can never be made to unite by peaceful means"—to accomplish this, he said, one had to search for some conflict.

It was true that, since his victory over Austria, Bavaria and Württemberg had turned away from him. In Munich a "Bavarian Party" was seeking to ensure that its country would remain permanently neutral during any wars Prussia might undertake in the future, and the King and Queen of Württemberg demonstrated a similar failure to think "German," for they had openly assured the French ambassador to their court that they hoped France would be victorious . . .

Thus, for Bismarck, the placing of a Hohenzollern on the Spanish throne was not only an end in itself, but a path leading to his principal goal, the unification of Germany. Therefore, he opposed the well-meant intervention of Lord Clarendon, who in the spring of 1870 suggested that Germany and France should both disarm. (He did this at the instigation of several French ministers who wanted to remain in the background.) The "idealistic Lord," as Bismarck called him, addressed to Bismarck several imploring letters, but nothing was farther from the Count's mind than to promote disarmament, which he called "humanitarian sentimentalism."

Despite all Bismarck's efforts, Prince Leo withdrew as a candidate for the Spanish throne, and Napoleon would have won his longed-for victory if he had been content with this. Instead, he listened to the raving of irresponsible members of the press and German-haters in his country, who were not satisfied with the Prince's withdrawal because it had been the "private decision of the Hohenzollerns" and thus could be revoked by the Prussian government at any time. Thus, Napoleon ordered his ambassador

Benedetti to obtain from the King of Prussia his promise that he would expressly forbid any member of his family to assume the Spanish throne for all time to come, through which clumsy and unnecessary provocation he delivered himself directly into Bismarck's hands.

For King Wilhelm had no choice but to refuse to enter into this overly subtle, dictatorial agreement that had been inspired by fear, and Privy Councillor Abeken, who represented the Foreign Office, sent a telegram to Bismarck notifying him of this fact, in which he said, employing the circumstantial language of officialdom: °

Ems, June 13, 1870. After the Government of the Emperor of France had been officially informed by the Government of the King of Spain about the renunciation of the Spanish throne by Prince Leopold von Hohenzollern-Sigmaringen, the French ambassador Count Benedetti addressed to His Majesty the King of Prussia the petition of his sovereign, Emperor Napoleon III of France, that he guarantee that the house of Hohenzollern would not accept the throne of the King of Spain at any time in the future. However, the King was forced to reject this petition, for he had not yet received official confirmation of the Prince's withdrawal and the French ambassador appeared to be better informed than he was about the events which had occurred. Later the King sent his adjutant to officially inform the French ambassador that he could not receive him until he had received detailed official information about these events . . .

° The Ems Dispatch is here quoted from memory. The text actually reads:

"His Majesty writes me: 'Count Benedetti intercepted me while I was out walking, and in what in the end became a very importunate manner he demanded that I authorize him to immediately telegraph the message that I promised never again, at any time in the future, to give my consent if the Hohenzollerns were to renew their candidacy. Finally I refused his demand somewhat sternly, for on no account may one or can one enter into undertakings of this kind. Naturally, I told him that I had not yet received any information and that, since he had been informed sooner than I about what was going on in Paris and Madrid, he could easily understand that my government had nothing to do with the matter.' Since that time His Majesty has received a letter from the Prince. As His Majesty had told Count Benedetti that he was waiting to hear from the Prince, His Majesty, in view of the aforementioned unreasonable demand, and upon receiving the report of Count Eulenburg and myself, has decided not to receive Count Benedetti again, but merely to inform him through an adjutant that His Majesty has now received from the Prince confirmation of the news which Benedetti had received, and that he has nothing more to say to the ambassador." (Source: Gerhart Binder, *Geschichte im Zeitalter der Weltkriege*, Stuttgart 1977)

However, Count Bismarck rigorously reduced this official language to a text that was designed to hit like a grenade and to raise nationalistic feelings to fever pitch in Germany and France. Thus his revised version of the telegram from Ems read as follows: *

Ems, June 13, 1870. Today, France's Ambassador Benedetti intercepted the King of Prussia when he was out for a walk and importunately demanded that he promise to forbid the Hohenzollerns to assume the throne of Spain at any time in the future. In view of this unreasonable demand, the King of Prussia refused to reply to the French ambassador and sent his adjutant on duty to inform him that he had nothing further to say to him.

In this way, Count Bismarck made an ordinary dispatch read like, and imply, a sharp official insult, which it, in fact, was not; and which had not, as Bismarck well knew, been the intention of his King. But that was not all. The very next day he published the text he had devised in special editions of all the German gazettes, whipping the populations of Germany and France into a frenzy of patriotic fury. In addition, Count Bismarck informed all the German and foreign courts of the wording of this text and intensified its effect by adding that Benedetti had "addressed the old and sickly King of Prussia, against his will and in a provocative manner, on a public street" (in reality, in accordance with protocol, the King had addressed the ambassador!).

The results were everything Bismarck desired. When his thunderstruck King read the morning newspapers, he cried, "But this means war!" He recognized too late that his Chancellor had usurped the right, which the constitution of the North German Confederation expressly reserved to him alone, to declare war. There was nothing left for him to do but go through the formalities, for the government of France could have only one re-

---

* This text too is quoted from memory. The actual text reads:
"After the Government of the Emperor of France had been officially informed by that of the King of Spain about the renunciation of the Prince von Hohenzollern, the French ambassador in Ems demanded that His Majesty the King authorize him to telegraph Paris saying that His Majesty the King promised never again, at any time, to give his consent if the Hohenzollerns were to renew their candidacy. Thereupon, His Majesty refused to receive the French ambassador again, and sent the adjutant on duty to inform him that His Majesty had nothing more to say to the ambassador." (Source: Gerhart Binder, *Geschichte im Zeitalter der Weltkriege*, Stuttgart 1977)

sponse to Bismarck's actions: a declaration of war against Germany!

While Simson, the President of the German Parliament in Berlin, was still reading announcements and conducting the business of the day, Count Bismarck bounded in with youthful élan, his eyes sparkling with triumph. He had scarcely reached his seat before he demanded to be heard, and when stillness had settled over the assembly, he shouted a single sentence, "I hereby inform this great House that the French *chargé d'affaires* has just handed me France's declaration of war!"

He had scarcely uttered the word "war" when a thunderstorm that had been hanging over us throughout that sultry morning, broke loose outside, and a dazzling flash of lightning streaked to the earth accompanied by a crash of thunder. But before the thunder had rolled forth, it was swallowed by the clamor of a hundred voices proclaiming their boundless rejoicing. Applause and shouts of "Hurrah!" roared through the hall, everyone present had risen from his seat, and in the diplomats' box old Bancroft, an historiographer from the United States of America, wiped his eyes with a lace handkerchief—apparently moved by the thought of that day when his fatherland had made a similar decision to fight for unity and freedom.

After that there was silence, while outside the storm sent down the pattering rain, and it grew so dark that someone quickly lit a candle and placed the candlestick at Bismarck's side. But the Count remained laconic and merely said that he did not want to anticipate the statement that His Majesty the King intended to address to the Parliament. Another dazzling streak of lightning descended from the clouds, followed by a clap of thunder, and again the sound of the thunder was drowned in the general enthusiasm, in the cries of "Hurrah!" and "Bravo!" that issued from all sides of the hall.

After the breach in diplomatic relations—which appeared to be the fault of France alone—had thus become irrevocable, the mobilization of German troops followed with lightning precision. Now it was revealed what a powerful weapon those "offensive and defensive alliances" that Bismarck, looking toward the future, had forged after his victory over Austria, had placed in the hands of Prussia! For now they guaranteed that the armies of all the states of southern Germany would immediately be placed at his disposal for use in his war against France.

PART FOUR

The Franco-Prussian War began with an unprecedented demonstration of German solidarity: All the nations of southern Germany, including Bavaria, immediately joined the North German Confederation, all their sovereigns signed orders to mobilize their troops, and with equal unanimity, took the necessary measures in their countries to prepare for war.

As in the last war against Austria, General von Moltke once again came to the aid of King Wilhelm I by serving as Chief of the General Staff, and all the German troops were divided into three armies:

1. An army of sixty thousand men under General Friedrich von Steinmetz,

2. An army of one hundred and ninety-four thousand men under Prince Friedrich Carl of Prussia,

3. An army of one hundred and thirty thousand men under Crown Prince Friedrich Wilhelm of Prussia.

In all the history of the world, no one had accomplished what Prussia accomplished now. Within a period of only fourteen days, an army of almost four hundred thousand men had not only been mobilized but was in position and ready to attack. This was a triumph of Prussian discipline, order and energy.

Not only did Germany mobilize its troops with the enthusiastic support of the nation, but the French, too, expressed their delight that the war had finally begun! Whereas our German soldiers jubilantly cried out, "On to Paris", my agents in the country that was now our enemy reported that the French soldiers were exultantly shouting "À Berlin!" In front of the royal palace in Berlin and in front of the imperial palace in Paris hundreds of enthusiastic supporters of the war stood and waited, their eyes riveted on their respective sovereigns' windows, and burst into ecstatic applause if the one monarch or the other betrayed his presence by so much as a shadow.

Actually, no one in either of the enemy countries, Germany and France, paid the slightest heed to the dangers, the sacrifices and the suffering involved in every war. Such joy and jubilation reigned in both nations that it seemed as if the coming struggle were already at an end and that both parties had been blessed with victory (which, of course, was impossible). If the two sovereigns had shown the slightest opposition to the ecstasy of their subjects, they would probably have risked losing their thrones!

The German newspapers, as well as the French newspapers

(my agents continued to supply me with all of them) outdid each other in goading their people into a frenzy of warlike zeal, in France by calling the Germans "barbarians," in Germany by boasting that "The entire world will thank us when we have driven the megalomaniacal specter of Caesar from the French throne!" Moreover, in both countries, even in the most distinguished and fashionable quarters of the cities, the shopwindows displayed the most hideous caricatures of all the civilian and military leaders of the enemy nation, caricatures which mocked the French as "sans-culottes" and the Germans as "sauerkraut-eaters."

An operetta entitled *The Prussian Eagle on His Flight of Vengeance* was hastily composed and adorned with verse by the German historian Heinrich von Treitschke. Among other things, the lyrics said:

> When the hate-filled Frank
> Impudently mocks with his coarse brawling
> The majestic being of our King—
> Rise up, valiant German avengers:
> Strike the French felons on the head
> And liberate the German Rhine . . .

During the premiere performance of this operetta at the Royal Theater in Berlin, the public demonstrated for several minutes in favor of the war when, in the last act, S., a singer in the royal opera, dressed in the costume of the German dragon-slayer Siegfried, hit "high C" and intoned in a shattering tenor: "Thus cuts the sword of Germany!" As he sang he struck a papier-mâché anvil bearing the inscription "LA FRANCE" a blow with his stage-prop sword, whereupon the anvil was supposed to split in half. However, apparently the mechanism inside it failed to function, and despite the furious blows rained upon it by the singer in the Siegfried costume, the recalcitrant block stubbornly remained in one piece and did not move from the spot.

The King, who left his box, perhaps as a result of this fiasco, did not return until the theater public burst into frenetic cries of rejoicing, and, deeply moved, he thanked them for their tribute.

However, at the same hour, the public at the Paris Opera were celebrating just as stormily the "French answer" to the German song, "They shall not have it, the free German Rhine!" This answer was Alfred de Musset's battle hymn: *Across Your Rhine River, Frank, Which Your Father Crossed Before You, Will Now Storm the Son!*

Only a group of workers (I was immediately informed of this) dared to speak ill of the war, called it a "purely dynastic quarrel," and made the following public resolution: "We demand for all peoples the exclusive right to choose war or peace for themselves and thus to determine their own fate!" However, when the Social Democrat August Bebel subsequently took an equally public stand and condemned the coming war in the Parliament as "genocide in the interests of those in authority," his words were greeted by the unanimous indignation of all the members of Parliament, all those who had voted for him withdrew their support, and he barely escaped being arrested.

In France, too, only one voice was raised against this war: "You will not be victorious in Germany but annihilated in France—I know the Prussians!" French politician Prévost warned his countrymen, who were confident of victory and did not listen to him—and he shot himself!

By order of the Cabinet I was ordered to the King's headquarters expressly to take charge of "guarding its security and order for the duration of the hostilities," just as I had done during the war with Austria, but now I had much greater authority and a larger apparatus at my disposal, expanded primarily by the addition of French-speaking officers. This time, the following were also expressly included among my duties: "The support of German army leaders with information from the enemy nation, defense against enemy spies, the supervision of all postal traffic and of those members of the press who travel with the army, as well as the policing of foreigners, the cordoning off of territory, requisitioning, etc."

Long ago, while we were still at peace, I had submitted an almost imploring memorandum to the Chancellor Count Bismarck, pleading with him that in any future war a special "security police force" should be established for the personal protection of the King and his advisers. At that time I pointed out that in "unseasonable times like the present" it was to be feared that more attempts would be made to assassinate these persons in the field than in peacetime. Indeed, almost in a tone of desperation, I warned him that in enemy territory such distinguished individuals represented magnetic targets for assassins of all descriptions, and complained that, in the past, the regular police had shown that they were helpless to combat assassins. Honest constables, accustomed to capturing thieves and swindlers, were not prepared to cope with this completely new type of criminal, whom, in addition, if they were to prevent him from carrying out his crime, they were required to track down and arrest—not, as they were accustomed to doing, after, but before he had committed it.

To serve in a police force such as I envisioned one needed great skill in observation, a profound knowledge of human nature, considerable analytical powers, the ability to dissimulate or, in general, artfulness and cunning—qualities rarely possessed by an ordinary policeman. Trained to act only in accordance with regulations, he learns these skills, if he learns them at all, from his own mistakes and omissions. And if, yes, *if* he survives them, to deal with assassins he must confront murderers who are capable of anything and who will grant no mercy!

Thus my concept demanded a specially trained troop of guards who, instead of obeying orders, were free to take any action they believed was required by the situation in which they found themselves at the moment. To be sure, I could use only extraordinarily intelligent and daring individuals in this troop, but I was confident that I could find them!

However, Count Eulenburg, the Prussian Minister of the Interior, who, as was appropriate, was given my memorandum, did not want to hear about any such "hysterical puffing-up" (as he liked to call it) of the police force that had always served in the field in the past, and he was convinced that the ordinary police were quite capable of continuing to meet our needs. At the same time, despite their present enthusiasm for the war, the German press, apparently at the instigation of my old enemies, once again attacked me for my long-forgotten past and branded my character as "non-liberal, inhumane and cynical."

But Count Bismarck ignored all these intrigues, expressly declared that he agreed with my plan, and appointed me (the appointment was to take effect immediately) head of a new "field security police force" whose orders were to be obeyed by all personnel at the King's headquarters. Officially he justified his action by saying, "In the past, Stieber's recommendations have often proved invaluable to us!"

He quickly gained the King's approval for this decision, which was also supported by War Minister von Roon, and Count Eulenburg was forced to give in. The first words Bismarck spoke after this victory seemed to me representative of his blunt, direct nature: "Now that you have made these proposals that arouse the mistrust of your enemies," the Count rumbled at me, "please get busy and carry them out immediately!"

The first thing I did, with the aid of a dozen carefully chosen plainclothes detectives—the best and most experienced I could find at such short notice—was to keep the King, the Chancellor and their most important advisers and aides under perpetual guard both day and night. This had to be done very quickly, for King Wilhelm and his retinue were already preparing to take to the field. In addition to a considerable number of princes of German states, the monarch was accompanied by War Minister von Roon; von Moltke, the Chief of the General Staff; Count Bismarck, the Chancellor of the North German Confederation; and a large escort. But when, before their departure, the King publicly embraced his son, the Crown Prince, weeping as he did so, all my guards were present and only reluctantly permitted the crowd to press towards him and try to kiss his hands.

Count Bismarck, on the other hand, had taken Holy Communion in his home and mockingly asked the men I had sent to guard him whether they wanted to take Communion too. However, they—each of them dressed in plain clothes that concealed the fact that he was armed with a dagger, a club and two pistols, and that he always kept his hand on one of the pistols—were forced to refuse. In the presence of my officers, the Chancellor made out his will, thus "arming himself for all eventualities," and then, accompanied by his wife and daughter, and also, less conspicuously, by my guards, took a coach to the railway station, where he attached himself to the field headquarters of his King as he had done in the war with Austria.

At the same time, my agents in France reported that Emperor Napoleon III—quoting Friedrich Schiller in fluent German (for he had attended the Anna Gymnasium in Mayence!)—intended to emulate the Spartan Bonaparte: All he took with him into the field was a servant and a hard soldier's bed, even though he was tortured by a kidney stone and even make-up and hair dye could not conceal the fact that he was as pale as a corpse. And when his son "Lulu," dressed in the elegant uniform of a lieutenant and cutting off locks of his hair so that he could throw them to the ladies of the court, asked his father whether he did not at least wish to take along a tent, the Emperor replied, in a voice which could be heard some distance away, "I am going to conquer a country where I shall find plenty of houses!"

Meanwhile our headquarters rolled out of Berlin in six long special trains. The King travelled in the drawing-room car with Prince Carl, who was general master of ordnance, the generals, and those of their aides-de-camp who were on duty. The compartments were crowded with members of the general staff, the supervisors of the artillery and the military engineers, the members of the military and civilian cabinets, the field postal service, the field telegraphers and field police—a total of eighty-six high-ranking officials and officers, fifty-four upper-grade officials and one hundred and eighteen subordinate officials, fifty-two non-commissioned officers, six hundred and seventy-one troops, seven hundred and eighty-two horses and eighty-four vehicles—almost one thousand men, the strength of a cavalry division!

Our journey into the field resembled an endless triumphal procession! None of us, from the King down to the lowest "maintenance man," had ever experienced anything like this or even believed it possible. All the railway stations were a single sea of flowers and were filled with jubilant crowds packed shoulder to shoulder. This was true even of the stations where we did not stop. Besides this, we received the ceaseless homage of magistrates and university students; indeed, along the open track were walls of people singing and applauding, and even the roofs and the trees were filled with them. Again and again, the King had to step with his generals to the windows of the long train, to be greeted by the boundless rejoicing of patriots, by cheers and shouts of "Long live the King!"

The enthusiasm of the people appeared to be truly inexhaustible, for every day around twenty troop trains had passed by before we arrived, and each of them was welcomed and sent on its way again with equal zeal!

From the outset, our existence at headquarters unfolded within the confines of strictly demarcated circles formed by the King and his court, then the staff of the Crown Prince in his role as commander of the Third German Army, followed by Count Bismarck and his aides, and finally Generals von Moltke and von Roon with their staffs and the proud princes of the Confederation with their royal households.

In appreciation for his services, the King had long ago raised Bismarck to the rank of Count and Major-General, as well as making him Premier, the Prussian Secretary of State for Foreign Affairs, and Chancellor of the North German Confederation—but despite all these dignities, he was apparently not yet of equal rank with the "demigods" of the general staff! I involuntarily overheard a dialogue which shed some light on this matter, between no lesser figures than Generals von Moltke and von Roon. Von Roon said in a voice that was unabashedly loud, "Have we taken steps to ensure that the Civilian Club (the soldiers' nickname for Bismarck's office) won't take over the whole show again?"

Whereupon von Moltke grumbled in an equally audible voice, "Let us hope so!" (In the war with Austria, Bismarck had prevented the victorious army from enjoying their triumph to the full by marching into Vienna, for he was already thinking about the possibility of war with France and wanted to ensure that in this event the Austrians would remain neutral, which they now did in gratitude for the fact that the boots of Prussian soldiers had not "profaned" their capital. I believed that such foresight was so rare a phenomenon in history that I should gladly have heard people express more appreciation of it!)

Whereas my agents in enemy territory reported that the French were so confident of victory that the French commanders were given maps of Germany but no maps of France, at first I heard our leaders express little confidence that we should win a swift victory. On the contrary, King Wilhelm and his generals feared the new French *chassepot* or army rifle, and only General von Roon sought to encourage us by saying, "Prussia's ancient god of battles will not allow us to be defeated!" Whereas Count Bismarck assured everyone who would listen that we were in a very favorable position because the world regarded the French, not ourselves, as the aggressors, King Wilhelm was still indignant: "Did you ever see such impertinence?! I am supposed to suffer for an affair that was not my fault but Prim's!" (Prim was the Premier of Spain.)

The "headquarters" of my field security police crossed the border along with the headquarters of the King, and did so very inconspicuously, for apart from myself, it consisted of only a few aides, who, despite their small number, quickly became the center for order and security throughout our headquarters.

We always rolled along in front of the King's cars, and between dawn and evening we often travelled long distances of up to seventy kilometers; once we travelled for forty hours without stopping! No sooner had we taken lodgings than I always had our quarters hermetically sealed and cordoned off and set up a "security bureau" that never lacked for something to do. Here, after the field telegraph had reached us, I again became what I have always been, for I have never been anything else: a dedicated detective!

Even when we only stopped travelling for a few hours, I kept my aides busy and alert. Couriers arrived with reports and questions and left again carrying my answers and instructions; things had to be confiscated and areas cordoned off; letters, telegrams and press publications had to be supervised; and I had to make decisions about them and usually make arrangements relating to them right away. All these activities were intended to facilitate my one goal, which was to provide for the maximum security and ensure the undisturbed functioning of every person at the headquarters of my sovereign while he waged his war.

Usually, the reports from my agents arrived during the night or very early in the morning, so that I had to work during the night and often did not get to bed until 3:00 A.M., only to be forced to rise again at 5:00 A.M. Thus soon I acquired the ability to fall asleep at any time of day whenever the opportunity presented itself.

Let me describe the kind of demands that were made upon me almost daily. At 2:00 A.M. I would get to sleep, then at 3:00 A.M. my agent would arrive from O. with a long report. I would wake up the secretary and give him orders that were to be carried out immediately, to put messages in code, to send out the necessary messengers, etc. All this would take place at around 4:00 A.M. I would barely have time to go to bed, where I would stay until 6:00 A.M., when Count W. would arrive punctually bearing orders from the King that had to be carried out at once. I would be forced to get up, ride almost four miles accompanied by my officers, and, once we had arrived at our destination, issue the necessary orders from horseback and make sure that they were carried out. I would arrive back at headquarters too late to eat with the others, would gulp down some cold food and in the evening would finally find time to wash myself for the first time that day.

My tireless aides and I always concealed our identity by wearing civilian clothes or the most inconspicuous army uniforms. On the other hand, to our deep concern, our high-ranking charges—even those who had never worn them in Germany—sparkled in the most striking dress uniforms.

Thus, throughout the entire campaign, Count Bismarck wore a gleaming silver helmet and the yellow coat of a cavalry division, decorated with the sparkling Order of the Eagle, or a gleaming white field service cap that could be seen from a long distance away. When he rode to observation posts or to the battlefield he wore topboots, carried a telescope in his swordbelt, and sported a gleaming dress sword that was hardly of any use in self-defense (instead of a loaded revolver, that would have afforded him much more protection). And even King Wilhelm was clearly visible everywhere he went because of the gleaming cape he wore, as well as the royal helmet, which everyone knew by sight. Indeed, he looked very heroic in this uniform when—with a skill astonishing in one of his age—he rode along on his battle charger. And I believe that he knew this and was proud of it!

Besides the King and his Chancellor, all the rest of my charges exposed themselves by dressing, as if they were going on parade, in splendid battle dress, sparkling gold and silver braid and gleaming patent-leather boots. Indeed, besides all this, Count Bismarck had arranged for the civilian personnel attached to our headquarters to wear the same kind of fancy-dress, so that now even secretaries and chancery clerks, cryptographers and servants strutted around wearing uniforms, gold buttons and daggers with silver sword-knots.

From Saarbrücken, King Wilhelm I issued a proclamation to the French people which read as follows: "People of France! I have assumed command of Germany's armies, to defend Germany from attack, only because your Emperor Napoleon declared war on the German people, although the German people desired and still desire to live in peace with France. However, I am waging war only against the soldiers of France, not against its citizens . . . !"

Emperor Napoleon III of France seemed to share the same opinion, only in reverse, for in a proclamation to the German people which sounded very similar to King Wilhelm's he assured us:

"I am not waging war against you Germans, but am only doing my duty by restoring those conditions which will guarantee the security of France throughout the future . . ."

We in command headquarters had scarcely left the borders of Germany when it was discovered that there were not enough men in my field security police, and all at once, I was forced to triple their number.

For the natives we encountered were so stubborn and so hostile that the field police had to be used to procure the supplies we needed every day to stay alive. To be sure, the countryside resembled a magnificent park, but all we saw were old women—all the men and the young women had left. And the filth! At least a dozen people had slept in my bed before I arrived, and yet I was given the cleanest quarters available!

The French had plundered their own country and the remaining natives were amazed at the strict morality we observed in every area of behavior. Everywhere, the French authorities had ceased to function and left no one to supervise public affairs, so that my field police also had to take over the reins of the civilian government in all the places occupied by our headquarters.

Wherever our headquarters settled, I had to proclaim martial law, appoint myself prefect of the county in question, and also serve as mayor of the deserted village where we wanted to stay.

Thus, we were thrown out of our well-ordered homeland, which seemed to us like Paradise, and straight into the chaos of war! As the German troops approached, almost all of the three thousand inhabitants of the wretched village of Faulquemont fled, and suddenly at least one hundred thousand hungry and freezing German soldiers descended onto this tiny spot that was completely without resources. The troops literally broke in from all sides and choked all the thoroughfares.

A pouring rain and the kind of cold one experiences in late autumn ate away at our strength; streams of water flooded the bivouac huts that the troops had managed to construct with foliage in the fields, and our headquarters were shifted to Pont-à-Mousson, an equally forlorn little town that had been the home of eight thousand people. However, only thirty thousand of our troops were encamped here, and were suddenly joined by the special train that arrived unannounced with the *crème de la crème* from German headquarters.

The soldiers who had raced here ahead of us had long ago consumed all the available food, so that the remaining natives, most of whom were old and sick, were starving to death. My host, a blind, retired French colonel, the nephew of the famous Marshal

Davoust who had served under Napoleon I, and his aged wife came to me to beg for bread because they had nothing more to eat. Even Count Bismarck had nothing but a piece of cold meat that he was generous enough to share with me in my lodgings; he also warmed me up with some cognac from his canteen.

All the kitchens, stables and storehouses had been broken into and emptied out long before, and I found the mayor of the town, who threw himself at my feet in despair, in jail, where he had been locked up by the previous German commandant for hiding French deserters. German soldiers were sleeping on straw in every room of the town hall so that it looked like a barn. But when I ferreted out two members of the town council, I took possession of the town hall, cleaned it up and set the town government in motion again. I released the mayor so he could help me with this task and because I could not blame him for having acted as he had, for after all, he was a Frenchman.

But in other areas I had to take severe, even ruthless action. Just the day before, a local citizen had shot at our wounded, killing six men. Two other men who were still fleet of foot captured him, and when the killer was led before me, I immediately had him hanged, without ceremony, from the gable of a house and left him hanging there for three days, guarded by two sentries, as an example to others. I also had forbidden the ringing of any bells in the town and for a distance of three leagues around it, under pain of death, so the enemy could not receive any secret signals. The French (Catholic) priests were our bitterest foes, and I was forced to rip the bellrope out of their hands and have the stairs leading to the churchtower destroyed in order to finally ensure our security. I ceased to feel compassion where matters like these were concerned!

I also took rigorous action in cases involving German soldiers who had begun looting, and was on the point of shooting with my revolver four German thieves who refused to obey me. Prince Carl himself captured six Hessian looters and turned them over to me, for we were determined to preserve the honor of our troop and wanted to bring this disgraceful stealing to an end. (However, later I did not make a great fuss over what these Hessians had done, for if I had, they would have been shot without mercy; and besides, before they arrived in the abandoned town, they had spent three nights lying in the rain in the open fields!)

Thus, although our behavior here was as unexceptionable as

possible, we nevertheless sucked the enemy land dry in a way that was terrible to see: Our armies carried off all money, tools, animals, food, stores, vehicles, the fruits of the field and the forest. Even the avenues of trees were cut down and burned in the bivouac fires.

It must have been terrible for the proud French people to see our soldiers living in their homes and their food being confiscated while they themselves were starving in the straw in their stables, and being forced to serve the intruders as well. But we too had to exercise self-control to get along in the houses of strangers and to take from boxes and crates the things that, in our present desperate straits, we could not do without.

I began to interrogate several suspected spies my officers had apprehended close to enemy lines. They turned out to be harmless but exceedingly brave reporters working for English and American newspapers, and their leader, an American who had formerly been a major, had even had an excellent education. Working together, they had spent five years covering wars in the course of which, one of them, a poet from London, had been wounded; and another, an American editor, had been killed. I not only released them all immediately, but even held a special conference during which I told them about the course of the war, to the degree that I was not betraying secret information.

Among the men we captured were also *partisans de guerre* dressed in woolen mantles and shepherd's caps, who literally rose up out of the earth. Most of them were wiped out in the open fields, and not until the rest proved that they were soldiers by displaying their soldiers' paybooks, did our soldiers cease firing and take them prisoner. Among the captured men were fourteen- and sixteen-year-old boys, but they too were already wild and ready to kill us if we let them out of our sight.

Now, for the first time, I really began to make use of my spies, most of whom were French, to spy on and observe the enemy troops. I always kept several of them near me so that I could put them to immediate use, and others were firmly installed in Paris, Bordeaux, Lyons and Orléans.

During the war, I was forced to accept some spies from the lowest social classes. Most of them plied their trade coldly, without thinking about what they were doing. Only a few exhibited pangs of conscience when they received their assignments and when they delivered their reports, and from the outset, I was able to find as many as I needed who were prepared to betray their country for five francs a day.

Every day, I also sent spies from headquarters to Paris and welcomed other spies back so that I could hear directly about all the events and changes taking place in the enemy metropolis, as well as examine all the newspapers, posters and other documents certifying the changes. These spying excursions were often so dangerous that we had to pay many spies several hundred talers to undertake one, but the expenses of this "high-risk service," like many other expenses, were paid out of the inexhaustible fund of the "Central News Bureau," alias Count Bismarck's confiscated Guelph treasure.

Twice a week, we met with the King to discuss all the data, aspects and eventualities of the war. The King usually asked me to summarize the most recent information from my agents in enemy territory. Quite apart from the information gathered by my agents, the French themselves, through their garrulous press, familiarized me with many of their most important and informative plans before they were carried out and made it possible for us to evaluate them thoroughly.

Our meetings told me a great deal about the esteem in which I was held at headquarters, for they always reflected my report of our situation at the moment. If things were going well, everyone present beamed with joy, but they darkened just as promptly if I appeared with a gloomy face. But even when we did not seem to be making progress in our actions along the Loire and outside Paris, I had only to make an encouraging remark (such as, that Paris now possessed only so much food and would necessarily fall at such and such a time), and at once the sun began to shine again on everyone. Since, thank God, I had never been mistaken in my predictions, everyone was quite willing to believe them and they worked miracles by way of calming people down and spurring them on.

During our very first discussion with the King, I pointed out that the *Grande Armée* of France that Napoleon had once led to one victory after another, now existed only on paper. Its degeneration had been proven now that it had been forced to mobilize again after a long period of peace. Its antiquated system of recruitment by lot, and the fact that one could always buy one's way out of the army, had long ago reduced it to a troop of the poorest citizens, those who could not afford bribes.

Even in peacetime, our armies were already divided into corps and divisions, whereas France did not form its corps and divisions until after its troops had been mobilized, and as a result, the men who had been called up had to engage in a laborious search for their units (which had already marched into the field). Thus, a ghostly army of reservists wandered around the country, choking the railroads and the thoroughfares, and not all of them tried to find their regiments as fast as they could; in fact, many never reached them! Even newly appointed commanders searched in vain: "Have arrived here, can't find my brigade, can't even find my division—don't know where my people are!" said a telegram I intercepted, sent from Belfort to Paris by a General de Michèle. Whole battalions marched into the field still missing hundreds of soldiers, ammunition, horses, vehicles, and tents. I was even able to display the telegrams sent to Paris by Marshal Bazaine on July 30, a cry for help in which he begged to be sent some money so he could pay his soldiers wages. As a result of this chaos and confusion, hungry Frenchmen everywhere who had been called up for military service were eating their iron rations and even begging on the streets!

"Leboeuf (The Chief of France's General Staff) has no plan of operation," said General von Moltke, interrupting me. "First, he wanted to cross the Rhine to carve up the South Germans, then, he intended to defend France from the fortresses of Alsace. But once the campaign has begun, one cannot make up for the delay in arranging the disposition of one's armies."

Often the King himself asked me, instead of simply reporting the facts, to take a look at the future and predict what "surprises" the next month or even the next week would bring. For example, could one count on the longing for peace that ostensibly had suddenly broken out among the French people, or not? Did they have enough power to influence the decisions of the French government?

But even the best-informed chief of the best secret intelligence service can never predict the future! The best I could do was to guess what, in view of all the information I had received, would be the most probable outcome. I felt proud when Count Bismarck graciously told a gathering at headquarters that he would not want to miss hearing my conjectures before he made a decision, because no country in history had ever had access to such a continous stream of secret information about its enemy as Germany had now.

To be sure, my field security police now had at their disposal one hundred and fifty specially armed and trained "guard officers" (and one hundred more were available when danger was imminent), but they were not enough to keep continuous watch over everyone at headquarters. Therefore, people were guarded alternately and on an irregular basis: for example, at one time, eighty people were being "shadowed" by my guards, at another time, only eight.

What worried and concerned me was the deluge of warnings and emergency messages that continually rained down on me from my agents and spies. No one could tell whether any of these warnings pointed to a serious problem or was merely a false alarm, so I had to examine each with the same attention, and always take appropriate security measures.

For example, I practiced "orbital observation," in the course of which my officers investigated, at irregular intervals, the zone surrounding a person who appeared to be in danger, searching for anything suspicious. Another technique was the "rotation squad," by which a man whose life had been threatened would now be guarded by one guard, and on the following day by ten or twenty; so that no potential assassin could plan ahead.

Once a week, the carriages of the King and Bismarck rolled through headquarters. Suddenly, another vehicle would roll directly at them, the barrel of a gun sticking out. But before it could acquire a clear field of fire, a fourth vehicle, containing my officers, came up and forced the would-be assassin off the causeway and into the ditch.

Thank God, this exciting scene was a mere performance and the armed "assassin" was a fake. They were homework for my field and security police, who used them to memorize, again and again, how they would pose in front of, beside and behind their charge to cut off a murderer's line of fire. Indeed, showing their contempt of death, they even practiced making themselves the target of the bullet when there was no other way they could save their charge's life.

They also practiced a lightning-fast "draw," even when they were in the saddle or a swaying vehicle, so that they could always use their weapons faster than an assailant, no matter how abruptly he made his appearance.

No, King and Chancellor could not have been better protected, even though King Wilhelm complained of the "exaggerated care" we took of him, and Count Bismarck, to the dismay of my officers, engaged in little escapades, as when, even though his quarters had been requisitioned, he would spend the night in some place of his own choosing. Once, after a long search, we found him on the floor of a half-open barn because, under the stress of his duties, he had not been able to find anything better quickly enough to suit him.

I also took care to prevent "impersonal" attacks: Field police were always the first to open all incoming mail at Royal Command Headquarters to remove any poison or explosive it might contain.

When our headquarters moved, I insisted on sleeping in the King's own quarters, and had my adjutant, a brilliant sharpshooter, sleep in Count Bismarck's quarters, so that we could be fully responsible for both their lives. Moreover, when headquarters moved into a town, I was very strict about making all the citizens who lived for some distance around—even German soldiers—move out of their houses so I could cordon off the place and hermetically seal it.

After this, we could be absolutely certain that no unauthorized person could penetrate to the King and his Chancellor, either in the train or in their quarters in the towns, for both were constantly surrounded by my multi-layered security cordon. Heavily armed security police not only blocked all the entrances and exits, but maintained an impregnable patrol around the borders of our charges' quarters, and if a suspicious individual failed to respond to a challenge, they would shoot to kill.

In response to my urging, the King and his councillors continually switched compartments, and, by an order which was to take effect immediately, it was decreed that these private train compartments were to be off-limits to everyone. All visitors had to pass through the adjacent compartments, where my guards were holding sway. They did not let anyone through unless brought by messengers, and even those who were legitimized by messengers were not allowed to move about at will. After a visitor had completed his business, my officers immediately compelled him to leave, regardless of who he was or how high his rank might be. (This continually led to quarrels with high-ranking military and civilian officials. But Count Bismarck himself had conferred on me the authority to take this precaution, and everyone had to obey.)

I simplified this procedure only for the most exalted visitors, such as princes and sovereigns. They were simply told to walk slowly past the guards so that the latter could get a good look at them.

During journeys and excursions on horseback, my officers, also on horseback, accompanied all persons who might be in danger. They had strict orders to avoid groups of people, so that they could prevent spontaneous assassination attempts. They held their weapons ready to fire, and the same route was never taken twice. Instead, they would travel by an unexpected route, even if they had to take the longest way to get where they were going.

As "Supreme Chief of Security" (this was Count Bismarck's nickname for me) I composed the following instruction sheet for my high-ranking charges, almost imploring them, for the sake of their personal safety, to obey it.

1. The basic danger consists in entering and leaving all quarters and buildings. Before entering or leaving a building, check entrances and exits for suspicious individuals.

2. Continually alter the paths along which you walk, ride or travel, as well as the hours at which you travel them.

3. Always take care, whether you are on foot, on horseback, or travelling in a coach, to notice whether you are being followed, no matter how innocent this appears.

4. Do not ever bring your horse or vehicle to a halt if a stranger asks you to (not even if he asks for your help). Instead, leave this place as quickly as possible.

5. Do not allow any strangers to enter your coach and do not make any appointments with strangers, or if (for example, for some reason connected with your work) you cannot avoid making such an appointment, make certain that you know the stranger's true identity.

6. Go out only when someone else accompanies you and avoid solitary roads and places.

7. Keep your doors and windows closed, hang some opaque material over the windows before you turn on any light, and make a point of not opening the door to anyone you do not know, no matter what reasons he offers you.

8. Make a point of distrusting any strangers who attempt to approach you and speak to you.

9. Never carry documents and records on your person, and burn carefully and completely any documents that you wish to destroy.

10. If you observe any phenomenon or incident that relates to

the foregoing instructions—no matter how insignificant it seems—bring it to the attention of the field security police.

Naturally, there was no way of proving that my efforts and the efforts of my officers were responsible for the fact that not a single assassination attempt was made against the members of German headquarters while we were in enemy territory. As a result, the strict precautions I took were often disregarded and even ridiculed by the very people they were intended to safeguard. They had no way of knowing of the extremely threatening conspiracies whose members openly plotted regicide and were trying to recruit assassins to kill both Bismarck and von Moltke.

I had cause to take these rigorous precautions, even if I did not make public my reasons for doing so. I was deeply troubled when I read in the Paris newspapers that preparations were being made in the enemy metropolis to assassinate the Prussian King Wilhelm I, his Chancellor Count Bismarck, and von Moltke, the Chief of the General Staff. A "popular subscription" of no less than four million francs was being publicly collected to serve as a reward: two million francs of it were to be paid in return for the assassination of the King, and one million each for Bismarck and von Moltke! One of the infamous advertisements literally said, "Appeal to sign up for donations to be used as money prizes for the man—or men—who mortally wound the enemy King and (or) his Chancellor and (or) the leader of his army . . ."

As a result of this threat I labored day and night to ensure that these exalted figures, who were thus endangered, were efficiently guarded, although I was unable to increase the personnel of my field and security police again. However, from now on I slept with three heavily-armed guards, who were periodically relieved, in the King's anteroom, and my adjutant slept with the same number of guards in Bismarck's quarters, whereas von Moltke rested under the protection of additional security police.

After we had spent seven days in Pont-à-Mousson, during which time our troops won a great and decisive victory at Cravelotte, our headquarters suddenly breathed a sigh of relief. On August 23 we advanced to Commercy, where neither French nor German troops had preceded us.

The civilian administration here was still functioning as well as it had in peacetime, and for the first time we were welcomed almost like guests by a genuine prefect of a French *département*. Moreover, the abundance of foodstuffs made us feel as if we were in paradise, and the people proved to be almost kind and obliging.

Here, for the first time, we saw the real France, blooming and whole as it had been before the war, with herds of grazing cattle and stately farms and inns.

On August 25 our headquarters advanced to Bar-le-Duc, and along the way King Wilhelm I met the Crown Prince and fervently greeted his son on the open road, surrounded by the princes of the German states, Count Bismarck, von Moltke and others. It was a peaceful and touching family scene, and the townspeople stood around watching the exalted gentlemen as cheerfully as the people who attended military parades in Potsdam, and were in fact crazy about Bismarck.

A refined lady was determined to see the *comte prussien* up close, and I assured her, "Madame, you shall even shake his hands if in return you will bring us butter, eggs and cheese!" Then she hurried away and returned with her maid, who was carrying a huge basket full of the most magnificent butter, the most fragrant cheese, fresh eggs, crisp white bread and fine wine. After starving for so long we thought it food fit for the gods!

I immediately kept my word and not only permitted this admirer of Bismarck to approach my famous charge but even to touch his hands, although she did not suspect that my adjutant Z. and I were secretly pointing our revolvers at her. When, immediately thereafter, we regaled ourselves, in the company of Count Bismarck, with the contents of the basket in Bismarck's quarters, I confessed the lucrative way in which I had "trafficked in Bismarck's flesh"—and we laughed uproariously like shoemaker's apprentices in Berlin who have just played a successful prank.

In Bar-le-Duc, a wealthy city with a population of twenty thousand, we found paradise itself. Not one soldier had marched through here either. In the hotels one could still relish gourmet food and delicate confections, and luxuriant pubs were open everywhere. For the first time since our advance we ate genuine French dinners in the evening, with innumerable courses and rivers of champagne. In short, we had happened on a smaller version of Paris!

However, the rumor that German civilians had been imprisoned here in order to protect them from the French people set me to work again for a brief time. I immediately inspected all the prisons so that I could free any of my fellow countrymen who might be languishing there, but, thank God, the rumor proved to be false.

On August 27 headquarters was moved through the Argonne

Forest to the mountain town of Clermont, and all at once we found ourselves back in hell. Here, once again, reigned the bitterest hunger and want. Moldy bread was worth its weight in gold, and we lacked even water and light. Thank heaven, we had to stay in this wretched town for only two days, and on August 29 advanced to Grandpréor, where conditions were better. The following day we moved to Busancy, and on September 1 to the city of La Vandresse.

I can scarcely describe the deprivations we suffered as we made our restless advance (some of the men with us were in their sixties and seventies)! Our supply column had not been able to keep up with us for a long time, and like our soldiers, we had to laboriously glean the means of subsistence from the enemy country. I could no longer protect the property of the local inhabitants anywhere we went, which was so repellent to me that I often preferred to go hungry rather than requisition food from the French. But all of us stole only what we really needed in order to keep ourselves alive, and even this against our will!

Up until this point von Moltke, the commander of our army, had believed that his French colleague, MacMahon, would make a stand at Châlons or withdraw to Paris. But suddenly a French agent I maintained on the Marshal's staff reported that MacMahon was determined to march north, make a wide detour around us and—supported by the French fortresses along the Belgian border—liberate Metz, which we had under siege.

When this news arrived von Moltke was playing cards with the officers on his staff. He threw down his cards and cried in triumph, "These fellows are really too stupid; now they're going to learn their lesson!" He immediately ordered our Third and Fourth Armies, "Swing to the right, get going!" Five days later we had MacMahon at bay!

Next morning at exactly 5:00 A.M. King Wilhelm wanted to travel, with Bismarck and von Moltke, to the site of the decisive battle. I was waiting outside his door with my officers when Adjutant Count Waldersee, who was the first to emerge, said in a jubilant and downright arrogant tone, "Today we'll encircle and kill our game; come on, let's beat the bushes!" Thereupon von Moltke, following hard on his heels, confirmed what he had said: "Now we have them in our mousetrap!" Then our aged King appeared, looking grave with a pale, weary face.

After a fairly long journey we paused on the heights of Frénois, whence we could look down upon the entire battlefield: the blue masses of the infantry, the flashing of the rifle and cannon muzzles, the bursts of artillery fire.

Since the dawn of August 4, when the Bavarian infantry surprised the French near Weissenburg while they were eating breakfast and defeated them with the aid of the Prussians who came storming after them, the French had suffered continual defeats: On August 6 a battle took place at Wörth and on the Spicher Hills, and then there was fighting around the fortress of Metz, which we had surrounded. On August 18 there followed the battles of Gravelotte, St. Privat and Mars-la-Tour—and the French were beaten everywhere!

When MacMahon withdrew to Montmédy on the Belgian border with the rest of his troops, he fell directly into our trap. Our troops surrounded him from the west, the south and the east, whereas the Belgian border, which was only ten kilometers away, pinned him down on the north.

"You are facing Bavarians, the worst soldiers in the world!" MacMahon said encouragingly in the last orders he gave his army. Then, despite the dense fog, the Bavarians attacked. He sent *mariniers,* his elite troops, to fight them, and for seven hours both sides fought for every house in the village. But the soldiers of the First Bavarian Army Corps, under General Ludwig von der Tann, fought like devils, shot, blasted, stabbed, set fires and killed every Frenchman carrying a gun—for civilians were also firing from attic and cellar windows. Finally everyone had been smoked out of the village, which was a pile of ruins; many of its citizens burnt. It was called Bazailles and was the eastern outpost of the fortified city of Sedan.

This city had a population of sixteen thousand, and in the market place was a monument erected in honor of France's Marshal Turennes, who was born here and who had once laid waste the German Palatinate. Now the French regarded it as a second-rate fortress, for it was considered difficult to defend: Its fortifications were antiquated and the city, as well as the citadel, was within easy range of modern artillery placed on the distant hills . . .

Our repeated attacks were all successful and our troops grasped the retreating French army like a giant arm which would finally crush it. During the night of August 30 to August 31, Mac-Mahon retreated with one hundred and eighty thousand exhausted, hungry soldiers to the almost defenseless fortress of Sedan, which was not large enough and did not contain sufficient provisions to accommodate such an onslaught. The result was chaos: men on horseback, supply wagons and cannons choked all the roads, and the soldiers went begging for bread at the doors of the houses.

For some time now, without leaders, they fled this way and that through the darkness and unexpectedly found themselves in Belgian territory. "We can't fight on with these half-dead men!" said their commanders, cursing, and surrendered.

Von Moltke's "mousetrap" had snapped shut. Once again the trapped army attempted a sortie between Sedan and Bazailles, but they could not break through the Second Bavarian Corps which opposed them, and then the Bavarians raced forward and drove the attempted escapees back into their prison.

When we had arrived at the highest point of Frénois, our cannons began to direct their murderous fire at the fortified city, now surrounded. A mighty cannonade issued from all barrels. It went on for hours, and gradually the Germans won more and more territory. No fewer than seventy heavy batteries of the newest breech-loading Krupp cannons bombarded the French, who were squeezed together in a space three kilometers wide. The German cannons were far superior, in fire power and accuracy, to the antiquated musket-loaders of the defenders. For hour after hour we heard nothing but the thunder of cannons and saw columns of fire rising to the sky.

We kept tightening the circles of our forces around the unhappy fortress: two hundred and fifty thousand Germans surrounded one hundred and eighty thousand Frenchmen! The French army, that had intended to free Metz from the Germans who had surrounded it, was instead surrounded itself.

Their commander, MacMahon, who had been wounded in the hip by a fragment from a German shell, could no longer stand, despite the furious attempts he made to do so, and was forced to turn over his command to General Ducrot, whose right to that position was immediately disputed by General de Wimpffen, who had hurried here to report that he had been expressly appointed commander by the War Ministry in Paris. (Incredible as it may sound, even during these chaotic hours my agents kept the German commanders continually and accurately informed of these facts, so that we always knew what was going on.)

And now the desperate prisoners began to bleed themselves to death by making counterattacks which were as heroic as they were hopeless of success. French cavalry divisions rashly attempted to break through our encircling troops, and showing their contempt of death, the *cuirassiers,* the lancers and the *chasseurs d'Afrique* dashed themselves again and again against the wall of fire formed by our cannons and infantry; each time hundreds were moved down. Riders fell from their horses, horses collapsed beneath their riders, and the wounded men, attempting to flee, fell to their deaths in the neighboring stone quarries.

Involuntarily King Wilhelm, who was observing this ghastly spectacle from our hill, cried in French, *"Ah, les braves gens!"* ("What brave soldiers!"), while von Moltke and Bismarck stood behind him in a half-circle with their staff officers, a dozen German princes and a British, Russian and American general who had come to observe the battle.

Then a gentleman dressed in civilian clothes walked up to me and politely inquired how I had been getting along since he saw me last. At first I did not know to whom I was speaking, but then I realized that he was one of the newspaper reporters whom I had had captured a short time ago in the belief that they were spies: the correspondents of the *Freie Presse* in Vienna, the *Tribune* in New York and the *Times* in London.

These newspapers were no more afraid of spending money in order to give their readers as graphic a report as possible of our campaign, than their reporters were afraid of effort and danger. The reporters carried Red Cross flags, military travelling kits and telescopes, but no weapons. Nevertheless they fearlessly walked or rode on horseback or in wagons among the artillery, cavalry and infantry formations and even took part in battles if something was going on about which they wanted to give an eyewitness report to their newspapers.

The presence of civilian "newspaper scribblers," as they were secretly called, at German headquarters aroused the resentment of almost all the high-ranking officers and camp-followers, but their resentment remained subdued because of Bismarck's official and well-publicized declaration that the press constituted "the newest world-power" and that we had to pay it due tribute.

After our cannonade had continued for hours, the resistance of the defenders gradually began to waver: we could see their formations begin to break up as the men fled into the villages and the woods. However, there was as yet no indication that the enemy wished to bring an end to their hopeless situation by surrendering, and thus we had no choice but to continue bombarding this fortress packed full of human beings, animals and equipment.

But in the end, the sight, from our vantage point on the hill, of the unhappy fortified city as more and more of it went up in flames, and of the many burning villages in the immediate vicinity, became so unbearable that our King Wilhelm reached a decision and ordered the murderous and annihilating gunfire to cease. He did so in order to send a member of his general staff, Lieutenant Colonel von Bronsart, into the burning fortress carrying a white flag, with an offer to save the lives of the brave defenders if they would agree to capitulate. But along the way he met a Bavarian officer who told him that a French intermediary with a white flag had already appeared at the fortress gate.

At once von Bronsart was admitted to the fortress, and when he asked to see the commanding general, he was, to his surprise, let into the presence of the French Emperor Napoleon III.

When the ruler of France asked the German negotiator what message he bore, he was told, "I am to demand the surrender of the fortress of Sedan." The monarch replied that he was not in command here. However, he, the Emperor, would dispatch his adjutant-general, Count de Reille, with a personal letter to the King of Prussia.

Not only had my agents informed us some time ago that Napoleon III was with the imprisoned army in the fortress of Sedan, which we were bombarding to such deadly effect, but they had told the commanders of our army every detail about why and how he happened to be there.

In view of the rapid succession of ill tidings he had received about the war, the ruler of France no longer felt safe; he had left his army under Marshal Bazaine, as well as his corps of guards, and had fled to Verdun incognito in a hired carriage. There he boarded a railway carriage, still dirty from the last time it had been used to transport troops, and retired to Châlons-sur-Marne.

Here he believed that he was finally safe in the midst of a French army still intact, composed of MacMahon's troops, reserve corps and members of the national guard—a total of one hundred and eighty thousand men.

During the march the Emperor of France, weakened by renal colic, slept on a baggage wagon, covered by an ordinary soldier's mantle. Not until he reached Sedan did he take heart again and issue a proclamation to his soldiers.

"Defenders of France! There is no reason why we should not be confident: Thus far we have prevented the enemy from reaching our capital, and now all France is rising up to drive him from the land. As a result I have preferred the role of soldier to that of monarch so that I may stand at your head victoriously defending the fatherland!"

After we had placed Sedan under siege, the Emperor joined in a council of war to determine how the French could escape the encircling troops, and he placed his hopes in a newly-constructed road not yet marked on French army maps (although it had been on our maps for some time). But when we began firing at the encircled fortress, Napoleon, more convinced than were his ambitious generals of the inevitability of defeat, rode up and down before its walls, his pale face covered with make-up that made it look tanned so he would not frighten his soldiers, hoping that a Prussian bullet would put an end to his inglorious existence. Perhaps he was thinking about his great prototype Napoleon I, who, likewise in vain, sought a soldier's death at the battle of Waterloo.

Instead a wounded Frenchman took aim at the solitary rider; immediately the loaded rifle was knocked out his hand. "Damn— let me kill that monster who is responsible for all our misfortune!," he cursed and clenched his fist at the Emperor.

But Napoleon did not notice the incident. As if in a dream he rode along the hill of Moncelle and attempted to fire at the enemy a machine gun abandoned by its crew. German shells exploded around him, shell fragments flew past him and his face was blackened with gunpowder, but he could not manage to make the French "miracle weapon" work, and there was no one anywhere around whom he could ask to help. Then he turned around, rode back without being wounded and ordered that the white flag be raised above the citadel.

On the evening of that eventful day we saw, from our perch on "Generals' Hill," three riders bearing a white flag. They came from Sedan, approached us quickly and turned out to be Napoleon's Adjutant-General Count de Reille, accompanied by two other men. Count de Reille laboriously dismounted, limped toward our King with the aid of a cane and handed him a sealed envelope, crying, "Sire, here is a letter from the Emperor of France!"

However, King Wilhelm immediately interrupted him, "I demand that your army lay down its weapons immediately!", while General von Moltke added, "The entire army will be considered prisoners of war, including the officers and the camp followers!"

Only then did King Wilhelm open the letter, while we stood around him in a circle. The letter from the French Emperor said:

"My Lord Brother! Since I was unable to die among my soldiers, the only course left open to me is to place my dagger in your hand as Your Majesty's good brother Napoleon."

Everyone took counsel together to prepare an answer. The Crown Prince, who regularly kept a journal, always carried writing utensils on his person, and Duke von Coburg hastily bent down so that King Wilhelm himself could write on his back the words which Bismarck dictated in a pure French:

"My Lord Brother! While I regret the cause of our encounter, I accept Your Majesty's dagger and pray you to authorize one of your officers to negotiate with us concerning the surrender of your brave soldiers. For my part, I authorize General von Moltke for this purpose. I am Your Majesty's good brother Wilhelm."

Meanwhile the Crown Prince was holding an extremely friendly conversation with Napoleon's Adjutant-General, who had been attached to the Prince's party during the recent Paris exposition, and then King Wilhelm too spoke with him as with a man he had known very well during the happy days of peace spent together only a short time ago.

However, Count de Reille had scarcely ridden away before the King and the Crown Prince fell into each other's arms. "What a turn things have taken through the providence of God!" cried King Wilhelm, with tears in his eyes, and his son answered, deeply moved, "This day cost France its Emperor, its army and its victory!" Then the King telegraphed his Queen in Berlin:

"Today, in my sight, France's army was crushingly defeated in a nine-hour battle at Sedan. All those who lived through this battle have a right to be proud! Praise and glory to God!"

For thirty hours the aged monarch had not been out of his uniform, and now, with some difficulty, a piece of meat was procured for him. As he chewed he leaned back, looking picturesque in his general's cloak, against a fallen tree trunk, felled some time earlier by a storm rather than by the shells of war. Around him crouched von Moltke, von Roon and Bismarck, feasting on soldiers' rations. A canteen proprietor brought some captured wine, and the victorious leaders of Germany drank in turns out of the same bottle, like the ancient Teutons, to this day's victory. A courier was sent to fetch Günther, a painter of war scenes, so that he could sketch this scene and later paint it, preserving its image for posterity.

Finally the King wanted to return to headquarters to rest, and I hurried ahead of him, had all the houses lit up with candles and the marketplace with a great fire, while the bivouac fires of our soldiers flamed up everywhere and the headquarters company stood to arms. Then our victorious monarch returned from the battlefield accompanied by roaring voices shouting "Hurrah!" and other voices singing "Hail to thee, wearing the wreath of the victor!" . . .

Meanwhile German and French negotiators gathered around the dining table in Chancellor Bismarck's quarters. On the wall, as if to mock us, hung a picture of Napoleon I in a victorious pose, along with a dusty wall-clock which—*nomen est omen*—was almost an hour slow.

"Which dagger did your Emperor give us," Bismarck asked the French ambassadors, "the dagger of France or merely his own?" Whereupon General de Wimpffen, the defeated commander of Sedan, quickly replied:

"Merely his own—His Majesty was not empowered to do so by the army and the government!"

But von Moltke gruffly interposed that such hair-splitting did not alter the fact that the Germans had captured the entire French army!

But de Wimpffen stubbornly refused to accept these harsh terms, and negotiations were broken off. France's intermediaries rode back to Sedan, carrying with them Bismarck's threat that the German artillery would open fire immediately if the French had not approved the surrender terms demanded by nine o'clock on the following morning.

At 6:00 A.M. Bismarck was awakened again by Count de Reille himself, who brought news that his Emperor wished to speak with the German Chancellor. Thereupon Bismarck jumped into his uniform and, without washing or eating breakfast, rode immediately to Sedan; but when he was only halfway there he encountered Napoleon's coach in the fog. The driver and the Emperor's retinue wore the livery of the French court, powdered wigs and lace gloves, whereas the Emperor was leaning back in his coach asleep.

The Emperor was awakened, Bismarck politely removed his cap and asked to know the Emperor's commands. Napoleon asked whether he might speak with the King of Prussia, whereupon Bismarck (in order to gain time in which to get the French to approve the terms of surrender, which they had not yet done), offered his own quarters as a meeting-place, and the Emperor agreed.

However, on the way Napoleon paused at an abandoned farmhouse where they would not be observed, and the Emperor of France sat in its filthy kitchen for more than an hour on a hard wooden stool opposite the Chancellor of Germany, passionately swearing that he had never wanted this war (this was what Bismarck told us later). Finally an escort of Silesian cuirassiers, which had been sent by von Moltke, arrived and led the captured French Emperor to a small castle nearby.

Meanwhile von Moltke had brought the French to the point of signing the surrender terms, according to which more than one hundred thousand of their soldiers, one marshal, forty generals, two hundred and thirty staff officers, and two thousand six hundred officers and army officials were to be transported into German captivity in long railway trains, and France was to lose Alsace and parts of Lorraine, as well as pay the staggering sum of five billion francs to defray the expenses that it had forced Germany to incur when it declared war.

Immediately thereafter we accompanied King Wilhelm to the little castle where his French adversary awaited him, and we saw the victor and vanquished shake hands. Beside our tall monarch the little figure of Napoleon looked even slighter.

King Wilhelm began by saying that God had given *him* the victory in the war started by France, whereupon Napoleon assured us again that not he, but the French public, which had been goaded on to do it, was responsible for the war.

"A public goaded on by a press hostile to Your Majesty!" King Wilhelm emphasized, glancing at the newspaper correspondents who were also present.

"That was it, Sire!" Napoleon assured us in relief. "If I had resisted I should have been eliminated, and no one could ask that of me!" He shrugged his shoulders helplessly and then asked what his "Lord Brother" had decided to do with him, whereupon our King generously offered him Wilhelmshöhe Palace in Kassel. Napoleon agreed at once. However, he asked to be allowed to keep his associates with him (the French generals de Reille and Moskawa, Prince Murat II, etc.), as well as his usual household, and our King generously granted these requests. Thereupon France's captive Emperor praised our new artillery, which he said had no peer, and the two sovereigns took cordial leave of each other.

Prussian hussars accompanied Napoleon to his comfortable prison, and German soldiers clicked their heels in front of the royally-furnished railway carriage which King Wilhelm had provided for him. But just before the train departed, a battalion of captive French national guardsmen trotted past with bags and began to shout disrespectfully that that "damned Louis" ought to take them and their baggage along.

The Emperor, who had wanted to greet his former soldiers one last time, closed the window of his compartment in terror, and his train departed for Germany in a cloud of smoke.

Our way back from the rendezvous with the captive French Emperor led past the still fresh battlefield where we had won our victory, and we saw sights there which beggar all description:

Before us rose up mounds formed of the corpses of the French Guards, and just a few paces away were mounds of Germans, although these were fewer in number.

All around, beside and on top of each other and twisted by the most horrible dislocations, were the corpses of men and animals, with their limbs torn off, their skulls crushed so that they were unrecognizable or completely severed from the rest of their bodies, bodies without arms, legs and heads, arms, legs and heads without bodies, entrails bursting out of red and blue uniforms, and in between masses of blood-drenched weapons, rucksacks, helmets, military equipment of all sorts, all crushed together as if in a giant cauldron and—as far as we could see—all exactly the same so that it made us tired to look at it. This was apocalypse, the other side of the coin of war!

King Wilhelm was the first to break the silence. "Those who initiate wars instead of preventing them," said the aged monarch, "like Gramont, Olliver (the chief warmongers among the French) and others of even higher rank, should be brought to see these horrific scenes!"

As far as those guilty of starting this war were concerned, Bismarck replied, he had for a long time cherished the notion of installing a world tribunal composed of one judge each from America, England, Russia, etc., who would pass judgment on the criminals who had started this war.

So far only a few of the enormous mass of victims had been buried. Therefore, under the orders of the victor of Bazailles, General von der Tann, long ditches were dug and filled with the corpses of friend and foe, but no matter how dense the layers of dead, they soon spilled over the tops. What could such ditches achieve against the masses of slain men and animals lying here under the open sky undergoing a natural transformation; for already a faint but clearly detectable scent of decay had pervaded the air, and in a short time we should be threatened with pestilence.

Thereupon I raised an alarm throughout nearby villages and towns, categorically ordering all of their citizens who were able to work to come to the battlefield with shovels and hoes and, in their own best interests, bury the dead as quickly as possible.

When people showed little inclination to obey the proclamations that my officers attached to the walls of all the houses (apparently they did not believe that the dead represented a danger to the living), I warned them that their houses would be bombarded if they persisted in their refusal to help, and was forced to show them an example of what I meant. With the aid of a Prussian cannon I fired a shell behind the nearest village, and it exploded with a deafening noise in the open fields.

This helped, and men, women, old people, young people—a whole army of gravediggers from all over the area—hastily made their appearance! In order to make the best use of their powers, I had them follow a precise plan, working from inside out, that is, from the middle of the grisly battlefield towards its edges.

Because there were thousands of corpses of soldiers and horses, it took too long to dig even the shallowest of excavations. Thus I had the dead placed in heaps on large carpets made of boughs and branches and dragged by yokes of oxen and cattle, that the local citizens had brought to the nearby forest ravines and stone quarries (already full of the corpses of men who had fallen in while attempting to flee), where they were thrown in.

Hundreds and hundreds of friends and foes who were snatched away in the prime of life were hidden together in this way in the natural abysses of the land, and then people on both sides of each ravine threw huge quantities of earth over them. Finally we had cleared even the remotest spots—the dense forests, the deep caverns, and even the trees—of the men who had taken refuge when they were wounded and had died there all alone.

How happy I should have been to have given them all, both friend and foe, a Christian burial under grassy mounds of earth with their names written on the crosses, but Godfather Pestilence lurked behind us with his drawn scythe and drove us to relentless haste so that we could prevent death from claiming any new victims and at least be of service to the living.

The transporting of our prisoners of war also threatened to turn into a nightmare:

No fewer than one hundred and forty thousand captive French soldiers crowded into the peninusula of Iges, which was surrounded by the Meuse River, so that they could be taken from there to Germany; but we did not have enough food waiting for them.

Thus I initiated the rigorous confiscation of food all around the country and arranged to have it transported swiftly in special railway trains. In addition two entire German army corps were placed in readiness to begin transporting the captives, in batches of two thousand men each, to Étain and Pont-à-Mousson, whence they were to be conducted into German lands.

I myself went to the prisoner-of-war camp to see General Lebrun, and had to ride through a crowded mass of defeated French soldiers who were standing shoulder to shoulder. They greeted me with hostile looks, but moved aside without offering any resistance, and did not threaten me with so much as a gesture or an insult until I arrived at the place where their general was lodged.

The General was a small, white-haired man who was clearly grieving over his country's misfortune, and who, with his spectacles and didactic speech, resembled a schoolteacher more than the daring defender of Bazailles, where he had ridden at the head of his troops when they made their desperate sorties.

With the amiability peculiar to the French he introduced me to the officers on his staff, but showed the greatest obstinacy when he began to bargain with me over every measure we had taken, trying, as much as possible, to improve the lot of his captive troops.

During the night the French troops had burned their flags. Now they had become our captives—more than one hundred thousand officers and soldiers. They arrived in an endless but disorderly stream, all the branches of the service mixed up together, on foot, on horseback, on mules and donkeys. Most of them were filthy, many drunk, some weeping with rage and shame, wearing decorations for battles at Sevastopol and Solferino on their chests.

It was a stirring sight to see the "Grande Armée," once so proud, wobbling along, beaten by the Germans everyone had mocked: the famous *chasseurs d'Afrique* sitting in melancholy postures in their saddles, the dark-skinned Zouaves, Turcos and Zéphyrs chattering like parrots. They were troopers from distant regions of the world whose small figures, with their torn stockings and bare feet, made them seem alien to civilization; they looked as if, instead of being trained soldiers, they belonged in an exotic "foreigner show."

Thus I was not surprised when French soldiers who had grown grey bearing arms and who had fought for France in many victorious battles, angrily refused to be transported with this "jungle rabble," as they called them. I understood equally well the ruthlessness with which they seized the food supplies we had brought. Afterwards a Turco officer complained to me in poor French that he and his troops had received nothing because his "white" fellow prisoners had stolen his share, throwing him rotten horseflesh in its stead.

Many of the soldiers were loudly shouting, "Trahison, trahison!" ("treason"), and when I asked a French corporal the name of his general, who was riding behind me, he replied, "I don't know the pig any more!" Indeed, a ragged French infantryman struck at his commanding officer with his crutch (he had been wounded in the leg), which made me so angry that I made my way over to him and struck the mutinous fellow a blow with my whip.

No, it was no easy matter to maintain order in that disintegrating, protesting procession of captives. Giving orders accomplished nothing, and I was forced to supplement them with blows and shoves, until finally the first two thousand troops, guarded by German infantry, were on their way to Germany.

It was my responsibility to question the captive French officers, and from their answers it soon became clear that even at the beginning of the war their mood was black and they had expected some great disaster. I also gained an illuminating insight into the nature and thought processes of the French army, especially those of their officers. They had been recruited from France's traditional officers' schools, St. Cyr and the École Polytechnique, and some of them had been *troupiers,* or noncommissioned officers, raised to officer's rank in recognition of their merits.

These two groups of men who came from fundamentally different backgrounds did not get along together at all! The *troupier* envied his educated comrade, who was usually younger than he, and the younger, better educated man in turn despised the older man, even though he was more experienced. Thus French officers had never possessed such an indestructible *esprit de corps* as we Germans!

Despite all proofs to the contrary, even educated French officers refused to admit that they had been defeated by Germany. Again and again I heard them say that the battle of Sedan had merely been a military tactic, on the part of the French, to lure us Germans into the country. Bazaine, France's victorious marshal, was now at our rear with his army waiting to exterminate us. Not one single German soldier, cannon or horse, they said, would return across the Rhine, for all of us, who were now so proud of our deceptive victory, were doomed to destruction.

How could I reply to these deluded men? There was much that was touching about their desperate, fantastical flight from the reality of their defeat, and I saw no reason why I should attempt to instruct them in the error of their ways. They did not even believe that the soldiers of Bavaria and Württemberg had fought on our side of their own free will. The French officers believed that the Bavarians and Württembergians had been forced to fight by Prussia, and that they would secretly serve as the allies of France in the "war of vengeance" which was to come and in which they had placed all their hopes. When I replied that the victorious battle at Sedan had been won by a united Germany, they simply smiled, unteachable like all fanatics.

I also found shady characters among their ranks. For example, a wealthy Frenchwoman came to me complaining that a French infantry captain had stolen her pearl necklace, and she would not rest until she had led me to the accused man.

As a police officer I found the matter too interesting to refuse to investigate. The officer whom his countrywoman openly accused of theft was a still youthful and intelligent looking man, but his features appeared jaded by indulgence in base living. Naturally he denied that he had taken the necklace, but he did so with little animation, while the complaints of the woman who claimed he had robbed her, on the other hand, sounded determined and convincing, so that even today I still believe the man was guilty.

After their troops had been taken away, it was time for us to transport the captive French officers to Germany as well, whereupon I gathered around me the leaders of the corps which had served under Lebrun, in order to inform them of the generous favor accorded them by King Wilhelm: Any officer who gave us his word of honor that he would not fight against us again in the course of this war, would be free to return home immediately, so only those who refused to give their word of honor would have to remain our prisoners.

Approximately one thousand French officers were standing around the platform from which I read the official proclamation. After I had finished reading it, I asked those who agreed to sign, in my presence, written pledges of their word of honor. But fewer than one hundred officers signed, and these were only sick, elderly men, along with a number of bandmasters, who in France were given officer's rank.

However, scarcely had one of them signed his name when he was punished with the contempt of the others, for the majority greatly preferred enduring German captivity at their soldiers' sides to pledging their loyalty to the hated victor. Their proud and inflexible attitude filled me with respect!

I was seized with compassion when I saw the leaders of the enemy troops, wearing their exalted decorations, who had been victorious in many areas of the world, bowed down in humiliation as they entered captivity! They had to remove their sabres and swords, and many a man had tears in his eyes as he threw his weapon on the heap, whereas others broke their weapons in impotent fury. But there were also officers wearing sparkling decorations, the victors of battles in Italy, the Crimea and Mexico, who walked up with their heads held high and, as the vanquished, chivalrously greeted the victors, playing the perfect cavaliers.

Every French officer was allowed to take his servant with him into captivity. Each group of four officers was to be followed by the four servants who belonged to them, but it proved impossible to guarantee this order! In vain my officers shouted their "Marchez par quatre!" ("Walk in groups of four!")—no one obeyed and chaos resulted. I ventured to doubt that master and servant always arrived at their prison together!

The last man to arrive at the last train was General Lebrun, who personally handed his sword to General von Bernardi, our director of prisoner transport. With an emotionalism typical of the French he sobbed like a child as he did it, and von Bernardi found it difficult to console him, swearing by all that was holy that he would faithfully preserve that sword, as the honorable weapon of a brave fellow officer, until after peace had been concluded.

When the news reached Berlin that French captives were about to arrive—so I learned—it triggered a migration of curious citizens to the railway stations.

They eyed the Turcos with especial greed, and the glances of the upright Berliners went first to their shoulders: There, according to an old wives' horror tale which no one could convince them was untrue, was the seat of bloodthirsty cats which, during close combat, leaped at the enemy's face and so prevented him from fighting.

Concerned by this "unworthy curiosity," Queen Augusta sent her private courier to her husband to ask him whether it was proper to send captive Negroes to Berlin, to which our King replied by return post:

I consider it politically unwise to prevent the citizens of Berlin from seeing French prisoners of war altogether. For that very cannon fodder drawn from foreign continents lets them see France without its halo. However, if, despite the police barricades, something unseemly should occur, steps must be taken!

However, no incident involving rude familiarity or its opposite, hostility, was ever reported to me from Berlin or from other German cities, and thus the authorities were never forced to take action anywhere in Germany.

The French captives had left behind almost six thousand horses which we gathered into wild and raging herds—the stallions had of necessity been mixed in with the mares. They were still wearing their bridles, but their saddles had slipped down onto their bellies or were being dragged along behind them, and again and again herds of several hundred horses would attempt to break free. Our brave light cavalry risked their lives to drive them back with whips and clubs.

They had a difficult order: select the best specimens from the fenced-in herd to replace those of our animals which had been killed or fallen ill. More than forty per cent of the stock of cavalry and artillery horses that we needed to continue our advance into French territory was replaced with the former property of our defeated enemy.

When my field police caught eleven venturesome Belgian traders driving away groups of the captured horses during the night (after having bribed one of our sentries), with the intention of selling them back to France from Belgium, I immediately had all of them, including our disloyal sentry, shot by a firing squad. Afterwards I shot an equal number of sick horses and had the corpses of the executed traders fastened to their saddles, whereupon I ordered that the dead horses and their riders be thrown into the river.

Thus the Belgians received such a reprimand—in the form of the "riding corpses" of their wicked tradesmen who came swimming toward them along the Meuse—that all attempts to steal our horses abruptly ceased and we were left in peace.

After the surrender of Sedan and the capture of Napoleon, Prussian headquarters were moved to Reims, the capital of Champagne, where we received an unexpectedly splendid reception, in stark contrast to the hardships of war suffered thus far.

I had hurried to Reims before our headquarters in order to make all the necessary arrangements for its reception. At this time the city was occupied by only a few German troops, who had driven away the French soldiers there only the day before. Guarded by a squadron of dragoons I made a splendid entrance into Reims to assume the post of German prefect, and immediately quartered my troops so almost every house contained at least one armed soldier and each district of the city housed several cannon. When the King arrived in the city with Count Bismarck and his retinue, I lodged these exalted gentlemen in the archbishop's palace next to the famous cathedral, in the same rooms the kings of France occupied at the time of their coronation.

All the pubs and shops had closed when our headquarters entered the city. I ordered that they be opened at once, renewed postal traffic, which had ceased, and also put the town newspapers (one conservative and one democratic) back in business, for they too had ceased to function some time ago. This latter task involved a great deal of work, that I did not, however, perform from unselfish motives; after all, without newspapers how could we communicate with the public?

As soon as I assumed office as prefect of the city of Reims, I intervened with our soldiers on behalf of its citizens. A shot was fired from one of the houses at the German hussars, who were the first to enter the city, and as a result it was ordered that this house be razed. The desperate owner owed it to my intercession that the order to destroy his home, already issued, was rescinded. Thereupon the entire city of Reims expressed its joy by presenting our squadron of hussars, who had been shot at from the rooftops, with two hundred bottles of the finest champagne, and my police officers and I were given lodgings in the home of the (female) owner of a champagne firm with a world-wide reputation, who was a millionairess several times over.

From then on we alone had at our disposal her splendid palace, along with the gigantic park, for the "champagne princess" (as we called her) was glad to give us her entire property to live in, as long as my officers and I would stay there and she would not be forced to accept common soldiers into her home; and in return she gave us as much of the finest champagne as our hearts desired. This generous lady, a widow who was still beautiful, was all alone with her daughter and trembled with fear because when our troops marched in someone accidentally shot at her.

The first night we spent in her palace was also the first night in a long time that we slept deeply and soundly. We slept in gilded four-poster beds with silk curtains, surrounded by mirrors that reached to the ceiling, costly paintings and priceless marble and alabaster statues. What an inconceivable contrast to all our days of deprivation!

On the following evening the lady of the house regaled us with a dinner fit for a king, to which Count Bismarck and Count Waldersee, the King's adjutant, were invited, along with other high-ranking persons. We had fine wines of a sort which we scarcely dreamed existed, every one of which had won several prizes. The splendid palace contained a special room for almost every type of wine, furnished in a characteristic style: one for champagne, one for bordeaux, one for burgundy, and so on. We were served by servants dressed in gold-trimmed livery.

Then the owner of all this wealth, speaking fluent German, made a sensitive toast: "You victors have, to be sure, taken weapons from the men of France, but not from us women! We shall continue to employ against you the woman's weapons of charm and irresistible kindness, until you have changed from the victors to the vanquished!"

The proclamation in Paris of the "Revolutionary Republic of France," which followed hard upon our dinner party, caused a revolution in the political parties of Reims as well. The republicans in the town council removed from office the man who had been mayor and replaced him with a "democratic convention" made up of ten citizens. When I learned about this matter I intervened and issued the following orders to the deposed mayor:

"In my function as prefect of this city and this *département*, conferred on me by His Excellency Count Bismarck, I allowed you, with a view to maintaining law and order, to continue holding your original post as Mayor of Reims. As you are therefore under the protection of Prussian arms, events in Paris cannot have any effect on you here, and no change can be made in the government of this city without my approval. Therefore I order you to remain in office and to immediately dissolve the so-called convention which replaced you. If you do not, we shall force the city of Reims to pay large punitive reparations until its regular government is restored."

Immediately after its publication, this declaration, which left nothing to the imagination, caused the opponents of the former mayor to restore him to office and speedily dissolve their convention, whereas the decisive action taken by the German prefect and head of the Prussian field police with regard to the revolutionary forces in Reims produced a startling effect: French citizens began to develop a good relationship with us Prussians, and indeed, the French seemed to be quite eager to make friends with the conquerors of their city!

For the first time the French appeared to recognize that we were not cannibals but rational people, and that it was quite possible to get along with us! The result was that soon trade—which had come almost to a halt—was renewed, artisans and entrepreneurs got busy again and before long our city was almost as it had been in peacetime. Prussian discipline and order, as well as our unflagging energy, restored to its citizens their sense of security and trust.

Obviously the members of the powerful conservative party, which included a number of millionaires, feared the new French republic more than they feared us Prussians, and openly pleaded that we protect them from their own "revolutionary" government in Paris by leaving a strong German garrison in their city for as long as possible.

Certain "liberal" newspapers in Germany were the only ones to condemn my "affair with the mayor of Reims" as reactionary intervention in the internal affairs of France. (My officers immediately reported these statements to me and supplied me with the relevant newspaper clippings.) I took my revenge by sending a circular to all newspapers talking such drivel, not knowing what was really going on because they had been far from the danger zone. In this circular I stated:

"Newspapers like yours have written and repeatedly write about Germans murdered and poisoned in France. Under orders from the King I have investigated every single such case, and the report always turned out to be a lie. In reality the people of France have treated us well so far, and the new *régime* in Paris is the only group that now continually commands them to revolt. If they were to revolt we should be lost, for we cannot fight thirty million Frenchmen. The only way to maintain the present conditions, so far favorable to us, is to preserve, if necessary with great obstinacy, the status quo in enemy territory!"

Shortly thereafter our headquarters moved from Reims to Château-Thierry, and a short time later to Meaux, only four leagues from Paris. From there we moved to Lagny, and the King, along with Bismarck, von Moltke, von Roon, and I, as well as my officers, took up quarters in the palace of Ferrières, that was not far from the city and belonged to the Parisian Baron Rothschild.

The brilliant splendor of this palace made such an impression on our frugal King that when he first saw it he shook his head and remarked, "People like us wouldn't dare to own something like that; only a Rothschild could own it!" He did not intend this remark to express his admiration so much as his contentment with a more modest way of life. Another example of his frugality was the following: After news of the surrender of Sedan and the capture of Napoleon had reached Berlin, some enthusiastic young men had climbed up on the equestrian statue of Frederick the Great opposite the royal palace, to place a laurel wreath on "old Fritz's" head. When the King, while at Ferrières, saw a photograph of this improvised decoration, he was beside himself with rage that the costly, irreplaceable statue had been endangered, for it could easily have been damaged when several people climbed up on it. He wired the Queen of his "extreme displeasure," and sent an even more stringent telegram to the Chief of Police, ordering him to prevent any repetition of such mischief, which "might inflict costly damage."

On the day when our King arrived in Ferrières, Jules Favre, then Foreign Secretary in the "Revolutionary Ministry" in Paris, accompanied by two embassy secretaries, arrived at our outpost in the role of intermediary and asked to speak with Count Bismarck. The first attempt on the part of the French to negotiate the peace had begun!

The negotiations between Bismarck and the ambassador of the "new France" began immediately and continued all night. Our demands remained fixed from the outset: We wanted the German parts of Alsace and Lorraine, and for France to pay the expenses we had incurred in the war. Negotiations were not broken off until dawn. When Favre approved the Prussian demands but stated that the French did not wish to give up any of their provinces, Count Bismarck simply declared, "I must have the German part of Alsace and Lorraine, even if I have to wage war with five armies for another three years—Germany must finally be left in peace by France!"

But for me this event did not bring the excitement to an end. One intermediary and confidant after another kept arriving. Sometimes several of them were here at the same time and were not supposed to know about each other's presence. Jules Favre was succeeded by a messenger from the French Revolutionary Minister Gambetta, then by a confidant of Napoleon, then by an ambassador from the Pope and finally by delegates from the Tsar of Russia and from France's "Democratic Party." I was responsible for welcoming and supervising every one of them and was not to permit entry to the palace until a time had been appointed for a conference. After that I often had to arrange for their accommodations and transportation and ensure that they could communicate by letter or telegraph, as well as to observe whether, when, and where, they actually took leave of us again.

Besides all this, I received one set of secret instructions after another and was often forced to confer with the King, Bismarck and their councillors in the dead of night. Moreover I always had to be on the alert, for we were in the middle of enemy territory, among dangerous people and very close to Paris.

Finally our headquarters left Ferrières, or rather Lagny, and transferred itself to Versailles, where it remained for more than five months, until the end of the war. Becoming prefect once again, I assumed control of the city and its environs, a district of several square leagues with a population of over one hundred thousand, and headed a fairly large administration. Under me were a mayor, two police chiefs, ten police inspectors and thirty *sergents de ville;* I also commanded German personnel consisting of three inspectors, a secretary, five sergeants-major, seven constables, forty-four mounted military police under the supervision of two mounted-police captains and fifty members of the army service corps—a total of more than one hundred men and sixty horses.

In Versailles we received a wonderful surprise. The people, strict legitimists, therefore hostile towards Paris, Napoleon and the new Republic, had not fled the city. The shops and pubs were all open, the streets were brightly lit, and there was as much food as in peacetime. People strolled, and elegant carriages rolled along the avenues, and the women paraded around in beautiful dresses.

The local citizens treated us with friendliness and even invited our officers to lodge with them, and brought fodder for our horses on their own initiative, so that we were not forced to take harsh measures or declare a state of siege.

We felt as if we were in heaven, safe from the things threatening us for so long. Our troops moved into the town barracks, and the only thing that had changed was that now German troops rather than French made up the garrison.

Our King held a splendid parade in the palace square, as if he were the Emperor of France. The regimental bands played, and afterwards, in the King's honor, the fountains were set to playing in the park at the Palace of Versailles. (This amusing spectacle costs ten thousand talers each time it is performed, and thus disconcerted our frugal monarch again.) The entire city turned up for the occasion, and the King of Prussia and Bismarck circulated among the French as if they were at Sans-Souci.

Nevertheless I did not abandon caution; I stayed alert, and at my instigation the troops who were covering us had taken up secure positions. However, my wish to cordon off the palace did not meet with approval. Secretly I had taken precautions here as well, but this did not prevent me from being very worried all day, for my life was at stake if someone succeeded in playing a nasty trick.

The cooperative attitude of the citizens of Versailles began to dissipate as, day by day, it became a more oppressive burden for the city to feed our troops, and this burden finally began to create ever-increasing poverty and deprivation.

It cost two thousand francs a day to support our officers alone. Besides, there were a great many Frenchmen in Versailles who were living on a pension or who had limited independent means, people to whom no one was any longer paying so much as a penny of support. Also, all vehicles, fuel, medicine and tools were gradually removed. In addition there were close to one thousand wounded men in the city and close to three thousand out-of-work laborers with their starving families.

No wonder relations between our headquarters and the townspeople became increasingly critical and the scene had changed competely: Once again we found ourselves in enemy territory, and the ice-cold wind of battle was blowing from nearby Paris.

As each day passed we Germans were living in a more isolated and dangerous position, and I was forced to pay more attention to our personal safety than to the government entrusted to me. Sometimes I actually shuddered when I saw the hatred with which the French people looked at me, and involuntarily I reached into my pocket to feel the loaded revolver I always kept there. But my concern for my own safety was the least of my worries, for every hour I was afraid that some disaster might befall which, despite all my alertness, I could not prevent.

Some time ago I had tightened security precautions. To achieve closer supervision of the French population, who were growing more recalcitrant from one day to the next, I ordered strict police supervision of strangers, drew up a careful written record of all persons in the city and, using this record, conducted a "citizens' registration office" as I had done in Berlin. Whereas the French police were confused by such contrivances and orderliness, the genteel ladies of Versailles raised a hue and cry over that ungallant *préfet prussien* who had threatened them with severe punishment if they did not tell him their true age.

But that was not all I did. I had precise descriptions drawn up of all buildings and of all the roads along which our headquarters travelled and conducted its business, along with details such as whether this or that house had more than one entrance or an inaccessible courtyard, or whether that road was a dead end. In addition we had to identify, check out and keep under surveillance potential assassins, and if necessary to take the precaution of removing them from the scene. My industrious officers collected all important data relating to such potential assassins (names, addresses, habits, etc.) in a secret list of over one hundred persons, who if necessary could be arrested immediately.

The Versailles police did not have the slightest suspicion that to make up this list my officers not only employed their criminal archives but also the list of members of the "Democratic Party" in Versailles and even confiscated the index of subscribers to the party newspaper *Liberté*. And strangely enough, I turned over the task of compiling my records to a Frenchman: the writer Saliggré (a well-known composer of farces), because he knew Versailles like the inside of his pocket and was acquainted with everyone down to the last beggar. We had captured him at Sedan, where he was serving as an artillery officer.

Soon I had placed a field officer at the corner of every street in the city, placed every house and every window under observation, and manned every gate. Any person who looked the least bit suspicious was immediately searched down to the bare skin, and anyone who looked the least bit refractory was immediately arrested. No wonder that we often had up to fifty prisoners; I, as president of the investigation committee, used to officiate half the night in the overcrowded jail, clearing space so that we should have room for the people we arrested next. And throughout this whole affair I was forced to admit that most them had committed no other "crimes" than to be French and to act as if they were!

On the afternoon of October 21 the troops of Paris attacked Versailles and raked it with gunfire, but after just a few hours our troops succeeded in repulsing them and inflicting heavy losses. However, this unexpected attack, of which I had not received the slightest warning, enabled them to capture, like a school of fish, a whole troop of general staff officers from Bavaria, Baden and Württemberg—twenty men in all.

On the other hand, we had captured three aerial balloons and grabbed their navigators from their gondolas at the last moment, except for one Englishman, who did not know what was going on and who wrung his hands in despair as he fled. The captured balloonists were immediately shot in order to halt the danger of aerial espionage, and because they were supposed to be carrying secret dispatches from Paris to the South.

While their fellow countrymen were attacking Versailles, some of its citizens demonstrated such an openly conspiratorial attitude that I suspected they had secretly been in communication with Paris and had known about the attack ahead of time. A short time later I succeeded in tracking down mail which had been secretly sent from Paris to Versailles, by intercepting a letter the public prosecutor of Versailles received from his wife in Paris. Probably this guileless lady did not realize what misfortune she was causing her husband by sending him this letter. As a result of it I immediately had the public prosecutor arrested, along with the chief of postal service in Versailles, who had also been a party to the plot, and the prosecutor was locked up in his own jail (how he must have felt there, I knew from my own sad experience!).

I was also forced to arrest the sweetheart of the postal chief, a genuine countess proud of her country, and the divorced wife of one of Napoleon's ambassadors (although she was Italian by birth). Hundreds of letters and other mail from Paris were found in her possession; they were confiscated immediately. I was not unmoved when I reported these arrests to the commanding general of our troops and learned that the people we had arrested would probably be court-martialled and sentenced to death.

But I could not behave otherwise! It was wartime, and I was in charge of maintaining security; I had to keep in mind that such enemy contacts with the French metropolis as these letters could result in a surprise attack!

Up until this time I had behaved with great indulgence, but now I had to take stern measures. On October 22 the entire district around Versailles was declared to be under a state of siege, and a proclamation was published ordering all French citizens to return to their homes if an alarm were issued to our troops, failing which we should shoot them without mercy. However, this proclamation did not appear to have the slightest effect on the citizens, who—like all French—were accustomed to disobeying their police.

Only a few hours later, when the Parisian soldiers we had captured were being led through the city, the citizens formed into a threatening crowd. At once I dispatched officers who arrested one hundred of them. That evening three battalions of our infantry marched through Versailles in the company of two squadrons of dragoons and a battery of cannon, a total of five thousand men. On my advice our General von Voigts-Rhetz marshalled these troops and publicly told them to search all the houses in town, one district at a time.

The gates of the city were closed, a sentry placed at the door of every house and no one allowed to enter or leave. Throughout the period of the search our dragoons rode through the city and detained every passer-by. In addition all the main arteries around Versailles were in the hands of our troops; this was designed to nip in the bud any thoughts of rebellion on the part of its citizens.

As a result of our thorough and energetic action we discovered more than three hundred suspicious persons and many more rifles with live ammunition, as well as revolvers, bayonets, daggers and long knives. During that same night and into the morning a hearing of the arrested people was conducted by a commission that I hastily formed of German lawyers and over which I presided. However, I had Frenchmen observe the proceedings in the expectation that this would act as a deterrent, but also to prove that we were employing correct procedure. I released many of the arrested parties after we had established their identities, but others were thrown into jail. My investigation did not prove with any degree of certainty whether the people of Versailles had really intended to rebel against us, but the measures I took had achieved their purpose by warning off possible evildoers in time.

In the course of our search we captured unexpected prey: Le Sourd, the First Councillor of Napoleon's embassy and the agent of Benedetti, who had played a major diplomatic role in Berlin and who, after Benedetti had already been sent away, handed Bismarck France's declaration of war with genuine malice, was staying in Versailles incognito at the home of his mother, a citizen of Versailles and a distinguished and wealthy lady. He had not known where to go, for he would not have been well received in Paris and hoped no one would recognize him in Versailles. He had grown a luxuriant beard and was pretending to work as a nurse in a French military hospital.

Nevertheless my officers succeeded in unmasking him, and I personally arrested him and had him taken to our fortress at Mayence, accompanied by a cavalry escort. When he complained bitterly of his fate, I asked him coldly what fate his countrymen would have chosen for Solms, our First Councillor of the Legation, if he had had the notion of turning up in Paris just now.

My massive investigations also turned up several secret emissaries of the Revolutionary Ministry in Paris, who, like Le Sourd, had been hiding behind the Red Cross and apparently serving as nurses. Thereupon I ordered all members of the French ambulance corps who were not residents of Versailles to leave the city, and suggested that they travel to southern France, for on the way to Orléans they would find many wounded Frenchmen who were not yet receiving adequate care.

But there were also French priests among them who did everything they could to spy on us and conspire against us, and therefore I compelled the Bishop of Versailles to identify all the accredited clergymen in the city and drove all the others out. Only a few days previously I had been forced to court-martial a French priest who had attacked and stabbed a Prussian officer.

On the following day Count Bismarck organized a pheasant-shoot, taking advantage of the absence of the King, who had travelled out to see our siege troops and who had refused to allow anyone to hunt in his presence. The palace park contained as many pheasants as other places had sparrows, and they were as large as peacocks.

I had removed all hunting rifles from the French, who were forbidden to have one in their possession on pain of death, and so I had a large supply of weapons for our high-born hunters. I gave Count Bismarck a valuable Lefaucheux musket whose hiding-place I had discovered only a short time before.

Soon we were driving the pheasants before us like herds of sheep, and in the course of the hunt I suddenly found myself alone on the slope of a hill, in front of a villa hidden behind the trees. I found the doors unlocked and I entered, filled with curiosity, but no one answered; apparently the people who lived there had fled.

A deathly silence surrounded me in the hall, and the gloomy portraits of ancestors hanging on the walls heightened my impression that the place had been abandoned. In the library I found books on literary and scientific topics lying open on dusty tables as if someone had just been reading in them, and when I climbed a broad staircase to the next floor and walked out onto a wide terrace, I suddenly saw on the horizon at my feet the metropolis of Paris!

I felt anything but comfortable when I saw this unexpected sight. What if I were captured so deep in enemy territory? It would be awkward to be sent to the enemy metropolis in return for a reward of five *louis d'or!*

But everything remained still and abandoned, and only the setting sun infused the scene with life: It made the countless domes and crosses in the city glow. From my vantage point I could dimly hear the din of the metropolis. I saw the many streets, roads and paths that led into the center of the city from all directions, but I knew that they had all been cut off by our troops so no one could enter or leave the beleaguered city. We had hermetically sealed, surrounded and locked up the "hub of the civilized world," as the Parisians had in the past been so fond of calling it!

When I glanced behind me I saw on the roof a mast with several wooden sails which appeared movable, and then, in the room behind me I found a desk on which there was a telescope and a list of code signals. Through the ceiling above me extended wooden levers, and when I pulled on them, the sails on the roof moved. It did not take much imagination to realize that I was on the trail of a secret communications station.

Each position of the sails on their mast signalled a different letter on the code list, apparently to another station of the same type located within the sight of someone looking through a telescope; however, eagerly as I scanned my surroundings with the telescope, I could not find any such place. In any case, someone located at the other station would shift the positions of similar sails on a mast and thus transmit the information in code to a third station, and so on. There was no doubt: Here, quite by accident, I had probably discovered a previously undetected means of communication with Paris!

I hurried back into the library and lit a match—but then it occurred to me that if this house went up in flames before I got out of the area, I might be seized as an arsonist. I proceeded more cleverly; I removed a candle from a candlestick and placed it on several pages that I had torn from a book. The pages would not catch fire for some time, not until after the candle had burned down and I was long gone from the place.

Before beginning my labor of destruction, I involuntarily set aside costly editions of Rousseau, Voltaire and Montesquieu, and tore up nothing but a romantic novel, that appeared less valuable.

(But even the author of this novel—if he were dead—would certainly have groaned in his grave at the barbaric crime to which I was driven by war!). I placed my candle on the paper "funeral pyre," lit it and left the house.

As I was walking home, five figures dressed in brown jackets and hats literally rose up out of the earth before me, pointing their rifles: they were partisans, irregular French troops! For one instant I started to defend myself with my hunting musket, but they had me outnumbered. Their leader ran over to me, grabbed my weapon, glanced around him and, when he saw that I was alone, gestured at my civilian clothes:

"What are you, as a non-soldier, doing here in enemy country?"

"I'm a hunter at the court of the King of Prussia," I answered without hesitation, "and a game-keeper by profession—if I hadn't been, I should have had to become a soldier!"

"You are not here to kill Frenchmen?" asked my interlocutor.

"Oh no—my target is game!"

The Frenchman nodded, looking satisfied, and I secretly prayed that he would not have me searched. If they found my police identification, they would execute me immediately. Instead this remarkable partisan began to discuss the advance of the German army, and our conversation continued for almost a quarter of an hour, during which time I kept casting glances back at the villa: As soon as the fire I had started there began to take hold, they would connect it with me and . . . ! But nothing happened; the building stood peacefully and unchangingly on its slope, and there was not the slightest trace of smoke.

Then the leader, looking hungrily at the pheasants I had shot, which were dangling plumply from my hunting bag, asked:

"Could you please leave us the birds you've bagged?"

"Gladly!" I answered promptly, and handed them to him, whereupon he, to my amazement, gave me back my hunting musket after he had unloaded it and appropriated my ammunition. "Thank you very much—I shall not rob you unnecessarily!" he said politely.

I was so surprised that I bowed to him politely, but my adversary also bowed as he took his leave, as gracefully as if we were on the dance-floor. Was he the owner of the abandoned villa?

Naturally I could not ask him this question and began to walk away at a measured pace. "Don't hurry, keep it slow," I told myself as I walked along, "otherwise they'll start shooting at you after all . . ."

But nothing happened, everything remained still, and when I finally took a covert glance around me, my friends had disappeared. But at the same moment I saw flames rising on the horizon from the communications station I had set on fire, and sparks began to shoot in all directions. Apparently the library worked like a huge detonator. The roof of the villa was already bursting open with a crash, and the projecting mast crashed along with the roof into the inside of the blazing house.

Thereupon I instituted an investigation of secret communications between Versailles and Paris, and the investigation was to assume dimensions which I never dreamed. The innkeeper of an inconspicuous inn, which was licensed to sell liquor, and also located on a hill, had been, my agents now discovered, running a second communications station with the aid of movable sails on the roof, that he had been using for weeks to signal Paris all the movements of the besieging army.

Entirely by accident my spies tracked down an extensive and many-branched system of subterranean passages beneath Bagneux and Bourg-La-Reine, a system which doubtless ended in the Paris catacombs. By means of this underground network of roads the city that, above ground, was surrounded by our troops, had not only secretly obtained news whenever it chose, but had also been host to processions of wagons filled with food. On bright moonlit nights my observers counted up to three hundred supply vehicles, wheels wrapped with cloths to prevent noise, sinking invisibly beneath the earth.

All this obeyed a precise ceremonial. First they spent a long time observing and scrutinizing the perimeter of the city, looking for any changes which might endanger the vehicles. Then at night these vehicles were removed from the hiding places—the trenches formed by streams, valleys, bushes, and so on—where they had been waiting—so that, travelling beneath the earth, they could cart into the "belly" of Paris the nourishing fruits of the surrounding countryside.

In its subterranean reaches the supply officers were already waiting for the men who would bring the city the longed-for food, and would hastily order the soldiers in their supply units to unload the precious cargo, for often a vehicle had to travel in and out of the city as many as five times a night!

Even before we discovered all this, my spies had stated that Paris contained vast stores of provisions, which, however, we believed were acquired solely by absorbing possessions of fugitives from the countryside. All the inhabitants of the villages around Paris had abandoned their homes and fled to the capital, bringing their produce and livestock with them. It was for this reason alone—so we had previously believed—that Paris contained abundant food supplies, all of which, nevertheless, would one day be consumed by the masses of people in the great metropolis.

Since the siege began, cattle, sheep and pigs had been grazing in the city parks, and wethers and rabbits were tended in the gardens, where, instead of exotic, decorative plants and flowers, the feudal orangeries and greenhouses in the city contained vegetables, potatoes or scratching poultry which laid masses of eggs.

To be sure, the price of food had gone up, but nevertheless the Parisians still had turkeys in their pots, fish from the aquariums and, as was reported to me, even oysters. And "gourmets" even ate animals from the Paris Zoo—lion, bear and elephant steaks masterfully prepared by the most famous restaurant chefs. No, in view of all this I was firmly convinced that it would not help us at all to try to starve the Parisians out, that placing the city under siege would not enable us to conquer it, and that the center of France would not suffer the pains of an empty stomach for a long time yet!

Count Bismarck seemed quite alarmed when I reported that Paris still had enough food supplies to last for an indefinite period. "Great God!" he cried. "And we have hardly an ounce of patience left!"

It was true that no one at our headquarters had a very clear idea about what would happen in the future. It was said that the King had stated that we should not be home before Easter, but his adjutant, on the other hand, said that the monarch would be home by New Year's. The Crown Prince's circle claimed that we should be in Paris in a fortnight, whereas Count Bismarck believed that this would not happen until the end of January. It was no wonder that gradually we all became very nervous, for despite the fact that it was under siege and cut off from the world around it, Paris still did not surrender.

The King appeared to develop a more and more intense need for peace, to long for rest, as was natural at his age. In this respect he seemed to be of one mind with the Crown Prince, who sorely missed the pleasures of being with his family. In short, our leaders were suffering from exhaustion! This exhaustion was compounded by the fact that it was becoming more and more difficult to keep the wheels of government bureaucracy turning, and by growing interdepartmental jealousy between men in civilian and military posts. Anyone who conducted his affairs in such a confused manner in civilian life would have been done for a long time ago! But here no one thought about whether he might adversely affect the lives of others and the war effort as a whole. Everyone did what he wanted, the way he wanted it: Men who were the bravest heroes in the pursuit of the enemy quarrelled like schoolchildren when they were forced to wait and do nothing.

Morever, the cold was almost unendurable, for we could not actually creep inside the chimneys of the old palace, that gave off little heat. None of us could any longer bear sitting still and doing nothing; many of us had gotten sick because of it or were struggling with its effects, and the ground, slippery with ice, and the bitter east wind, made it real torture to take a walk, go horseback riding or driving.

During this period of idleness and waiting the civilian newspaper scribblers began to take a hand in our affairs. In the absence of other goals, their dammed-up stream of ink began to flow over our headquarters, and dissatisfaction and calumny now began to penetrate the German press back at home. The impermeable darkness that shrouded our future gave rise to speculations: could we, and in the end would we, for political or moral reasons, choose to go no farther? And soon false doves of peace were fluttering around.

The newspapers claimed Napoleon was no longer the ruler of France, and therefore Germany had no reason to continue the war. Indeed, there was, they said, no longer legitimate cause for war, and anyone who continued to wage it was subject to punishment by "international law." Instead of perpetuating the war we should offer the new France an honorable peace, and refrain from committing more atrocities of war. It was unnecessary to humiliate our adversary by taking Paris! To do so involved a waste of human lives, time and money, and so forth and so on.

Meanwhile, though Paris had been bottled up since autumn, the members of the French government concerned with national defense did not intend to surrender their capital. "There is nothing which could compel us to surrender—Paris will never surrender!" they proclaimed, and again and again spurred their citizens on, with patriotic phrases and falsified reports of victories, to continued resistance.

"Paris is the sacred hub of human civilization and thus is an eternally invulnerable city—remember this, those who defend it!" read an appeal to hold out until the end. The agents I still had working for me in Paris reported that the walls were covered with hundreds of posters describing French victories that had never taken place, and messages stating that the King of Prussia and the Crown Prince had been killed by French shells and that Mac-Mahon was now hurrying to liberate Paris at the head of a vast army. But the Parisian newspapers, blind with fury, declared that it was advantageous to the French that their attackers had penetrated so deeply into their country, for none of the enemy soldiers would return to his homeland alive.

No—until the more than two million Parisians began to suffer the horrors of true starvation, none of them would dare to consider surrender!

The French capital, that we had surrounded, was the greatest fortress in the world: The vast girdle of its trenches and fortifications measured almost sixty kilometers, its ramparts were forty kilometers in circumference and were fitted with one hundred bastions, there were circular roads and circular military railways, and two thousand five hundred cannons of the heaviest caliber adorned the whole, always ready to fire, and equipped with abundant supplies of ammunition.

Every day we lost soldiers to Parisian cannon fire. The Parisians, with the most incredible waste of ammunition, used to fire at random or when we were still leagues away. According to our calculations every shot they fired cost more than five talers, a shot from one of the huge cannons ten times as much. Three hundred and fifty thousand guardsmen, one hundred and fifty national guardsmen, sixty thousand *lignards* and fifteen thousand *mariniers,* as well as twelve thousand gendarmes, toll collectors, gamekeepers and firemen simultaneously fired their rifles at us as soon as they saw us leave cover.

And every day balloons with soldiers on board, carrying masses of mail, floated out of the beleaguered city of lights. Of course we always fired at them, but succeeded in shooting down only a few. Not until Krupp had sent us the "special anti-balloon cannon" did we begin to do better. But now the balloonists almost always plunged to their deaths, so that I could no longer interrogate them as I had done in the past, when their balloons, struck by a few bullets, sank slowly to earth.

Swarms of French carrier pigeons also began to take to the air, until we countered by releasing hunting hawks that descended on the slower, defenseless pigeons and pulled many of them down from the sky, along with the often informative and revealing messages carried in capsules fastened around their necks.

These ceaseless calamities led us, at first secretly and then ever more openly, to discuss whether it might not be necessary for us to fire on Paris, a discussion which led to the most violent divergences of opinion we had evinced at any time during the war.

Our military leaders advocated immediate bombardment, so that we could put an end to all resistance. From what I heard I knew that not only von Roon, but Bismarck too was doing everything he could to ensure that the bombardment took place.

"The world is not waiting for our benevolence, but for our victory," the Count told all the civilians among us, who rejected his proposal on humanitarian grounds. And he publicly stated that he and von Roon were already sick with rage over this "irresponsible delay."

General von Moltke was opposed to the bombardment of Paris, not, to be sure, because this would inevitably result in heavy casualties among the Parisians, but because one could not predict with any certainty whether the success to be derived from such an unprecedented bombardment of a modern metropolis would be worth the effort we should have to put into it.

The King was against the bombardment because it would violate "international law;" destruction, he said, was not our intention, and to inflict it would be a reversion to barbarism. The Crown Prince was even more strongly opposed to the bombardment than his father because—as he said—he did not want to have to deal with the hatred of France throughout his entire reign. And so we passed the time in discussion and nothing happened.

Before our first Christmas Eve in enemy territory I released, without imposing any fine, several French civilians whom I had placed under arrest, whose lives were at stake and whose families had been besieging me all day. Then I secretly went to an abandoned house where I knew that a cooper who had fled the area had left a well-equipped workshop, and there, with my own hands, constructed a stately Christmas tree out of wooden poles and fir-tree branches, fetched from a long distance away. I had also procured apples and nuts, French wine and German Christmas stollen.

At first I knelt beneath the quietly glowing tree alone. Then Count Bismarck was attracted to its bright lights, and we sat devoutly side by side like the first Christians in the wilderness (for the French do not have Christmas trees).

Then we began an intimate discussion of our past lives. The Chancellor was as honest and open as I was, and we discovered that we had many things in common. Ever since his stay there the Count had loved England, the land of my ancestors (even though he abhorred the puritanical English Sundays). And he had completed his examination at the same Berlin gymnasium as I had, and had even studied under many of the same schoolmasters who had taught me, so that now, like many people when their schooldays are past, we amused ouselves by describing the pranks we had played.

Count Bismarck concluded his description of his life with the words, "See what can become of a Pomeranian lout!" And concerning me he said, "It is very refreshing, for a change, to talk with someone with a clear, completely ruthless mind. Too many of the high-ranking gentlemen here are weak and without principle!" Whereupon I cheerfully replied, "Your Excellency—no one so far has ever accused me of a lack of ruthlessness!"

Then Bismarck allowed me to see more deeply into his heart and, among other things, said about the French, "When you get to know them they are not the cultivated people everyone takes them to be at a distance. Instead they resemble certain members of our own lower classes. They have strong muscles and big mouths and brutally force those of their own kind to respect them, and all the time they haven't the slightest idea of what things are like outside their own country. They learn nothing about these matters in their schools; that is why they suffer from such overweening presumption. Unfortunately their Emperor—not to mention his councillors, who were all asses—was no better, or at least not much better. Although he was educated in German schools, he remained basically ignorant. The fact that he spoke German merely served to conceal this fact—."

Then later the Count promised me the Iron Cross, and I immediately began to wonder whether he could really get it for me, a non-combatant, when (as I had secretly learned) he was on anything but good terms with the military leaders here.

Bismarck had just complained to the King that von Moltke, the Chief of the General Staff, possessed inadequate information about our military situation, and as a result that most gracious gentleman, without listening to von Moltke's side of the story first, had given him a rather ungracious order. I knew that General von Moltke had angrily protested that Bismarck, a "civilian in the uniform of a cuirassier," was trying to "take charge of and interfere in" military matters, which, given his lack of military knowledge, could easily lead to awkward *faits accomplis*.

Soon it was reported to me that a "disastrous shift of mood and feeling of depression" was apparent in Berlin and the German provinces. To be sure, the German people still believed that Germany was bound to be victorious, but the elation they felt at the outbreak of the war against France had given way to a feeling of sobriety. Sorrowing mourners dressed in mourning clothes, bewailing fallen soldiers, were everywhere, and for the first time the people seemed aware of what it would mean if the war continued much longer. Clearly no one had expected that the struggle would persist into this ghastly winter and that, moreover, at the end of the first year of war no one would as yet be able to tell when it might end.

What I said about these matters in my "report on our situation" at least achieved one effect: Suddenly von Roon was permitted to give the command that we fire on Paris. Hastily leadership of the engineering attack was assigned to General von Kameke and of the artillery attack to General Prince Hohenlohe, whereupon it proved that our batteries had already been in position for some time, as if all the men down in the ranks had always assumed that we would decide to shell Paris.

Four hundred locomotives and almost two thousand freight cars had transported, along France's excellent rail system, two hundred and fifty German cannons, complete with ammunition, some of them of the heaviest caliber available, and punctually at eight-thirty on the morning of December 27 our cannons opened fire. At first a snowstorm made it difficult to hit precise targets, but the French fortresses of Avron, Nogent and Rosny responded swiftly and energetically and our batteries lost officers and soldiers. Several of our gun-carriages collapsed under the shock of their own thrust.

Nevertheless an indescribable sense of exultation swept not only through our army but through all of Germany when the first German twenty-four pounders finally crashed into the sea of houses inside the obstinate city. Immediately thereafter the weather cleared up, giving us a precise target to aim at, and our cannon wrought fearful destruction among the garrisons of the Parisian fortresses; the fortress of Mont Avron grew completely silent, whereas the others returned only weak fire.

Naturally morale at our headquarters improved immensely, and we experienced a sense of liberation because we were finally able to act and knew just where we stood, and could cling to this certainty from now on.

My agents, who, as in the past, sent us their eyewitness reports by the most adventurous routes, were responsible for the fact that we always knew exactly what was going on.

However, neither reports nor documents revealed how boldly these spies broke through the barricades set up by the enemy and how deeply they penetrated into his territory. Unarmed and unprotected, equipped only with intelligence, cunning and the consummate ability to deceive, they survived hair-raising threats in the form of enemy patrols and more than once were exposed to the fire of their own side, that is German guns, and the French never succeeded in unmasking a single one of them—.

Paris was paralyzed by the first shots we fired. That very morning its citizens had read in their newspapers that the Germans had already despaired of victory and only intended to hold out a short time longer because they were afraid of marching home without having succeeded in their quest. But now abruptly all the lights in the city were extinguished and its boulevards were shrouded in an uncanny darkness.

Horrified, frightened, but also furious, the startled Parisians ran through the city and gathered into groups shouting, "Revenge; they have lied to us!" Meanwhile the corpses of those hit by fragments from our shells, sank to the ground. It was in vain that people sought to bury them at once, for German bullets fell remorselessly around them and pursued even the victims they had already slain as these were on their way to be buried.

Already parts of the city were catching fire, and the suburb of St. Denis was shrouded in flames. Military and civilian hospitals were soon filled to bursting, and there were not enough doctors and medicines to treat the victims. All activity, indeed all movement ceased, and no one dared to leave his house. Half-grown boys and fathers of families who were well along in years were drafted to defend the city, and the roar of our cannonade went on and on. Relentless and inexhaustible as the blows of a hammer, the explosions smashed into the crowd of houses inside the French capital, until now spared the ravages of war.

The citizens of Paris implored that the city be surrendered so that the horror would end, but the commanding officers remained as hard as iron. "Let them shoot, then at least they'll find nothing left but a heap of ashes!" they replied to the citizens' committees, and the citizens were already falling victim to martial law: Anyone who so much as appeared on the roof of a house along the line of defense was instantly shot as a traitor or an advocate of surrender.

In addition to everything else, the Parisians were tortured by the most quixotic rumors. Their hearts already wrung by the destruction, they feared that the defenders of the city, in their blind rage, would prefer to blow up Paris rather than surrender it, and would do so with the masses of powder with which the still intact fortresses were so abundantly equipped.

Most of the subterranean supply tunnels and huge quantities of meat, grain and produce of all sorts—almost all the food reserves of the unhappy city—had been burned and choked with rubble by our bombardment. Bread had to be rationed: three hundred grams a day for adults and one hundred and fifty grams for children. Women stood about in queues to get half-charred meat and scorched vegetables from the storehouses we had riddled with gunfire. In fact, with their own eyes my spies saw people killing dogs and cats so that they could eat their meat.

I particularly asked them to confirm something I was unable to believe: that a rat market had been established in what had once been the metropolis of epicures, where these monsters who aroused man's disgust leaped around inside big cages until they were slaughtered by the dealers and sold at high prices to hungry buyers.

In view of these facts, there was no longer any doubt: As a result of our bombardment Paris could not survive for much longer, and it was destined to fall very soon. Now the spectre of starvation had awakened within its walls and was threatening with its bony and relentless fist: surrender or death!

From then on everyone at our headquarters engaged in a passionate discussion of the "conceptions of emperor and empire."

Our military leaders declared that it would be very easy to

create a "united Germany with an emperor at its head!" Now that the sons of all the German provinces had fought the battles of this war together, they claimed, the union of these provinces had, to all intents and purposes, already been achieved, and their victorious Commander-in-Chief, the King of Prussia, was now the "natural heir to the title of Emperor."

On the other hand, the debates taking place around the tables of the King and Count Bismarck centered on the activities of a political group in our homeland, namely the "National Liberal Parliamentary Party," whose leader, a Jewish lawyer named Lasker, enthusiastically and categorically demanded the union of Germany.

King Wilhelm protested vehemently against such "popular agitation," which savored of the "carrion scent of revolution." If he had to become Emperor of Germany, then he would accept the crown only from his peers, from the princes who ruled the German states.

Count Bismarck, on the other hand, seemed to have concentrated all his thoughts on the idea that, no matter what happened, this war had to win the crown of the Emperor of Germany for the Prussian ruling family; but at the same time he was aware of the enormous difficulties involved in realizing this goal.

In any case he summoned me to his presence and remarked that unless he had precise and up-to-date information about all the public and private attitudes, views and intentions of people in all the German states with regard to the question of German unity, he could not and would not act. And he assigned me no less a task than the immediate and confidential investigation of the attitudes of people, in all areas of Germany, of whose views he stood in doubt.

Fortunately, ever since my investigations of Communist plots I had maintained secret informers at the following German courts:

The courts of Their Majesties the Kings of Bavaria and Württemberg, Their Royal Highnesses the Grand Dukes of Hesse and Mecklenburg-Strelitz, His Highness the Duke of Brunswick, Their Serene Highnesses the Princes von Waldeck, von Schwarzburg-Rudolstadt, von Schwarzburg-Sondershausen and von Reuss Younger Line, as well as His Majesty the King of Saxony, His Royal Highness the Grand Duke of Mecklenburg-Schwerin, and His Serene Highness the Prince von Schaumburg-Lippe, Their Royal Highnesses the Grand Dukes of Baden, Saxony and Oldenburg, Their Highnesses the Dukes of Saxe-Meiningen, Saxe-Altenburg, Saxe-Coburg-Gotha and Anhalt, and Their Serene Highnesses the Prince von Reuss Older Line and the Prince zur Lippe.

My informants in these places were almost unanimous in their view that people everywhere were firmly opposed to the idea of a "German Empire" under the rule of a "German Emperor." As was quite natural, the most impassioned resistance to this idea existed in Hanover, where a "Guelph party" had managed to maintain its integrity and its allegiance to its dethroned king; it was led by the King's former minister Ludwig von Gerlach. This party, as it always had, regarded Prussia's treatment of King George V, that resulted in his loss of his throne, as a "crime against the monarchical principle," and the people of Hanover also believed that a bitter injustice had been done them.

(At this point Count Bismarck interrupted me with the sarcastic comment that it was this same King of Hanover who, in 1853, had wanted Bismarck to serve as his minister and who had Bismarck write down the stratagems which he should employ in order to abolish the liberal constitution which his people had struggled to win from him.)

On the other hand, the throne of Bavaria, the largest of the states of southern Germany, was occupied by the young dreamer Ludwig II, who was more interested in art and science than in the dry affairs of government. The only political matter which concerned him was the splendor of his house of Wittelsbach, which he wanted to outshine all other German dynasties, including the Hohenzollerns. The idea of the former King of Prussia's acquiring the German imperial crown was particularly repellent to him.

By the same token, my agents in the kingdom of Württemberg did not detect the slightest inclination on the part of the people to welcome a united German "Empire." Instead, both publicly and in secret, the King, and even more so the Queen, tried in every way they could to maintain the status quo in Germany. The people of Württemberg were also firmly opposed to a "Prussian soldier-emperor," for they had inherited the Swabian's traditional hatred of soldiers, which expressed itself in refusal to grant any soldier a position of power in civilian life.

The reports I received from Dresden clearly revealed that the court of Saxony also rejected the idea of a Prussian emperor. Indeed, the King of Saxony's aversion to "Bismarck's obsessive notion of an emperor" seemed quite insuperable and as intense as that of the Grand Duke of Hesse-Darmstadt and that which reigned throughout the Rhineland, where ever since the "fraternal war" of 1866 my agents had verified the existence of an overt and massive hatred of Prussians.

No matter how extensive the promises and concessions of Prussia, almost none of the courts of the various German states appeared to want to have anything to do with the notion of a united Germany, quite simply because they feared it might result in a reduction of their hereditary powers of sovereignty over their subjects. They presented Count Bismarck with a chilling picture of hostility and rejection of his plan, for Germans everywhere would still have preferred Austria to regain its ascendancy and Prussia to submit to it.

At first Count Bismarck questioned the accuracy of the extremely uniform reports from my agents, but I corroborated these by showing him documents taken directly from the cabinets of the various courts and even instructions and orders written by the sovereigns themselves to their foreign ministers.

All this made the Count so furious that he swore at the top of his lungs that he could do nothing to counteract these princely foxes who had not yet learned to do their duty by their German fatherland as a whole. Yet in a short time, while still in Versailles, he had succeeded in coming to agreements with the representatives of almost all the German courts, agreements that paved the way for the establishment of the "Empire" and its "Emperor."

In order to ensure that the most mighty sovereign Ludwig of Bavaria would offer the new imperial crown to the King of Prussia in the name of all the other German princes (which would also satisfy the King's claim to accept only if the crown were offered by his peers), Count Bismarck employed the following tactics: From the "Guelph treasure" of George V, the exiled King of Hanover, who in 1866 had been the ally of the King of Bavaria in their war against Prussia, and from the private fortune of the electors of Hesse, acquired by selling their subjects as soldiers to the English, he offered to grease the palm of the Bavarian sovereign with seven millions in compensation. He made the offer quite openly through Bavaria's ambassador in Versailles, Count Holnstein, for the construction costs incurred by the extravagant young sovereign, that I had learned amounted to some four millions. Moreover he did not hesitate to offer Count Holnstein an additional ten per cent of this fee as a commission in return for acting as go-between.

To simplify matters Bismarck gave Holnstein the draft of a letter which he had himself composed for Holnstein's hesitant master, a letter which emphatically offered King Wilhelm of Prussia the imperial crown. An agent who had been working for me for many years at the Bavarian court disguised as a paid footman, told me what happened.

No sooner had it been reported in Bavaria that Count Holnstein had returned from Versailles, than King Ludwig II took refuge in his sick-bed, pleading that he was suffering from a "paralyzing toothache," and was completely unaware that my spy was listening at the keyhole.

Before the eyes and within the hearing of my spy, Count Holnstein reported to his sovereign, shrouded in blankets, about Bismarck's offer as well as the "imperial letter" which Bismarck had already written. The allegedly sick man groaned and declared that he would never be able to write.

Thereupon the Count sought to pressure him by suggesting that the King would become Emperor of all Germany without Bavaria's help and Bavaria would be isolated as a result, whereupon the King whispered almost inaudibly (addressing Count Holnstein in the familiar), "If this horrible thing must be, then let it once again be *thou* who dost perform it!" (This remark seemed to suggest that Count Holnstein had often performed such royal commissions in the past!)

Uttering a curse (!) the Count sank down at the King's writing desk and began—rapidly and with assurance, as my informant assured me—to copy Bismarck's rough draft and finally, after a brief hesitation, sign it himself. Clearly he had mastered his young King's handwriting. Meanwhile the King lay motionless on his bed and, throughout the time Holnstein was writing, did not so much as move his little finger, not to mention a pen!

Thereupon Count Holnstein concealed the finished letter in his pocket and left the chambers of his King so abruptly that he almost flung the doors in my eavesdropper's face, but my informant saved himself at the last moment by leaping behind the door curtain.

After a hasty six-day journey during which he did not rest and even made use of a locomotive that he had requisitioned, the

King's inexhaustible messenger Count Holnstein returned to Versailles. Here Count Bismarck immediately received him in his bedroom and shortly thereafter sent for champagne; at this time I saw him looking more pleased and high-spirited than ever before.

On the other hand, King Wilhelm, to whom Bismarck had read the Bavarian "imperial letter," brought by Holnstein, immediately after dinner, looked completely thunderstruck and devastated, and clearly had no idea that the letter itself had originated here in Versailles, so that I several times felt the urge to reveal the double fiction to which he had been subjected. However, such action would have resulted in virtual assassination or mass murder and would not have been legally binding because the verbal request the King of Bavaria made of his agent to write a letter in his name, signified that he had given his consent.

King Wilhelm was afflicted by the most acute sorrow at seeing his "God-given" title of King of Prussia replaced by what he regarded as an "empty title that would appear to confer on him more power than he really possessed," and seemed less reconciled to it than ever! He also claimed that this offer had arrived at exactly the wrong time, for he did not believe that the Germans had won a clear victory and he still regarded their position as insecure.

Immediately Count Bismarck replied that the selection of a German emperor had nothing to do with the continuation of the war and that it would remain valid even if Germany were hurled back behind the Meuse. As I left the King's table I suspected that despite everything, today the German Empire had become a reality!

Shortly thereafter a thirty-man delegation from the German Parliament, led by its President, Simson, arrived in Versailles to offer our King the imperial crown in the name of the German people.

However, for two days King Wilhelm refused even to see these representatives, because "a crown offered by the people was tainted with the carrion scent of revolution," to which he did not want to bow a second time. Only with great difficulty did Bismarck succeed in getting him to change his mind so that he could avoid an open scandal. Then at last the "chosen representatives of the German people" were reluctantly admitted by their future Emperor—to "make their obeisance" to him, as I myself heard his aide-de-camp call it.

My police were kept very busy arranging the whole thing and guaranteeing security, and almost my entire personnel were going about their business on foot, in the saddle or on wheels, as if we were arranging a party at the court in Berlin. However, the "coaches" in which our guests arrived were a strange mixture of Prussian supply wagons, requisitioned French carriages and farm wagons. In place of coachmen dressed in livery the vehicles were driven by uniformed cannoneers from the regiment of guards.

Nevertheless it was an impressive moment when these vehicles, carrying the delegates of all the German people, drove up to deposit them before the royal palace of Versailles, occupied by the King's troops, so that they could visit the victorious King of Prussia and offer the imperial crown of Germany to his house, the house of Hohenzollern. At that moment heavy fire was coming from Mont Valérien, and several Prussian batteries were moving past; the soldiers happened to be singing "What is the German's fatherland?" and their vigorous warrior's voices, mingling with the distant thunder of cannon, created a heroic scene.

President Simson handed the King a document written on parchment and bound in red leather, the "most humble plea of the German Parliament that by accepting the imperial crown His Majesty the King of Prussia might perfect and consecrate the labor of uniting Germany."

Without altering his expression King Wilhelm took the document and passed it on to his aide-de-camp (the one who had said to me that the members of the delegation wanted to "make their obeisance" to the King). As I knew, the spiritual author of the text was a Member of Parliament, Professor Julius von Stahl, who, although from a Jewish family, had converted to the Protestant faith, and of whom it had been said that people listened to his enthusiastic speeches in Parliament about the creation of an Emperor as if they were listening to our forefather Moses himself.

The leader and spokesman of the delegation, the Prussian judge Eduard von Simson, was also Jewish; he was the son of a Jewish merchant and was married to the daughter of a Jewish banker named Warschauer. Once before—exactly twenty-one years ago—he had entered St. Paul's Church in Frankfurt, as a delegate of the German people, to offer Friedrich Wilhelm IV, who was then King of Prussia, the imperial crown of all Germany; but he had offered it in vain. Now once again he appeared before the King, made an exquisite bow and began to express the "enthusiasm of the entire German people for the reverend person of their sovereign Wilhelm I." in such solemn and moving words that patriotric tears filled the eyes of everyone present, especially the Crown Prince.

Through my police connections I knew that this well-set-up speech had been drafted by the lawyer Eduard von Lasker, whom I have mentioned before and who—like Karl Marx the scion of a middle-class Jewish family—in 1848 had incited the people to "armed revolt against its princely oppressors," and who, for this reason, had been sentenced to prison.

However, at this historic moment no one noticed the fact that it was men of Jewish ancestry who thus movingly expressed the "ancient longing of all German people for their ultimate union under a German Emperor and Commander-in-Chief." Even our high-ranking general officers, all of whom were present at this solemn scene, seemed moved by these "genuinely German and patriotic speeches and documents," as the Crown Prince called them, tears running down into his blond beard.

However, when King Wilhelm, deeply moved, hesitated to read the reply which Bismarck had already composed for him, Bismarck drew aside the door curtains because he believed that his King needed more light to read.

Later Friedenthal, an Independent-Conservative Member of Parliament (and likewise a Jew) asked Count Bismarck to read once again the imperial letter from the Bavarian King Ludwig II. At first Bismarck was unable to find it, then he read it in the driest, most official tone as if it were some routine document from his chancellery. "No wonder!" I thought. After all, I knew about the somewhat dubious origins of that letter.

At the dinner party that followed, the representatives of the German people sat beside the King of Prussia. Among them was a Member of Parliament from Frankfurt, Karl Mayer-Rothschild, a well-known Jewish banker, who pointed out during the conversation that six thousand Jewish soldiers of all ranks were fighting under Prussia's flags and so far three hundred of them had fallen for King and country (at the end of the war the number was four hundred and forty-eight).

After that the King joked with the citizens of Berlin about the "depot-ful of martial vehicles" which they had brought him, and here, once again, Simson demonstrated his ready wit by courteously replying, "Once again we owe everything to the soldiers of Germany!" Grinning, the King took his revenge by conferring on him the Star of the Order of the Red Eagle, Second Class, which he personally pinned on Simson's breast. However, Simson was soon compelled to take it off again because this particular decoration belonged to Councillor of the Legation von Abeken, who, eager to do his duty, had merely lent it to him because there was no other available at the time.

After the "New Imperial Constitution" had been printed and appeared in Berlin, the "German Empire" was considered a legally valid entity as of January 1, 1871, and yet it was not capable of taking any action because its executive organs had not yet been formed. On the evening preceding the day when the Empire would become legally valid, those in our headquarters were not even able to find out *whether*, *where* and *how* this significant first step would be followed by a "celebration of the proclamation of the Emperor and the Empire" (as the Crown Prince mockingly expressed it).

Our Prussian King, who, according to the text of the Constitution now in force, was already the "German Emperor," declared categorically that he "wanted absolutely no public fuss" until the outcome of the war with France had been decided and the war had come to an end. He preferred that his "inauguration" should wait until after peace was concluded!

On the other hand, Count Bismarck pleaded that they should hold a "solemn coronation" on January 18, the historic birthday of the Prussian monarchy, the day in 1701 when the Elector Frederick III of Brandenburg placed a king's crown on his head.

But our Crown Prince angrily demanded, now that we had gone this far, we at the head of government should make some kind of official statement to Germany's princes and people on January 1, the day when the new Empire would actually come into being. If we did not we should place ourselves in a legally impossible position because the German people would possess a constitution that would not be fully implemented and, in addition, possessed clauses providing for an Emperor who remained hidden from view. The Crown Prince claimed that such a lack of decisiveness made him sick to his stomach!

His father, the King of Prussia, whose opinion ultimately counted most, continued to emphasize in private conversations what horror he felt at the idea of accepting that empty and purely formal title in place of the legitimate title of King of Prussia, and seemed to be on the point of withdrawing and allowing this doom to fall on his son. Indeed, on the day before the coronation was to be proclaimed (we had finally decided on January 18), Wilhelm I refused to be raised to the rank of "German Emperor"—for if he must be an emperor, he wanted to be "Emperor of Germany."

Bismarck objected that this latter title suggested that Prussia had an inadmissible claim to the non-Prussian land of Germany which would never be tolerated by the princes of Germany, and that "German Emperor" had already been printed in the new Constitution; also, one said "Roman Emperor," not "Emperor of Rome," and "Russian Tsar." Likewise the word *Borussorum* ("Prussian"), and not *Borussiae rex*, was printed on the coins of Frederick the Great and Frederick Wilhelm II.

But Bismarck's weighty defense of his position angered the old monarch so greatly that he pounded on the table and declared, "Even if what you have said is true, now I am commanding it to be otherwise!" Having said this, he walked over to the window and turned his back on everyone present, which brought any further debate concerning the title to an end.

Nevertheless the indefatigable Count Bismarck left the date for celebrating the coronation unchanged and told me that he was no longer the slightest bit concerned about the matter. On the morning of the appointed day, January 18, he paid a visit to Grand Duke Friedrich von Baden, the highest in rank of all the princes now in Versailles.

They quietly came to an agreement about how to smooth things over. At the coronation of his stubborn father-in-law the Grand Duke was simply to cheer "Emperor Wilhelm," rather than "the German Emperor," which was not favored by the King, or the suspect "Emperor of Germany."

On January 18, 1871, King Wilhelm I was proclaimed German Emperor in the Hall of Mirrors in the royal palace at Versailles.

However, the invitation to the ceremony spoke of it simply as a "jubilee in honor of the Order of the Black Eagle," for this was not only the anniversary of the day, one hundred and seventy years ago, when the first Prussian sovereign had himself placed a king's crown on his head, but also of the day when he had founded the "Order of the Black Eagle."

By the same token, no solemn procession, customary at coronation celebrations, took place, but King Wilhelm's carriage, which, thank God, was quite inconspicuous, made its way to the splendid palace of the former sovereigns of France through a crowd of military vehicles, wagons carrying food supplies and herds of livestock being driven along by farmers—the everyday traffic of Versailles—accompanied only by the field police I had ordered to protect the monarch, supplemented by twelve soldiers on horseback.

Far away the cannons thundered from the fortifications of Paris and were answered by our German batteries, for even on that day we continued our bombardment of the beleaguered French capital!

Beneath the statue of le Grand Condé King Wilhelm stood beside an honor guard with the flag that Major von Kaisenberg had taken from his slain standard-bearer at the battle of Weissenburg, and had carried with him when he attacked the enemy and was himself killed. After him two more of his officers, who were also killed, had carried the flag during that first victorious but deadly battle of the war.

The King reverently took hold of the bullet-riddled flag, noted the traces of blood left on its shaft by those who had defended it, and then gave it to its present bearer, an extremely young non-commissioned officer entrusted with the colors, and said, "Always hold it high, my son!"

Princes, officers and deputations sent by the German regiments drawn up around Paris, as well as fifteen Russian generals and eight chaplains, were already waiting for him in the great Hall of Mirrors in the palace of Louis XIV. Almost all the German commanders were present except von der Tann; he had remained with his corps outside Paris, for a sudden sortie from the beleaguered city would have disrupted the celebration!

Standing erect, his gaze firmly fixed on those who were awaiting him, the image of venerable nobility, the aged monarch ascended the dais where he would be crowned, displaying no weariness despite his age. There he stood on the very place once occupied by Louis XIV's chair of state, dressed in the uniform of his First Regiment of Foot Guards, adorned with the ribbon of the Order of the Black Eagle as well as a number of other orders, commemorative decorations and other decorations designed to honor him.

His coronation as the new German Emperor was preceded by

a religious ceremony which took place near an improvised altar. The altar stood near a statue of a nude female, for there were so many of them around here that it was impossible to cover them all.

The Crown Prince energetically commanded, "Remove your helmets to pray!", whereupon Rogge, the court chaplain, recited the liturgy according to Prussian military usage, followed by a performance by a soldiers' choir under the direction of the court conductor, Goldschmidt. Wilhelm I had expressly asked them to sing the sixty-sixth Psalm ("Thanks be to God for His wonderful guidance of his people!").°

Then Bismarck, his face pale, wearing tall riding-boots so that he looked like a giant, bowed deeply before the approaching Emperor. On his shoulders he wore the epaulettes of a lieutenant-general, for he had just been promoted to that rank. In his left hand he held his massive helmet, in his right hand the coronation charter, which he read in such a business-like tone that in the vastness of the hall I could not understand a single word. Then, likewise failing to hear what was said, I saw the newly-crowned Emperor murmur something and receive a brief reply. Then I heard the Grand Duke von Baden shout in a loud voice, "His Majesty Emperor Wilhelm the Victorious, long may he live!" Three times a thundering "Long live the Emperor!" issued from innumerable throats, as vigorous a cry as would have been heard in a barracks square; flags fell, sabres were drawn from their sheaths, helmets were waved in the air. Again and again the soldiers roared "Hurrah's," almost drowning out the three regimental bands playing "Hail to thee in the victor's wreath!" as loud as they could.

The historical drama was over, and once again, after sixty years, we had a German Empire with an Emperor at its head! But as the Emperor descended from his dais he turned to his generals, without so much as glancing at the waiting Bismarck, who had made all this possible.

Not until later did the Count explain this ill treatment, which at the time I attributed to the press of the crowd after the ceremony. Those present had pressed closer and closer to the dais in order to be as near the drama as possible, until monitors (my

° This is a very innacurate translation of Psalm 66:5. Stieber is probably quoting—or misquoting—from memory.—Tr.

police officers among them), inconspicuously but energetically, refusing any resistance, stopped them in their tracks.

"His Majesty blamed me for that maneuver (as he called it) to have him celebrated as Emperor Wilhelm instead of Emperor of Germany!" Bismarck told me, and added that the Emperor had obstinately persisted in this rejection for several days, until gradually, under pressure of their duties, their relationship resumed its accustomed character.

At the dinner party that followed the table was set for one hundred and twenty people, but we ate modest fish, beef, butter, ham, sausage and wine (everyone could have as much of the latter as he wanted), while a band played the favorite pieces of the man who was now the German Emperor: Schubert's song for trombone, *By the Sea;* the overture to the opera *Agnes von Hohenstauf;* the *Hohenfriedberger March* composed by his ancestor Frederick the Great; and—as if to confirm his identity—the aggressive song "I'm a Prussian and Prussian are my colors!"

But the music did not resound for very long. The monarch ordered it to cease because he failed to understand a mark of homage tendered him by his dinner companions: They said, "Wilhelm the Great!" He did not thank them but responded, "Those who flatter me today will tear me apart tomorrow!"

On the following day all the windows rattled while the fortresses of Paris ceaselessly thundered and lightened. The besieged Parisians were firing salvo after salvo as a preparation for their great sortie, that my agents had warned me about some time ago.

We moved all our regiments forward and left only two companies of militia in Versailles to protect our newly-proclaimed Emperor. Although Count Bismarck, for the first time, addressed his daily bundle of documents "To His Majesty the German Emperor" and received it back again with the inscription, "To His Excellency the Chancellor of the German Empire," I heard at court that no one expected any real changes because in the future everything would continue to be "strictly Prussian."

In fact the man who was now the German Emperor worked exactly as the King of Prussia had done, i.e., from early morning until (usually) well into the night, in his office with its spartan furnishings, laboring over documents, military maps, calculations, orders. His meals continued to be frugal and he never smoked. Early in the morning he washed with ice-cold water and in the evening, even after tea, he continued to work, studying newspapers, listening to reports and receiving visitors.

Oh, I admired our tireless Emperor who paid so little attention to his age and could outstrip many younger men. Moreover, he had an astonishing memory and could often remember things forgotten by men young enough to be his grandsons!

A short time later I intercepted two secret letters (that is, my agents immediately presented me with copies of them). The first was sent from Versailles to Munich and had been written by Prince Otto of Bavaria to his brother King Ludwig II; the second was sent from Berlin to London by none other than our Crown Princess herself, the consort of the man who was the "German Crown Prince," and was addressed to the Princess's mother, Queen Victoria of England.

In the first handwritten note I read: " . . . I confide in you how deathly ill I felt when I beheld these presumptuous proceedings [the coronation of Wilhelm I as Emperor], how I rebelled and raged inwardly against everything I heard and saw: so greedy for greatness, heartless and false! Such beginnings always give rise to nothing but new evils and ultimately to the downfall of Germany . . ."

In her letter to England our future German Empress declared: "I do not believe in the stability of this Empire, for it is not a good thing to owe the creation of such an Empire to the humiliation of one's neighbor. Because it was born of a victorious war, in the future we shall thirst only for wars and victories. Oh, Mother—I fear that Germany will soon be crushed between France and Russia!"

I turned these missives over to Bismarck, but he did nothing about them except to file them with the other documents. He claimed that he did not wish to "enervate" his new Emperor with any more letters, for His Majesty had already been disturbed by a letter he had just received from his imperial nephew, the Tsar of Russia, which, according to Bismarck, stated:

"The monarchical principle has been wounded by Germany, which has wiped whole dynasties off the map. Such calamity is not lessened by the fact that it was the work of a King and not of a revolution . . ."

"For the worst thing about it is that in his heart His Imperial Majesty sympathizes with these impossible views," Count

Bismarck explained to me, looking annoyed and weary. And he called our newly-proclaimed Emperor "the most unteachable particularist of them all," and said that the Emperor did not care a straw for the Empire and would rather give it up today than tomorrow.

Thereupon Bismarck complained to me that he could no longer endure all this obstruction. Immediately after peace was concluded, he said, he intended to leave office, and then Wilhelm I could look for another workhorse!

The coronation which we, so confident of victory, had held in the palace of their kings, seemed to imbue the Parisians with a desperate will to resist, and mustering, with the last of their energies, a total of one hundred thousand troops, half of them recruited from the citizens of Paris, they attempted a sortie to liberate their city. However, they did not penetrate beyond our outposts, and we responded by riddling with gunfire the entire district of St. Denis, where huge fires broke out.

A short time later during that dark night, lit only by the flashes which came from our thundering cannons, I received a message from my agents in Paris stating that a high-ranking French intermediary was on his way to see us.

I immediately hurried to Count Bismarck and was ordered to prepare well-guarded lodgings for this messenger of peace, whereupon I decided to shelter him in my own quarters at once (without letting him know that he was with the police).

Not long thereafter, none other than Jules Favre, Vice-President and Secretary of State for Foreign Affairs in the new French government, arrived in a coach whose windows were draped and on which the coat-of-arms of the French Emperor had been painted over with black paint. He was accompanied by his stepson Martinez del Roi, a famous artist, and sat with Count Bismarck on his sofa as if he were an old friend whom Bismarck had not seen for a long time.

But I could not have imagined a more striking contrast: The Count in his cuirassier's uniform, tall as a lamppost and beaming with health, and beside him the pitifully pale and starved-looking Frenchmen, whose clothes hung loose on their bodies.

I hurried home, had my offices transferred elsewhere, two beds made ready, all my officers put on civilian clothes, and laid in a large supply of food, including many delicacies, because the

French always imagined that we Germans were living in abject hunger just as they were.

An hour before midnight the unsuspecting messengers from the besieged city of Paris were given lodgings with my field police, and I even gave Jules Favre my feather coverlet to use in his bed so he could keep warm. Count Bismarck, at this late hour, was hurrying to the Emperor to take part in a council of war with all the leaders of the army.

Meanwhile Jules Favre, whom I ordered my officers to keep under constant surveillance through a hole in the wall, was still awake at dawn and, instead of sleeping, paced up and down with his stepson in my room, waging a tireless and violent debate. At dawn he finally asked for ink, a pen and some paper and began to write most eagerly—if I was not mistaken he was writing his offer of peace—not suspecting that he was writing it with the pen of a Prussian policeman.

After taking a brief nap I ordered the wretched Frenchmen a breakfast of beefsteak, ham, eggs, cake, wine and Mocha, which they devoured with a keen appetite. At the same time, as if by accident, I had a herd of some three hundred fat wethers and pigs from our storehouses driven past the window; designed to let the French know how long we could hold out here without wanting for food!

At noon the Count stormed up, driving his coach himself and bringing with him our terms for peace. The gentleman bargained for an hour or so, and when I accompanied the Count to his coach, I felt a surge of joy: judging by his features, which I had been studying for such a long time, peace was close at hand!

Inside my guests replied, "Unfortunately we shall not be able to dine together, reverend sir, for we wish to travel home to Paris immediately!" However, both of them asked for meat, bread, sausage and a huge piece of cake to eat during their return trip, and I generously packed all this up for them.

Later, when I expressed to Count Bismarck my conviction that Jules Favre appeared to be in a hurry to get our peace treaty signed and to bring it back with him again, Bismarck told me that as long as none of the generals accompanied the civilians, we could accomplish nothing but orientation. Favre, he said, had asked for a month's truce, as well as thirty-six thousand head of livestock and even more in the way of provisions, all of which

Bismarck had refused. "We'll keep them on scanty rations unless they agree to the peace terms we choose to set!"

The very next day I once again received word that several negotiators were approaching: Jules Favre and various councillors and generals! With great eloquence the former lawyer sought to mitigate Bismarck's harsh terms. The Count treated them all to smoked goose and bacon, and this time curiosity-seekers gathered in front of our house until I had the police drive them away.

One of Jules Favre's companions was General de Beaufort, a hoary firebrand who pushed away the well-filled plate offered him by Bismarck and growled, "It is merely good will on the part of France which allows us to engage in these negotiations! Our troops can always fight on and drive you away from here!"

Bismarck rose to his full height, walked over to Jules Favre and said cuttingly, "If you bring this gentleman here again, I shall break off the negotiations!", whereupon the lawyer smoothly apologized and the General sat there and did not say a word until the meeting was over.

On January 28, 1871, Count Bismarck and Jules Favre signed the cease-fire agreement; thus Paris had surrendered after one hundred and thirty-two days under siege. Its fortresses were occupied by our troops, and the city turned over all of its armaments: six hundred and two cannons, one million seven hundred and seventy thousand rifles, one thousand ammunition wagons, one thousand three hundred and sixty-two fortress cannons of the heaviest caliber, three hundred thousand shells, three million five hundred thousand cartridges and four million four hundred thousand pounds of gunpowder.

Where the fortresses were concerned, I took hostages: members of the city council, newspaper editors, merchants, even priests. They were forced to walk ahead of our soldiers until the latter were sure that the fortresses were not mined and that they were not about to be blown to bits. The black, white and red flag of our new Empire was raised above Paris, and the "Grande Valérie," the largest of its giant cannons, was loaded onto a railroad car to be taken to Berlin.

"Revenge at the Spree River!" the soldiers of the French fortresses cried, filled with hatred, when we entered their cellars and casemates, which had already been largely destroyed by our shells.

Paris paid us a "contribution" of two hundred million francs, and in return was allowed, for the first time, to procure provisions. I was named head of the commission which supervised traffic between the city, still surrounded, and the countryside. Then the Parisians engaged in a mass exodus: They applied for almost thirty thousand travelling permits on the first day alone, and then, with empty pockets and bundles they stormed into the food-filled countryside which they had not seen for so long, only to return packed and loaded like mules with meat, potatoes, sausages and bread.

My new house-guest, replacing Jules Favre, was the Director-General of all the French railroads, who wanted to make arrangements with me about getting as many express trains as possible on the rails to gather food. For weeks, he told me, all the infants in Paris had been dying because there was nothing more to eat but rotten horsemeat and rancid bread, and he added that if we kept trains on all the tracks night and day, we should barely be able to procure the food which the giant city consumed in a day. Although soon thereafter endless trains full of food arrived, pulled by as many as three locomotives, we were still unprepared to think about other equally important problems such as how to procure fuel and illumination for the city that had been under siege for so long.

At the same time a great many people wanted to go to Versailles, so I had my hands full trying to cope with them. Distinguished and wealthy people from Paris wanted to visit their houses there, which we had confiscated, were still occupying, and had cleared of their furnishings. Besides all these responsibilities, which scarcely left me time to eat and sleep, I was in charge of determining the rights to compensation of Germans who had been driven out of France; I cooperated in this task with our consul from Bamberg.

Thank God, peace was finally concluded with Adolphe Thiers, the newly-elected head of the French government, in return for France's cession of Alsace, Strasbourg, German Lorraine, Metz, and the fortress of Belfort, as well as six billion francs in reparations and the entrance of our troops into Paris.

Previously Count Bismarck had showed me a map of France showing the location of French- and German-speaking areas, and he wanted up-to-date information about the attitudes of the people who lived in the areas to be ceded to Germany. Nothing could have been easier, for these areas were literally swarming with our agents, and once again I was able to be of service in supplying accurate data:

The people of Alsace and Lorraine felt alien and in many areas hostile to the Germans, and had no economic or ethnic ties with them. To be sure, most of the Alsatians spoke our language, whereas the citizens of Lorraine spoke German only in isolated pockets, but the people of both regions felt friendly only towards southern Germany and not at all towards Prussia. Indeed, they felt more strongly than ever that they were French and did not want to have anything to do with Germans. The citizens of Metz were all French-speaking and felt as if they lived in the heart of France. We were taking over both provinces against the will of their people, violating all their thoughts and feelings on the subject . . . and so on.

Count Bismarck appeared to have expected all this and commented on my report only by saying that he was being forced to act this way: The German newspapers demanded that God punish France, and the "professors and beer-drinking patriots" were screaming for Alsace and Lorraine. "Even our revolutionary democrats led by Engels," he claimed, had categorically demanded "one" Empire in which "our flag waves over Strasbourg, and our fleet lies safely outside Kronstadt. They all want these border regions we lost centuries ago, which have become completely alien to us since that time," Count Bismarck said, sighing, and claimed that "in violation of his own reason" and "without hope" about the outcome, he was forced to "take their wishes into account."

Of course his intentions were not quite as pacific as they sounded. Like our military leaders, he believed that it was absolutely essential to guarantee our security against France. For example, as long as Strasbourg provided a gate through which a perpetually prepared army of hundreds of thousands of French soldiers could attack, we should never be in a position to move an equal number of troops to the Upper Rhine in time to fight them there; the French would always arrive before us!

After France, to our joy, had approved and signed our terms of peace, Count Bismarck appeared at the table dressed in civilian clothes—for the first time throughout our entire campaign. The Emperor embraced and kissed the War Minister and the Chief of the General Staff and then, finally, the Crown Prince, but he merely drank a toast to Bismarck's health. Was that not unjust?

On March 1, after I had freed all the political prisoners in

Versailles and had restored the police administration to the French, I travelled to Paris with our troops. A young hussar lieutenant named von Issendorff raced prematurely into the city, leading his equally stormy troop of cavalry. He left behind him a cloud of dust from which the countenance of General von Blumenthal, red with anger, emerged, and the General poured out over the poor hussar the flood of his magisterial rage. He spoke of demotions and expressed curiosity as to who was commanding Germany's entrance into Paris, the Lieutenant or himself, the General. For it was only eight o'clock in the morning! According to the agreement we were not allowed to enter the French capital until eight-thirty!

With Prussian down-to-the-minute punctuality we arrived in Paris at the appointed time, bayonets fixed, flags waving to the resonant music of the 1814 "March of Entrance into Paris," and went on to the *Arc de Triomphe;* which Napoleon I had had constructed after his victory over Prussia.

Exactly thirty thousand German soldiers held a parade before Emperor Wilhelm I at Longchamps; they filed past as snappily and with as much precision and order as if they had been on the drill square. In the evening there was a general tattoo, and our warriors sang hymns and wished our Emperor long life. Then they bivouacked to the right and left of the *Champs Elysées,* lighting a few watchfires with branches from the trees along the avenues.

There were almost no Frenchmen to be seen, hotels and shops were closed, and the venetian blinds tightly shut. Parisians had barricaded all the streets and bridges leading out of the areas we were allowed to occupy into those areas of the city that "remained free." All the news I received was bad.

My agents warned me about a resolute campaign on the part of the Parisians, amounting to a conspiracy, against the lives of the Emperor and his retinue. I regarded these rumors as all the more threatening because they mentioned names and suggested that the ringleaders of the plot were the Frenchmen Palmié and Durand, whom I knew to be fanatical nationalists.

Apparently because nothing had happened up to this point, Emperor Wilhelm I belittled my warnings that he might be attacked, dismissing them as mere "hypochondria," and even Count Bismarck insinuated that I was imagining things. With a carelessness which afforded me great anxiety he rode along through the *Bois de Boulogne,* and when the rabble whistled and shouted in derision, he paused before the man shouting the loudest and mockingly addressed him in French, saying, "Ah, I hear that Monsieur is musical?" The man whom he had provoked went away, without, at least this time, doing any harm.

But I was ceaselessly on guard, and although, like a hunting dog, I always lay tensely in wait, it was only by chance that I succeeded in preventing a particularly cunning assassination attempt that came within a hair's breadth of depriving us, at a single blow, of everything we had achieved!

At a dinner party given by the Emperor and Count Bismarck in the palace on the *Champs Elysées* which the German Count Henckel-Donnersmarck had built for his wife (a former courtesan named Lachmann, as I had learned in the course of my police work), I was unnerved by the government officials who had been invited because they boasted, with far too much pleasure for my taste, of the hangings, shootings and burnings they had carried out during their occupation of France.

I hurried into the basement before the food was to be served—was it a sixth sense which guided me? In any case a door leading to the kitchen opened in the basement and I saw one of the cooks.

I felt as if I had been struck by lightning (for my memory for people has never yet failed me): This cook who was preparing the meal we were to enjoy—with his piercing blue eyes, pitch-black hair and bushy eyebrows—appeared to be none other than the French partisan who had taken the pheasants I had shot near Versailles, beside the villa I had set on fire!

How had this particular person gotten into this basement, and why? An inner voice deep inside me sent me such an urgent warning that—although I had no pretext for doing so—I called him to accompany me for some reason, then had him arrested by two of my officers and led to my quarters nearby.

He did not appear to recognize me, or at least did not reveal that he recognized me by any change of expression. In his cook's clothing we found a so-called "free pass" issued by the French War Ministry, of a sort granted only to important persons, and I grew even more suspicious.

On his person I finally discovered a small bottle whose contents had a strong scent; the arrested man explained that his physician had prescribed this medication for a cold. Nevertheless my aide, von Z., and I tied him up, and I even held him in check with my weapon, while von Z., who spoke French fluently, hurried to the apothecary shop with the confiscated vial.

He had scarcely returned and was standing in the door when

he shouted, "Poison, poison—enough for an entire dinner party!" whereupon the man, still tied up, executed a headlong dive, and, despite his bonds, tore the bottle from von Z.'s hands and swallowed its contents with the speed of lightning. The next moment he fell to the ground groaning and did not move again.

I immediately knelt beside him and tried to find his pulse, but failed, then raised his eyelid—and saw that his eye had turned blood-red and twisted upward.

"What's wrong with him; should I fetch a doctor . . . ?" von Z. asked in consternation.

"He is dead," I explained, "and that's unfortunate, because I wanted to interrogate him. Just as the Emperor and all the others would have been dead, if he had succeeded in putting his poison . . . !"

Then I looked at the clock and delayed our banquet, which was due to have taken place in one hour, until all the food which had already been prepared could be thrown away and more food could be prepared under the supervision of my officers.

I did not dare to leave the dead Frenchman in my quarters or risk attracting any attention to him in this city whose people already hated us so much. Thus, with von Z.'s help, I removed his cook's outfit and dressed him in neutral-looking civilian clothes of mine. When it grew dark we propped the corpse up in my coach (the black horse that pulled it shied at his scent), von Z. sat beside him, and I drove the coach as fast as I could to the *Bois de Boulogne.*

We encountered no oppositon as we drove through the deserted streets—deserted because we had occupied the western portion of the city—and I paused in the dark underbrush before a marble bench which gleamed palely in the darkness. Unseen, we placed the dead man on it, so that his body leaned backwards as if sleeping, and beside him we placed an empty bottle of champagne that I had brought along. Then we jumped into the coach and hurried away as secretly as we had come.

Thus my colleagues of the Paris police department were left to rack their brains in the morning over who this dead man was and where he had come from before he emptied a bottle of champagne and apparently perished all alone!

On March 17, 1871, I finally accompanied our new German Emperor home to Berlin, the future capital of his Empire, where I continued managing my "Central News Bureau," which had so clearly proved its value in peace and war.

INDEX OF PERSONS